Africa, UK, and Ireland: Writing Politics and Knowledge Production

Volume 1

Edited by

Tendai Rinos Mwanaka

Mwanaka Media and Publishing Pvt Ltd,
Chitungwiza Zimbabwe
*
Creativity, Wisdom and Beauty

Publisher:

Mmap

Mwanaka Media and Publishing Pvt Ltd

24 Svosve Road, Zengeza 1

Chitungwiza Zimbabwe

mwanaka@yahoo.com

https//mwanakamediaandpublishing.weebly.com

Distributed in and outside N. America by African Books Collective

orders@africanbookscollective.com

www.africanbookscollective.com

ISBN: 978-0-7974-9334-6

EAN: 9780797493346

© Tendai Rinos Mwanaka 2018

DISCLAIMER

All views expressed in this publication are those of the author and do not necessarily reflect the views of *Mmap*.

Contents Table

EDUCATION AND RELIGION AS SOCIOLOGICAL TOOLS FOR SOCIAL AND NATIONAL DEVELOPMENT IN NIGERIA: *Amali, I. O. O (Nigeria)*

Kate Middleton and White Femininity: Excess Transgresses: *Nica Cornell (South Africa)*

EDUCATION AND VOCATIONAL REHABILITATIVE ASPIRATIONS OF STREET BEGGARS IN BAUCHI STATE, NIGERIA: *Amali, I.O.O (Nigeria), Saleh S (Nigeria),* and *Amali S.E (Nigeria)*

You have struck women! You have struck a rock! A South African Perspective on International Women's Day: *Lynnda Wardle (South Africa/UK)*

IT TAKES A VILLAGE: *EDITH OSIRO ADHIAMBO (Kenya)*

Transcription of a Conversation: *Andrea Mbarushimana (UK)*

One Man and His Axe: *John Eppel (Zimbabwe)*
Jo'burg: *Valerie Southgate (South Africa/USA)*
A MODERN RWANDAN FOLK TALE: *Ashby McGowan (UK)*
The Eyesore: *Christopher Kudyahakudadirwe (Zimbabwe)*
Life Can Make You Cry: *Kiarie Nyambura (Kenya)*
Haven Hunters: *Yugo Gabriel Egboluche (Nigeria)*
Beasts in the Farmstead: *NURENI Ibrahim (Nigeria)*

iii

About editor

Tendai Rinos Mwanaka is a publisher, editor, thinker, mentor, writer, visual artist and musical artist with over 20 books published which include among others, *Zimbolicious Poetry Anthologies (Anthology series of Zimbabwean poets), Playing To Love's Gallery (poetry book), Keys in the River (short stories novel), Voices from Exile (poetry book), Counting The Stars (poetry book),* and many more here: *http://www.africanbookscollective.com/authors-editors/tendai-rinos-mwanaka.* He writes in English and Shona. His work has appeared in over 400 journals and anthologies from over 27 countries. Work has been translated into Spanish, French and German.

Notes on contributors

ADEWUSI RAODAT ABIMBOLA is a budding poetess based in Zaria-Kaduna State, Northern Nigeria. She studies English Language from the Ahmadu Bello University, Zaria. She sees world as an empty vessel and tries to document the reality into non-fictional essays.

Edith Osiro Adhiambo is a Kenyan pharmacist with a passion for writing. She is currently working on her creative fiction pieces and is an ardent blogger at http://edosiakenshi.blogspot.co.ke/.

Dr. Ismaila O.O Amali, is from Benue State, Nigeria. He holds a B.Ed (Arts); M.Ed. (Guidance & Counselling) from University of Maiduguri, Nigeria since the year 2000. He is currently an Associate Professor in the Department of Social Sciences Education, Faculty of Education, University of Ilorin, Nigeria. He is a researcher and scholar in the field of Sociology of Education with special interest in the development of indigenous Nigerian and African educational practices. He has served in Nigerian Immigration Service before transferring his services to the University of Ilorin, Nigeria. He is married with children.

Adjei Agyei-Baah is a language lecturer at the University of Ghana School of Distance Education, Kumasi Campus and author of two haiku books: *AFRIKU (Red Moon Press, 2016)* and *Ghana 21 (Mamba Africa Press, 2017)* and winner of several international awards. He is the co-founder of Africa Haiku Network (AHN) and Poetry Foundation Ghana, and as well doubles as the co-editor of Mamba Journal, Africa's first international haiku journal.

Ifeoluwa Ayandele studied at the University of Lagos, Nigeria. He has been published in *African Writer, Brittle paper* and *Kin Poetry Journal.* His poems are forthcoming in *Best New African Poet 2017*

Anthology and *Kalahari Review*. He lives in Lagos, Nigeria. You can follow him on Twitter @ifeoluwaDele

James Bell is originally from Scotland and now lives in France where he contributes photography and non-fiction to an English language journal. To date he has published two poetry collections: *the just vanished place* and *fishing for beginners*, both from tall-lighthouse. He has been publishing poetry in magazines for twenty years. He has recently began writing and publishing short stories again and is presently working on his first story selection.

Matt Black lives in Leamington Spa. He was Derbyshire Poet Laureate (2011-2013) and has successfully completed over 20 commissions, with poems on 15 benches, 20 milestones, a large glass panel, and in exhibitions and publications. In 2017 his pamphlet *Spoon Rebellion* was published by Smith Doorstop, and in 2018 a book of travel haikus, *Tales from the Leaking Boot,* is being published with Iron Press. His first play, *The Storm Officer,* is touring in 2018-2019.

Nica Cornell is a South African writer with her Honours in Political and International Studies. She has previously published in *The Times, Mobius: The Journal of Social Change, the Kalahari Review,* and *South African Foreign Policy Review Volume III* (in press). She has also been published by *The Good Cemetery Guide,* the *Good Men Project* and the *Africa Matters Initiative.* She is currently pursuing her Masters.

Troy Da Costa: "This has been a chance for me to highlight the emotional awakening of a person, like myself, who made the difficult choice, to leave his home in Africa (Zimbabwe) and pursue an uncertain future. Even though the links between Britain and Zimbabwe are still strong, in the sense we are the first generation born in Zimbabwe outside British rule, the cultural gap is huge. Therefore, I went with modern settings; to highlight the inner conflict between living in Africa or seeking your future elsewhere like so many have done."

Yugo Gabriel Egboluche is a graduate of the University of Nigeria, Nsukka. He writes from Nigeria where he works as a Development Practitioner. Together with fiction, he does poetry, non-fiction, screenwriting and copywriting. His works have been published in *Chapbooks, the Kalahari Review, Praxis Magazine Online, Words, Rhyme & Rhythm* and his stories translated into film. His short stories have been published in an *Experimental Writing, Africa vs Latin American anthology* and other webzines; and his poem featured in the *Best New African Poets 2017 Anthology*. He has also co-authored and edited more than two community development texts and guidebooks.

Born in South Africa in 1947, **John Eppel** was raised in Zimbabwe, where he still lives, now retired, in Bulawayo. His first novel, *D G G Berry's The Great North Road,* won the M-Net prize and was listed in the Weekly Mail & Guardian as one of the best 20 South African books in English published between 1948 and 1994. His second novel, *Hatchings,* was short-listed for the M-Net prize and was chosen for the series in the Times Literary Supplement of the most significant books to have come out of Africa. His other novels are *The Giraffe Man, The Curse of the Ripe Tomato, The Holy Innocents, Absent: The English Teacher, Traffickings,* and (awaiting publication) *The Boy Who Loved Camping.* Eppel's poetry collections include *Spoils of War,* which won the Ingrid Jonker prize, *Sonata for Matabeleland, Selected Poems: 1965 – 1995, Songs My Country Taught Me,* and *Landlocked: New and Selected Poems from Zimbabwe,* which was a winner in the international Poetry Workshop Prize, Judged by Billy g. Furthermore he has collaborated with Philani Amadeus Nyoni in a collection called *Hewn From Rock,* and with Togara Muzanenhamo in a collection called *Textures,* which won the 2015 NOMA Award. He has published three mixed collections of poetry and short stories: *The Caruso of Colleen Bawn, White Man Crawling,* and, in collaboration with the late Julius Chingono, *Together*. Eppel's short stories and poems have appeared in many anthologies, journals and websites

Beaton Galafa is a Malawian writer of poetry, fiction and nonfiction currently studying for a Master's in Comparative Education at Zhejiang Normal University in China. His work has appeared in *BNAP 2017 Anthology, Betrayal, The Seasons and Empowerment (all collections of poetry and prose by Robin Barratt), Love Like Salt Anthology, Fourth and Sycamore, The Voices Project, Birds Piled Loosely, Atlas and Alice, South 85 Journal, Rejected Lit, and First Writer Magazine, The Maynard, Literary Shanghai, The Wagon Magazine, The Bombay Review, Bhashabandhan Literary Review, Kalahari Review, Nthanda Review* and *elsewhere*.

Pushcart Prize nominee, **Abigail George** is a South African blogger, poet, short story writer and aspirant young adult novelist and playwright. She briefly studied film at the Newtown Film and Television School in Johannesburg followed by a stint as a trainee at a production house. She is the recipient of grants from the National Arts Council, the Centre for the Book and ECPACC. Her poems have been widely published in anthologies, in print in South Africa and zines based in Australia, India, Ireland, Finland and all over Africa. She has written a novella, books of poems and short stories.

Oscar Gwiriri was born on 15 June 1975 at Honde Valley, Eastern Highlands, Zimbabwe. He is a published writer featured in three indigenous language anthologies; *Shaurai Nduri Dzazuro Nedzanhasi, Gwatakwata reNhetembo,* and *Hodzeko Yenduri.* He is a Certified Forensic Investigation Professional, and holds a Master of Science in Strategic Management Degree, Bachelor of Business Administration, Associate Bachelor of Business Administration Degree, Diploma in Logistics and Transport, Diploma in Workplace Safety and Health, and a multiple of United Nations Peacekeeping Certificates. Oscar likes writing in Shona language to promote the Zimbabwean literal heritage.

Helen Harrison is a new Liverpool poet. She has had poems published in the following literary journals, *Bare Fiction, Prole Books, The Interpreters House, Ink, Sweat and Tears, Cake, Flash Journal* and an article in *Parisall.* She is currently studying for a PhD in Creative writing at Lancaster University. She lives in Merseyside with her husband and two children.

Tomas S Hidalgo (45) holds a BBA (Universidad Autónoma de Madrid), a MBA (IE Business School), a MA in Creative Writing (Hotel Kafka) and a Certificate in Management and the Arts (New York University). His works have been published in magazines in the USA, Canada, Mexico, Argentina, Chile, Venezuela, Germany, UK, Spain, Ireland, Portugal, Romania, Nigeria, South Africa, Botswana, India and Australia, and he has been the winner of prizes like the Criaturas feroces (Editorial Destino) in short story and a finalist at Festival Eñe in the novel category. He has currently developed his career in finance and stock-market.

Niall Hurley is a South African writer who spent his early childhood in Dublin, Ireland. He has a background in advertising and makes a living in digital media as a UX Information Architect. His poem *Shelley Point* was published in *Best New African Poets: 2016 Anthology* (edited by T. Mwanaka & D da Purificação).

NURENI Ibrahim writes from somewhere in Nigeria. He has published works in *The Mamba Journal of Africa Haiku Network; Shamrock Haiku Journal; Best New African Poets 2016 Anthology; Africanization and Americanization Anthology Volume 1, Africa Vs North America; Best New African Poets 2017 Anthology; Writing Language, Culture and Development: Volume 1, Africa Vs Asia; Poets in Nigeria Journal,* an lots more. One of his short stories was longlisted for Brilliant International Flash Fiction – Aftermath Contest and his poem *This is the Song for You and I* shortlisted for Ken Egbas Prize for Festival Poetry Calabar. He performed poetry in Purple Awareness Programme, Black History Month Programme, and Footprints of David Arts Festival. His poems have been spread across different countries and, his works have been translated into French and Arabic Languages.

Tola Ijalusi is a Creative Writer, Poet, and Reviewer who writes from Ibadan, Nigeria. His works appears on various online journals and magazine such as *Kalahari Review, Dissident Voice, Indian Periodical, New Ink Review, BlackBoy Magazine* and *elsewhere*. His poems have been published in anthologies such as *Peace Is Possible, Muse For World Peace II, The Sun Will Rise Again, Best New African Poets Anthology 2016* and *Best New African Poets Anthology 2017*. He is a recipient of PIN Excellence Award 2016. He is the Managing Editor of *PAROUSIA Magazine, An Online Christian Arts and Literary Magazine.*

Colin James was born in the north of England near Chester and is currently living in Massachusetts. He has a book of poems forthcoming from *Wundor Editions*. Another book, *RESISTING PROBABILITY*, is available from Sagging Meniscus Press.....

Samuel Kegwaro is a writer, teacher and Blogger. He has a degree in Linguistics, Media and Communications. He currently teaches English and Literature at River of Life Secondary School in Embakasi Nairobi, Kenya. Some of his poems have been published at *poemhunter.com*

Tralone Lindiwe Khoza is a South African female, Psalmist, and Prophetess. She is the Founder of *Leading Lindiwe Blogspot* and *Lindiwe's Folktales*. She is the Author of *Lindiwe – The Voice Amongst the Eagles*. She describes herself as a storyteller and she is passionate about changing the state of South Africa's creative industry. She holds a BA Communications degree and a post graduate Dipl in Marketing.

Christopher 'Voice' Kudyahakudadirwe is a Zimbabwean freelance writer, poet and teacher living and working in South Africa. One of his first short stories was published in 2013 in an e-book entitled *Ghost-Eater and Other Stories*. The first three chapters of his novel *Murmurings from the Anthill* have been published in one of South Africa's oldest magazine called *New Contrast* as a short story entitled 'Voices of the Ancestors.' Another short story entitled 'When the Rabbit in a Grade 2 Textbook Moved' was also published by New Contrast. Eight of his poems have recently been published in an anthology entitled *Harvest: The University of the Western Cape Masters in Creative Writing Poetry Anthology 2016* and he read them at the McGregor Poetry Festival 2016 in August. Two more of his poems were recently published in an anthology entitled *Best "New" African Poets 2015 Anthology*. He has also contributed three poems to the *Zimbolicious: An Anthology of Zimbabwean Poets*. He is currently running a poetry blog at: https://kudyahakudadirwe.wordpress.com

Enesa Mahmić (1989) from Bosnia and Herzegovina currently lives in Galway, Ireland; is a travel writer, member of PEN Center. She took part in more than 50 international festivals and conferences. She published 4 poetry collections. Her poems have been translated into German, Italian, Slovenian, Turkish and Hungarian- included in many anthologies. She received several international awards for literature: Gold medals Neigbour of your shore 2017 as best immigrant poet. Ratković's Evenings of Poetry 2016 and Aladin Lukač Award 2016 for best debutant book.

Rethabile Masilo blogs at Poéfrika and co-edits Canopic Jar. He's a poet from Lesotho and lives in France. His poems have appeared in various anthologies and magazines, including *Canopic Jar, The Bastille, With Our Eyes Wide Open, Seeing the Unseen, Tears In The Fence, New Coin, Botsotso, Badilisha Poetry,* and others. In 2014 his poem 'Swimming', published in *New Coin Poetry, Vol 49, N°1*, won the Dalro First Prize. The same poem won the Thomas Pringle Award for Poetry in Periodicals in 2015. In 2012 his first book of poems, *Things That Are Silent*, was published by Pindrop Press. The second book, *Waslap*, was published in 2015 by Onslaught Press. And the third, *Letter to Country*, by Canopic Publishing in 2016. In October 2016 he was part of the 20th Poetry Africa Festival, where he also represented The World Poetry Movement. That same year his book second, *Waslap,* was awarded the Glenna Luschei Prize for African Poetry. In 2018 his fourth book, *Qoaling,* was published by Onslaught Pres

You will find **Zongezile Matshoba** in your township or village or school or town or hall or open ground, and wherever there is a literary event for the young and old. His writings narrate the humour and hardships of township and rural life, and interrogates whether it is yet uhuru in people's livelihood.

Mandla Mavolwane: I am a student currently studying Psychology at the Midlands State University. Writing poems is a form of therapy and it also helps me to express my views on the things that take place in daily life.

Andrea Mbarushimana is a writer and community worker in the UK. Her short collection of poems, prose and urban legends 'The Africa in my House' was published last year with Silhouette Press.

Ashby McGowan: I live in Glasgow (Scotland) and love poetry and short stories. I am a Buddhist and a vegan. I campaign for human and animal rights. I am also on Twitter and Facebook. I have several websites:
https://humanrightspoetryashbymcgowan.wordpress.com/.
humanrightspoetryashbymcgowan.wordpress.com.
https://ashbyshortstories.wordpress.com/
ashbyshortstories.wordpress.com.
https://multivoicepoetry.wordpress.com/.

Maria Manuel Godinho Azancot de Menezes was born on June, 1957 in Lisbon, she's daughter of Manuel Pedro Azancot de Menezes, natural of S. Tomé e Príncipe and of Maria de Lourdes Pires Godinho, natural of Portugal. She lived in Timor-Leste in the early years and then in Angola, where she lives. She is pediatrician, married, mother and grandmother. She wrote the book of 100 poems "Magicmoon", edited by the publisher "Chiado Editora" and released in September 2017 in Lisbon. One of the poems, "Coconut tree of my beach", is part of the book "Between sleep and dream", VIII Volume of Anthology of contemporary Portuguese Poets. And two other poems, "What will my promise do?" and "Recommended on S.Tomé" will be part of the book *Best "New" African Poets 2017 Anthology,* edited by Tendai Mwanaka and Daniel da Purificação.

Mzomuhle Mkhabela, Swaziland is 20 years old and is currently a student at University of Swaziland. He grew up around books which is no surprise he love poetry and writing. He writes for the lowly, hopeless, heartbroken and the ambitious. He writes to bring hope and inspiration to many minds.

Sinaso Mxakaza is a young writer from South Africa who currently lives in Mthatha. She started writing in 2008 inspired by her love for books; her poetry is a collection of tales that inspire healing, change and finding one's voice. Her poems have been published online on sites as *Voicesnet, Fundza, Poetry Potion* and an online anthology *(Next Generation Speaks Global Youth Anthology).*

Chido J. Ndoro is a protest and women's issues poet who has been writing since 2009. She is a holder of a Bachelor of Arts Honours Degree in English and Applied Communication. She mainly focuses on protest literature that addresses the political, economic and social issues in Africa. She also addresses women issues, illuminating the difficulties women face in society.

All her life Kenyan born **Nyambura Kiarie** has had a passion for the written word and the telling of stories. She believes that life is a story just waiting to be told and everyone has their own. She is passionate about exploring the politics of psychology in the struggle for voice and identity: especially the powerful inner stories of minority voices capturing women and children. Nyambura has published both poetry and prose online in *Saraba Magazine, African Roar, The Princess Project Kenya, Make Every Woman Count, Tintota, Botsotso 17,* among others. She was among the winners of the 2013-

2014 Women's Domination Short Story Competition by The Forgotten Writers Foundation Egypt.

Kariuki wa Nyamu, a Kenyan poet, radio playwright, critic, editor, translator and educator, earned a Bachelor's in English, Literature and Education from Makerere University, Uganda. His poems won The National Book Trust of Uganda (NABOTU) Literary Awards – 2007 and in 2010, while in third-year, he won Makerere University Creative Writing in the Contemporary World Competition for the best collection of poems. He is published widely both in print and online, in anthologies such as *A Thousand Voices Rising, BodaBoda Anthem and Other Poems, Best New African Poets Anthologies; 2015, 2016, 2017, Experimental Writing: Volume 1, Africa Vs Latin America Anthology, Africanization and Americanization Anthology: Volume 1, Africa Vs North America, Writing on Language, Culture and Development: Volume 1, Africa Vs Asia Anthology, The Mamba Journal for African Haiku: Issue IV*, besides co-authoring a Children's poetry and short story anthology titled *When Children Dare to Dream*. He emerged the overall winner of Babishai Niwe 2017 Haiku Prize. He is presently pursuing a Master's in Literature at Kenyatta University, Kenya.

Nwoke Theophilus hails from Ekka community in Ezza-North Local Government Area of Ebonyi State, Nigeria in West Africa. An aficionado of literary works, he holds a Bachelor of Law degree from Ebonyi State University and Master of Laws (LL.M) from the prestigious University of Ibadan, Ibadan, Nigeria.

Diane Pacitti lives and works in London. In 2004, in collaboration with her artist husband, she co-published *Guantanamo*, which was described by the Nobel Laureate Harold Pinter as 'deeply impressive and very important'. Her poetry has featured alongside Antonio Pacitti's artwork in events like *In an Occupied Land* in Glasgow. In 2014, she was awarded first prize in the Bronte Society Poetry Competition, and has been shortlisted for other literary awards, including the Blake Tithe Grant award and the Jane

Martin prize adjudicated by Girton College, Oxford. Her first novel, which explores immigration and war, is being prepared for publication.

Gugulethu Radebe is a teacher and poet from Durban, South Africa. She has a strong passion for women empowerment, youth development and community building and these ideas are reflected in a lot of her written work. She has published an eBook on Amazon called *The Coffee-Stained Sticky Notes* and is currently working on her second anthology called *Learn to Love Her*. Her work reflects a diversity of themes from human dignity to the perfect sunset.

Amanda Sewani is a 27-year-old highly motivated woman with a Bachelor of Arts degree from the University of Zimbabwe and is currently studying towards a special Honours degree in Communication and Media studies. Her passion lies with Women Rights' Activism. She is also interested in issues to do with Religion, Feminism, Politics, History and Literature. Her poetry is more of a mixed bag, unlimited and raw. She is a Game of Throner, a sports fanatic, loves reading books, an animal lover and enjoys watching Crime investigation programs.

Ibinda Kayambu or perhaps **Hélder Simbad**, pseudonym of Helder Silvestre Simba André, was born on August 13, 1987, in Cabinda, Angola. He is a student of the 4th year of the Languages, Translation and Administration course at the Catholic University of Angola; Teaches Portuguese Language and African Literature. He is General Coordinator and co-founder member of the Litteragris Movement. Poet, prose writer and literary critic, with texts published in newspapers, magazines and blogs. He is the winner of António Jacinto 2017 Literary premious

Valerie Southgate: I live between South Africa and America. A molecular biologist working as a medical communications consultant, I write fiction whenever I find time. I have completed an MFA (Mountainview MFA, Southern New Hampshire

University). Born and raised in Johannesburg, I return every year to spend a month in the city. The rest of my time is spent between the South African Karoo and Denver, Colorado. When in South Africa, I make it my job to listen to the many voices I meet on the streets. My fiction preferentially explores the more marginalized, less represented socio-political perspectives that I hear.

AJ Taudevin (writer) is associate artist with the Tron Theatre in Glasgow and won the Playwrights Studio New Writers Award in 2010. Her written work includes *Some Other Mother, Untruth The YelloWing, Demons, The Jean-Jacques Rousseau Show* and *Chalk Farm*. Chalk Farm was co-written with Kieran Hurley with whom AJ has also collaborated on the creation of *Beats, Hitch and Rantin*. As an activist and community arts worker she often works as a Theatre of The Oppressed facilitator and popular educator. She has facilitated and set up women's groups across Glasgow and has been an active member of Glasgow's support network for asylum seekers and refugees since 2007. As actor Julia Taudevin she has worked for theatre companies including The National Theatre, The National Theatre of Scotland, The Traverse, Magnetic North, The Tron, The Arches and A Play, A Pie and a Pint and her screen work includes the feature film *Sunshine on Leith*.

My name is **Asekho Toto,** last year I just passed grade 12 and this year I have taken a gap year. I'm a full time writer I don't have any qualifications. I'm 18 years old, from George, Western Cape

Wilson Waison, Born on the 7th of January, is a Zimbabwean human rights activist and an advocate against Gender Violence. The editor of *Deem.lit.org,* he is also a flash fiction writer as well as a dramatist, inspired to scribe mostly by the prevailing violence and chaotic situations faced in life dilemmas.

Lynnda Wardle was born in Johannesburg and lives in Glasgow. In 2007 she was awarded a Creative Scotland New Writer's Award and was shortlisted for the Scottish Book Trust Next Chapter Award in 2015. She has stories and essays published variously in *thiwurd, Gutter, New Writing Scotland, Tales from a Cancelled Country Anthology, Scottish PEN magazine* and the *New Orleans Review*. She is currently writing a memoir. www.lynndawardle.com

Thamsanqa Wuna is a 26 year old Accountant and entrepreneur with a Bachelor of Business Administration degree from Solusi University. A keen human rights activist and gender equality advocate, he is keen on protest poetry with particular focus on the ordinary Zimbabwean perspective. He is an avid reader and he will always find time to read a book. He is loyal to his fiancee, Arsenal FC and his family.

Introduction

After over 500 years of contact between Africa, the UK and Ireland, and as Africa and her erstwhile colonial master, the UK, continues forging for a closer constructive engagement that's beneficial to all, I decided to do an anthology of writings (essays (both scholarly and general)), fiction, mixed genres, poetry and plays) that focuses on politics and knowledge production.

Knowledge production could be scientific methods of creating knowledge as you would find in *Amali. I* essay *Education And Religion As Sociological Tools For Social And National Development In Nigeria:* that begins this anthology, and his other essay *Education And Rehabilitative Aspirations Of Street Beggars In Bauchi State, Nigeria:* that he collaborated with *Saleh S,* and *Amali S.E.* Knowledge production could be on the aspect of managing knowledge you would find interrogated by *Nica Cornell* in her essay, *Kate Middleton and White Femininity: Excess Transgresses,* where she critically and personally dissects how the media, especially the western media, has managed to produce and managed the *Kate* we have come to know and accept as the real *Kate.*

It could be knowledge production on the aspect of processing and sharing knowledge between people, cultures, countries etc, or it could be looked at culturally, or even socially... like sharing ideas through communication with word of mouth, digital medias, internet systems which is highlighted by Edith Adhiambo's essay *It Takes A Village* that deals with globality, and how it has connected us all.

For example and not as argument but as a perspective point of view and questioning: An African writer/person has knowledge about the UK and her people, some Africans think of the UK as a subjecting authority, but is that the entire truth, and an Irish writer/person might think of Africa as strife-torn and disease ridden because that's what is produced in their medias, that's the knowledge she will have of Africa, but is that the whole truth.

They were several refreshing perspectives on politics depicted in this anthology. Whilst a lot of African poets, for example, *Mxakaza, Simbad, Ijalusi, Matshoba* tackled the political relationship between the UK and her former colonial subjects, quite a number of poets, like *George, Wuna, Nyamu, Ndoro, Mwanaka* in his play, *Rage of the Devils*, and *Kudyahakudadirwe* is his story *The Eyesore*, also focussed beyond the independence of African countries as they showed us how the liberators have turned to be our oppressors.

The other aspect is the migrant/exilitic condition which is tackled by several writers like *Mahmić, Egboluche* in his story, *Haven Hunters,* and *AJ Taudevin* in her play, *Some Other Mother,* where these dealt with the difficulty of asylum seekers living in the UK and Ireland, and a number of poets like *Da Costa, Masilo* etc inhabited that painful middle ground between longing for home and finding home far from home. In the interview with her husband who was also an NGO worker in Africa *Andrea Mbarushimana* who was a former NGO worker in Africa, in her piece, *Transcription of a Conversation:* dealt with the refugee situation in Africa and NGO politics.

It was also refreshing to see a number of UK writers writing their stories and poems based in Africa, or about Africa as one will find in *Ashby McGowan* historical tale *A Modern Rwandan Folk Tale,* and *Matt Black,* and *James Bell* poems, yet *Harrison* and *Pacitti* focussed on blackness in the Western World by going back to colonialism and how London has changed and is now full of several colours.

Eppel, Southgate, Hurley dealt with the political space for white Africans in predominantly black Africa, each from his or her own perspective. *Wardle, Sewani,* and others dealt with women's rights and I connected on a personal level with Wardle's essay on women's rights during apartheid South Africa, as it focussed on the city I have been staying in for over a year now, Pretoria, and ingratiating more, I stay in Lillian Ngoyi Street, named after one of the women who fought for women's rights during apartheid, and the Union Building is just a few streets over. I have seen statues of Botha, Kruger etc.

Nyambura in her story *Life Can Make You Cry* deals with knowledge production and politics from the perspective of sex, sexual identity and sexual abuse. *Khoza, Agyei-Baah, Ibrahim* harks back to traditional and or spiritual African worlds in trying to find solutions to political problems or to understanding their identity. A number of poets, *Radebe, Menezes, Toto* dealt with love politics, thus in all these writings we are reminded politics can be tackled from several perspectives, especially the personal one, not just only from the governance perspective.

The far-reaching idea behind *Africa, UK, and Ireland: Writing Politics and Knowledge Production, Volume 1,* was to create (produce) new knowledge between these worlds. I think in every contributor you will feel each believed and felt strongly that (re)imagining and (re)writing about these issues would help the UK, Ireland and Africa to find common strands to move beyond neo-colonialism and postcolonial discourses and structures into the 21st century and beyond; as mutual, respectful and beneficial partners.

Africa, UK, and Ireland: Writing Politics and Knowledge Production, Volume 1 is the fourth in a series of ongoing transactional and transcontinental anthologies.

The first one is *Experimental Writing, Africa Vs Latin America, Volume 1* which is in print here, http://www.africanbookscollective.com/books/experimental-writing-africa-vs-latin-america-vol-1. The second one we focused on Africa Vs North America writers, especially on race issues, entitled, *Africanization and Americanization Anthology, Volume 1: Africa Vs North America*, which was published by *Mwanaka Media and Publishing Pvt Ltd.* The third anthology focused on African writers and Asian writers, entitled *Writing Language, Culture and Development, Africa Vs Asia, Volume 1,* which was also published by *Mwanaka Media and Publishing Pvt Ltd.*

These anthologies also help us to create links/communities between writers, foster development of African writers and help us tackle issues we feel are pertinent between the regions we will be focused on, and this one will particularly help us produce new knowledge between these regions.

Africa, UK, and Ireland: Writing Politics and Knowledge Production, Volume 1 has work from upcoming poets and writers, and established and experienced poets and writers; it has work from academic scholars, essayists, poets, fictionist, playwrights, and thus it is invaluable to literary and language theorists, poetry collections, political sciences, social sciences and human sciences, general academia and readers, education departments and students

Non fiction

EDUCATION AND RELIGION AS SOCIOLOGICAL TOOLS FOR SOCIAL AND NATIONAL DEVELOPMENT IN NIGERIA.

Amali, I. O. O. (Ph.D)

Abstract

This study examines Education and Religion towards how they are used for Social and National development in Nigeria. It discusses education and religion as two benefitting social institutions that guarantee Social and National development in a multi-ethnic and multi-religion society such as Nigeria. Thus, it succinctly clarifies the conceptual terms, identifies and discusses the parity between education and religion in the Nigeria context, show the way forward and recommends a paradigm in the interface between education and religion as tools for Social and National development. Further, it advocates for an application of education and religion as tools in the examination of Social values for National development. In this respect religion is viewed from the prism of faith as a discipline while education and religion are viewed as institutions for facilitating social wellbeing for National development. Thus, it recommends among others, the promotion of education and religious philosophies that would bring about understanding and cooperation among communities with multi-religious backgrounds such as Nigeria.

Keywords: *Education and Religion, sociological tools, Social and National development*

Introduction

The need for social and national development is paramount to the existence of any nation. Education and religion have continued to play significant roles in the directions of social and national

2

development. They have influenced the lives of all Nigerians, where educational institutions and religious houses are on the increase daily.

In Nigeria, it is assumed that most Muslims and Christians are devoted to their faith as well as having great passion for education (western or Islamic). The traditional worshippers have no less passion for their faith and education (Dopamu, 2009). Ekanem and Ekefre (2013) asserted that Nigerians view every aspect of their lives on religious prism and that particularly for a good Muslim there would be no difference between religion, culture and education. Further, that religion has become the basic social element through which Nigeria societies are grouped. Thus, a disagreement relating to any aspect of social element is viewed as a disagreement of religious views or beliefs among Nigeria multireligious society. Education at the other hand has as its cardinal philosophy; that of the illumination and liberation of minds of the masses, which unchains people, from their darkness and corridor of illiteracy (Akinpelu, 1981).

Thus, Education and Religion have become the two benefiting elements that sustain the basic principles of security, freedom and other fundamental human rights as enshrined in the Nigeria Constitution (FGN, 1999) and the National Policy on Education (FGN, 2004). They are thus, social institutions that guarantee Social and National development.

Conceptual Clarification of Terms

Education and Religion: Fafunwa (2004) stated that in Nigeria before the advent of western or Islamic education, education was functional in nature, a guiding value upheld by elders that ensured an enduring society. That education in whatever form, was used to train the young and adult members of the society. To him education was a tool for disseminating or transmitting social values, knowledge and cultural heritage from one generation to another. This was why the Federal Government of Nigeria (2004) posited that:

> Education is an instrument for national development. To this end, the formulation of ideas, their integration for national development and the interaction of persons and ideas are all aspects of education. Education fosters the worth of development of the individual for his sake and for the sake of the general development of the society (pp. 6-7).

Religion is man's belief which centered around the sacred, the unknown Super natural power (Davis, 1988; Dopamu, 2009; Dzurgba, 2009). Dzurgba (2009) noted that Durkhein showed how religious beliefs and practices had shaped the course of human civilization and social life. Thus, he referred to Durkhein's Social theory of religion as functionalism. Fafunwa (2004) observed that Traditional, Islamic as well as Christian religions have the same functionalist prerequisite. Like Mahutta (2011) asserted, if Education and Religion are accorded their well deserved value and place, they would mean a lot to the society.

Social and National Development: In this study, social and national developments have been used as paradigm which intertwined in the thinking about the future of Education and Religion in Nigeria multi-religious society. This is because, Education and Religion hold a pride of place in environmental and economic consideration in the pursuit of approved quality of life needed by the citizenry for social and national development. Thus, as earlier posited, both Education and Religion have been presented as a fundamentally optimistic human endeavour characterized by aspiration for progress and betterment of societies (Dzurgba, 2009). They are both understood by many to be means of overcoming handicaps, achieving greater equality (or wealth) and social status. They are both social institutions where children can

4

develop according to their unique needs and potentials. They both connote the idea of pasture ship that would lead to the development of the individual society and the nation. Both invoke enlightenment and training as means to achieve the end.

The Parity between Education and Religion in Nigeria

The National Bureau of Statistics (NBS) portrayed 50.48% of Nigerians as Muslims, 48.2% as Christians while 1.4% was members of other religions. This typified Nigeria as a good example of two major religious societies where the bulk of the Muslims are in the North and the bulk of the Christians reside in the South. Education in this respect is to serve each society the freedom to practice their religion and to educate their young ones the practice of such religion. This has been spelt out in the Federal Republic of Nigeria Constitution (1999) where freedom of worship is enshrined and guaranteed for the citizenry, making Nigeria a secular state. Thus, Education and Religion cultivate and prepare individuals towards tolerance and cooperation which would facilitate freedom of worship and the promotion of peaceful co-existence among Nigerians.

Basically, the teaching of religion in Nigeria is faith oriented. In Nigeria schools, it is a means of getting people to embrace Christianity or Islam. This is why Christian and Islamic religious studies remain the only two religions of study in Nigeria schools particularly at the lower levels of Nigeria educational systems. In this respect, Education and Religion have brought together, Nigerians from diverse socio-cultural, ethnic and linguistic groupings to promote social integration. For example, Nigeria public schools have been known for promoting social harmony by admitting Nigeria children without bias to socio-cultural, ethnic, religious and linguistic considerations.

Education is thus the panacea for settling problems created by religion as it equips people with better understanding of the dynamics of religion. To this end, Achunike (2008) asserted that better education will equip religious adherents with better understanding of the dynamics of religion, making the individual to compromise or give up some religious or doctrinal rights for the sake of social change.

According to Akinpelu (1981) and Cobb (1997), it is within the realm of philosophy to raise fundamental issues and to question certain beliefs. Thus, in Nigeria, the interface between Education, Religion and Culture cannot be ignored. At the cultural level, the family and the tribal communities had provided the young ones (even before he got to know religion) education. But nowadays, when people talk about religion, their minds go to school education where the institutionalization of religious life precedes that of education for most societies. As such, religious institutions as asserted by Cobb (1997) had contributed to the development of education systems. This was true of Northern and Southern parts of Nigeria where the Mosques and the Churches spawned the early Western and Islamic schools (Dopamu, 2008). This was so because parents would like their children to adopt their values. The schools in this case provided personal development of pupils where the ethos of civil religious education continues to affect the overall personality of many youth in Nigeria schools.

Again, Education and Religion in Nigeria have become centres for importation of fresh ideas that create values for civic responsibility and civil order. This indicates that there exist epistemological relationship between Education and Religion which create the required awareness in the citizenry towards social and moral values needed for Social and National development. Therefore, the parity of education and religion is that of mutuality. This is because, the more Education and Religion work together and borrows the values of another, the more values that people shared together would affect their social life needed for national development. In this way religious education will continue to affect the overall climate of many schools in Nigeria.

Implications of Education and Religion as Designs for Social and National Development in Nigeria

Education and Religion serve as the instrument of social harmony for any society. But in Nigeria, Religion has caused insecurity due to either lack of understanding and misinterpretation of the various religious doctrines that have been sometimes fuelled due to religious rivalry or dogma. The issues of religion conflict have become common phenomena in the country, especially in the last three decades. The rivalry existing between Islam and Christianity sometimes lead to religious conflict, violence and terrorism. The latest ravaging the country is a sect known as Jama'atul Ahlus sunnab haddla'awati wal Jihad (Brethren unite in the pursuit of holy war), also known as Boko Haram; a group that sees western education as an extension of colonialism and imperialism (Omotoye, 2012). Thus there have been accentuations of regional and ethnic distinction attributed to religion differences in Nigeria (Dopamu, 1993; Achunike, 2008).

Further, Islam and Christianity are missionary in nature, that through education tried to connect people from their traditional religion that have been handed down from generation to generations of Africans (Dopamu, 1993). But today, religion has become one of the important weapons which selfish elites and leaders use in manipulating and dividing the people (Lemu, 2012). Consequently in Nigeria, access to Education and Religion thus became the dominant force used to control the lives and rights of groups and individuals. This has led to multiplicity of religious sects and educational institutions across Nigeria. This has implications for education that seeks to liberate the minds and remove all forms of mental cobweb gathered through cultural and religious activities and beliefs for parochial interests being exploited by religion bigots and fanatics in Nigeria toward social values (Lemu, 2012).

Again the interactive forces of Education and Religion have created unhealthy atmosphere for social and national development. This is because religion has become a very emotive issue among Nigerians, particularly in the institutions of learning where there are occasional break down of law and order due to religious differences (Alana, 1993). Amali (2009) attested that the opportunities created by the establishment of exogenous religious influences (Christianity and Islam) provided a new pattern of challenge to teaching and learning in multi-religious society. That, it is on the basis of this scenario that teaching and learning of religious tenets in schools are accorded a high premium and recognition in the life of the Nigerian people which are included in Nigeria educational curricula. The Nigeria Constitution (FGN, 1979) and the National Policy of Education (FGN, 2013) took cognizance of the values of Education and Religion and make legislative provisions to regulate and control the behaviour of the citizenry.

Thus, educational institutions in Nigeria stand the chance of reawakening and resuscitating the conscience of Nigeria people for positive endeavour. Religious education plays a crucial role in this respect. This has implication for teaching and learning in Nigeria where the consequences of religious teaching have sometimes negatively influenced the social wellbeing of the citizenry leading to ordeal, disorder, wanton destruction of lives and property. Similarly, Lemu (2012) observed that education and religion are the causes of the disparity that entrenched marginalization in terms of Social and National development in Nigeria. Achunike (2008) has asserted that the several religious conflicts in Nigeria have assisted in the accentuation of regional and ethnic distinction due to the pattern of education where there were differences between the North and South.

The Way Forward

The National Policy of Education and Religious curriculum did not spring from nowhere. They evolved as a reflection of the need, perceptions and historical development in Nigeria for Nigerians. Multiplicities of religion and strict compliance to religious dogma have become a challenge to cooperate existence of people in Nigeria. Education would serve to curtail excesses in the behavior of individuals. The essence of Education and Religion thus revolve around the interface between Education and Religion as presented as a recommendation in the paradigm below:

A Recommended Paradigm on the necessary Interface between Education and Religion for Social and National Development.

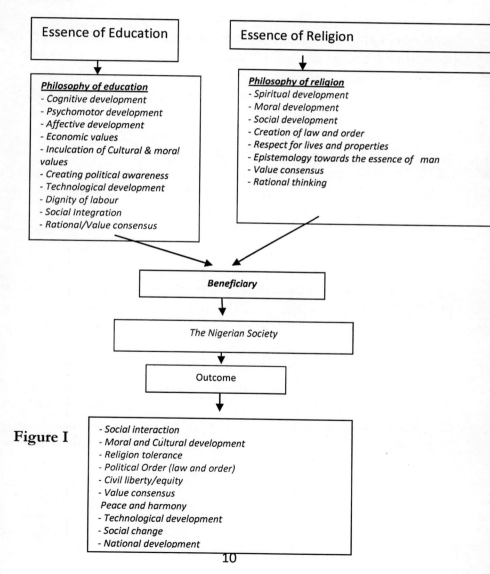

| Essence of Education | Essence of Religion |

Philosophy of education
- Cognitive development
- Psychomotor development
- Affective development
- Economic values
- Inculcation of Cultural & moral values
- Creating political awareness
- Technological development
- Dignity of labour
- Social Integration
- Rational/Value consensus

Philosophy of religion
- Spiritual development
- Moral development
- Social development
- Creation of law and order
- Respect for lives and properties
- Epistemology towards the essence of man
- Value consensus
- Rational thinking

Beneficiary

The Nigerian Society

Outcome

Figure I

- Social interaction
- Moral and Cultural development
- Religion tolerance
- Political Order (law and order)
- Civil liberty/equity
- Value consensus
 Peace and harmony
- Technological development
- Social change
- National development

10

As shown in figure I: there would be need for national initiatives to address religious challenges using Nigeria institutions of learning as forerunners to address excesses of individual behavior through dialogue, religious discourse, symposia, conferences etc. This would employ constructive education based on a sound philosophy of Education and Religion that would recover the minds and souls of those behind religious bigotry that at times result into rivalry which creates problem for Nigeria Social and National development.

This would also address the challenges posed due to low illiteracy level of religious adherents in Nigeria. Ekanem and Ekefre (2013) pointed out that what has been taken as philosophy of education in Nigeria, are policy statements and objectives of education. That there would be need for the creation of department of philosophy, particularly for the interest of northern part where they noted that no federal and state universities teaches philosophy as a course of study except University of Abuja. Again a combination of physical and spiritual dimension that would help to develop Social and National development is needed. In this regard, Education would help to re-educate and eradicate those vices that tend to retard the development of Nigeria people and the country.

Education and Religion should jointly help to promote peace, sound and appropriate meaningful social order required for national development. Thus Nigerians would use Education and Religion to enhance their living side by side as long as they do not insult or cast aspersion on one another's sanctities. Education and Religion should not conflict in social responsibility. Religious adherents should be taught how to discuss popular misconceptions about their beliefs without making it as an offence or with the aim not to convert but to develop a better mutual understanding that encourages social solidarity needed for national development.

Also Education can be used in the re-direction of misuse of religion for selfish ends. This would require correct teaching of religion that would facilitate common values for all persons irrespective of their religious differences.

Conclusion and Recommendations

This study advocates for an application of Education and Religion as sociological tools in examination of societal values for national development. Religion is viewed from prisms of faith as a discipline, while Education and Religion are viewed as institutions for facilitating social wellbeing for national development. Since the need for Social and National development is paramount to the existence of any nation, the collaborative roles of education and religion in Nigeria is essential because they would help to ensure unity, peace (within Nigeria religious diversity) required for social solidarity and national development. This has been enshrined in the Nigeria Constitution (1999) and in the National Policy on Education (FGN, 2013).

The following recommendations are thus drawn for this study;
1.   There should be a promotion of Education and Religious philosophy that would bring about understanding, cooperation among communities with multi-religious background.
2.   Education should encourage the publication and distribution of books about different religions that should be used in the various tiers of educational systems in Nigeria.
3.   Teachers of religion in Nigeria schools should be well grounded in philosophies of Education and Religion to enable them to understand the essence of education and religion in Nigeria.
4.   Government at all levels should be involved in the funding of education to promote and monitor religious activities in Nigeria.

5. Liberalism should be promoted both in religious and educational spheres of Nigerian national life. Components of Christianity should be included in Islamic syllabus and vis-a-visa. Thus teachers should realistically and objectively explain the basic principles of the religion they teach to promote social justice and national consciousness.

6. Education should discourage poor theological education in Nigeria and encourage inter-religious dialogues, interactions and discussions between two or more different religious groups with a view to bring about an atmosphere of social harmony needed for social and national development.

7. Institutions of learning should serve as cross-fertilization grounds for ideas about religious beliefs to various religions adherents.

References

Achunike, H.C. (2008), *Religious practices in Nigeria as a source of conflict. Journal of Liberal Studies, 12 (1 & 2) pg 286-295*

Adogbo, M. P. and Ojo, C.E. (2003), *Research methods in humanities: Lagos, Malthouse Press Limited.*

Akinpelu, J. A. (1981), *An introduction to philosophy of education. Ibadan, Macmillian Company Ltd.*

Alana O. E. (1993), *'The relationship between christians, muslims and afrolists in history with particular reference of to Nigeria". in Studies in Religion understanding in Nigeria, Rasaq D. Abubakre (ed), Ilorin Christy-David Printers.*

Amali, O. O. I. (2009), *The challenges of teaching and learning in a multi-religious society. Nigeria Journal of Sociology of Education. Vol. III.*

Cobb J. B. (1997), *Religion and education. California Claremont School of Theology. Lecture one.*

Davis, D. (1988), *The Study of Religion; In The World's Religions, (ed.) by R. Pierce Bearer, (Hert, England: Lion Publishing, 1988), pp. 10-11.*

Dopamu P. Ade (1993), *African Religion in Nigeria Society; Past, Present and the future in Studies in religion understanding. in Nigeria, Rasaq D. Abubakre (ed) et'al (Ilorin: Christy-David Printers).*

Dopamu A.T (2007), *Religious' pluralism in Nigeria; the example of the Yoruba" in dialogue: Issues in Contemporary Discussion, Ade P. Dopamu (ed) et'al Akure; Big Small books.*

Dzurgba, A. (2009), *An introduction to sociology of religion. Ibadan John Archers.*

Kanem, S. A., & Ekefre, E.N. (2013), *Education and religions intolerance in Nigera: the need for essencism as a philosophy. Journal of Educational and Social Research Vol. 3(2) may (published online).*

Fafunwa, B. A. (2004), *History of education in Nigeria. Ibadan. NPS Educational Publisher Ltd.*

Federal Republic of Nigeria (2013), *National policy on education Abuja. Abuja Ministry of Education.*

Constitution of the Federal Republic of Nigeria (1999), Publisher, Federal Ministry of Justice, Lagos.

Lemu B. A. (2012), *Religion education in Nigeria – a case study, Nigeria. Islamic Education Trust.*

Mahutta, M. G. (2011), *Education for morality. A panacea for rebranding the Nigeria Society. Nigeria Journal of Sociology of Education. Volume V. No I. Alaya. Education Trust Fund*

Omotoye, R. (2012), *Inter-religion dialogue as a panacea for national development in Nigeria. Centre point Journal: Ilorin. University of Ilorin Library and Publications Committee – Volume 15 No I.*

Kate Middleton and White Femininity: Excess Transgresses

Nica Cornell

Until recently, the walls of my room were plastered with images of the Duchess of Cambridge, or 'Kate' Middleton as she is known in global media, her husband Prince William, and their two children George and Charlotte. Despite living in Grahamstown, South Africa, for four years it is not home. I feel out of place and alone here, and this year has been particularly alienating as my political activism with the Black Student Movement has exposed me to the reality that my university is a stagnant and oppressive institution. One of the various escape mechanisms has been a continuous and compulsive fascination with Kate. This essay comes from the desire to understand that compulsion. What is it about images of Kate and her family that offers reassurance and familiarity? Importantly, there is a distinction between the person who was born Catherine Middleton and the media subject Kate, which is not a name she has ever used. This alone demonstrates the role and power of the media here —a nickname grants an illusion of intimacy. I do not know the private person that is Catherine at all. I know Kate, the subject based on Catherine and produced by the media, extremely well. I realized that there was a "double movement" (McRobbie, 2007: 720) within the narrative of Kate that makes her so globally appealing – she embodies the impossible neoliberal standard of white femininity that I feel compelled to meet *and* simultaneously seems accessible and relatable. She therefore makes it seem possible that I can do it too.

Having always felt that I breached the boundaries of womanhood by having 'too much body, too much brains, too much emotion,' here is proof that it is possible to get it right, to achieve the "ideals of neoliberal active womanhood and its qualities such as economic independence, self-regulation and happiness" (Repo and Yrjölä, 2015: 2).This essay, using Harding's three dimensions of gender, Brown and McRobbie's double movement, and Foucault's disciplinary power, will identify the false universal of the narrow unattainable definition of white womanhood being produced via the framing of Kate and how the effects of this reach as far as me, a young white South African woman. Imperatively, this is not intended to erase the devastating effect of the projection of a white universal in the first place. Instead, it focuses on white femininity to render the invisible visible, displace it as the universal, and disentangle the mechanics of its power.

"What script of white femininity was being so successfully spun and mediated such that this highly British woman became a simultaneous signifier of a national popular and a global popular?" This was the question asked by Raka Shome (2014: 1) about Diana, Princess of Wales, Kate's mother-in-law. When Diana died, Shome (2014: 1) was fascinated by how a media narrative of a "white heterosexual upper-class British woman was able to secure so many affective attachments of love and desire from people – white and not white, Western and not Western." The peculiar reach of Diana's death is demonstrated by Epainette Mbeki (cited in Gevisser, 2007: 362), mother of former South African Thabo Mbeki, telling her son's biographer that she cried her eyes out when Diana died because "She really was a people's princess." Diana's legacy is central to understanding how it came to be that Kate is a vehicle for the construction and perpetuation of white femininity – defined by Shome (2001: 323) as "an ideological construction through which meanings about white women and their place in their social order are naturalized." This definition is imperative to understanding that white femininity is an ideological discursive construct – just as the subject Kate is.

Jane Barr who writes the *From Berkshire to Buckingham* blog that is one of the four biggest blogs in the world following Kate (Barr,

Personal Communication, 26 September, 2015), argues that the fundamental changes in media and communication technology were central to Diana's popularity. Her youth and apparent naiveté at the time of her engagement to Prince Charles meant that she easily fitted the archetype of the virginal bride marrying Prince Charming. Her popularity only increased as she garnered public sympathy for her misery and isolation once married. Barr (2014) argues that "her very premature, dramatic and tragic death in Paris solidified her star status," which was then passed on to her sons and would inevitably affect whoever married William, who like his father would one day be king.

Shome (2001: 324) examines the underlying narratives at work in the same tale. In the years before her death, Diana disrupted boundaries of race and patriarchy of "'Englishness,'" (Shome, 2001: 324) and her prescribed script of white femininity as bride, wife and mother of the nation that is conceived as a (white, heteronormative, bourgeois) family. In 1995, she conducted a secret television interview about the royals with Martin Bashir, at the time an unknown black British man. After her divorce she had relationships with Egyptian playboy Dodi Al Fayed and the Pakistani doctor Hasnat Khan. According to Shome (2003: 326), these are examples of the "white female body constituting an excess, spilling out beyond the racialized boundaries of the nation, threatening to contaminate its essence, in ways for which there was no room in the imagined community of the nation, especially in the body of the future Royal Mother." This language of excess as transgression immediately captures the normative understanding of white femininity as one of containment and prescribed acceptable limits.

Sandra Harding (2008: 110) establishes that gender is fundamentally relational. This is central to understanding the way in which the meaning of white femininity arises through its "constructed relationality with white patriarchy" (Shome, 2001:

328). This shaped how Diana was framed, notably after her death when there was an "explosion of media and mass cultural narratives" (Shome, 2001: 324) representing her. Such a process of re-presentation is the construction of national memory and a clear national subject on whom the "masses can lodge their desires and affects" (Shome, 2001: 325). At a time when the borders of race, gender and nation are more openly contested and changing overall, and England was marked with an identity crisis due to the tarnishing of the monarchy, the handover of Britain's last colony and Scottish home rule, the re-membering of Diana became the "public screen onto which this crisis of identity was projected, and through which it was negotiated" (Shome, 2001: 326).

Shome (2001: 329) identifies three "visual narratives of domesticity: marriage, motherhood, and Diana's transcendence in her death" that were inscribed into national memory through her memorialization – returning her to the "fixed and familiar locations of white femininity" (Shome, 2001: 326). If white female bodies function as sites of the "symbolic reproduction of national patriarchy" (Shome, 2001: 324), there was nothing so powerful in the symbolic dimension of gender (Harding, 2008: 112) as the images of Diana that were re-inscribed during the outpouring of grief that followed her death. The "techniques of juxtaposition, replay, and repetition" (Shome, 2001: 330) displayed her as the bride who entered the cathedral on her father's arm to have her hand given to her prince, and then her coffin which was carried into the abbey by foot-soldiers, followed by the tragic figures of her (ex)-husband and sons (Shome, 2001: 329). She is once again, reassuringly, surrounded and contained by white men.

The centrality of the nation in this process of historical production does not limit its effects to the United Kingdom. It occurs on the landscape of globalization, understood to be a "complicated process in which the global and the local are mediated by each other" (Davids and Van Driel, 2005: 4). In the

19

1995 interview, Diana (cited in Shome, 2001: 337) stated that "When I go abroad, I have 60-70 photographers traveling with me. So let's use it [the media] in a productive way to help this country." This allows Shome (2001: 336-337) to conclude that there is a relationship between white femininity, the nation, the media and internationalism. As Diana travelled as an ambassador for England, she expanded the borders of the nation and as people encountered England through her caring and empathetic persona it altered the way in which England was perceived and defined. Kathy Deliovsky (2008: 49) states that white women are constructed by white patriarchy as the "benchmark woman" who simultaneously occupies a particular position of privilege in society while functioning as nothing but a site for white patriarchal society's reproduction of itself.

There is also a geographical location of that hegemony - the Global North. As already suggested, its reach is global both through local access to Northern media and local media's representation as the "global is always articulated with and situated by the local" (Davids and Van Driel, 2005: 11). Just as the global and local intersect, there is also a dialectical process between people's agency and life experiences and the way in which they respond to the prescriptions of social structures and the symbolic order (Davids and Van Driel, 2005: 7).The hegemony of white patriarchy and the identity crises within the Western world inform the way in which Kate, as part of the reification of reassuring gender, race and class boundaries, is currently acclaimed. Simultaneously, there are particular reasons that Kate appeals to me – a life-long love of fashion, an interest in the British royal family inherited from my grandmother, and a desire for stability and a happy family that is fed by my history of depression and years of unhappy family life.

When Barr (2014) states that Diana is a factor in understanding the contemporary global media subject that is Kate, she stumbles onto another truth –the construction of Kate is the continuation of the project of re-membering white femininity, and shoring up the anxieties of the Western modern world, that occurred when Diana died. This is supported by Jemima Repo and Riina Yrjölä (2015: 5) who state that Diana's legacy is a "necessary backdrop" to understanding how Kate's "emotional and behavioural attributes [are] a site for the transmission of white, neoliberal ideals of female self-care and self-governance." This is demonstrated on the *From Berkshire to Buckingham* blog in the same article regarding Kate's popularity, after asking the question of whether any person who came after Diana would have attained it or whether Kate is unique in some way. What Barr (2014) identifies as unique to Kate is that "She is a private woman who can be both publicly available and personally reserved." She contrasts this to Diana who, she says. "Failed at being a public princess. We knew her too well, she gave too much of herself to too many people, and she damaged the institution that initially had shone the spotlight on her" (Barr, 2014). This immediately demonstrates the same point I experienced –excess transgresses. As Barr (2014) concludes,

> We are fascinated by Diana and we are fascinated by Kate, but she presents a picture to which people aspire…Kate is a beautiful, emotionally healthy woman in a world of dysfunctional celebrities, and that stability that she brings, that simple and normal background – from her own happy family, to the new little royal family she is building with William – is her own 'particular brand of magic' drawing the masses. She is a personality that inspires emulation.

As someone who is fascinated by Kate, this neatly encapsulates how I feel about her, which only serves to demonstrate the success of the ideological "double movement" (McRobbie, 2007: 720) at work when "gender retrenchment is secured, paradoxically, through the wide dissemination of discourses of female freedom" and the violence of patriarchy "is not overcome but reorganized and resituated" (Brown, 1992: 23).This occurs as Kate is celebrated as the epitome of post-liberation femininity, beautiful, intelligent, caring and happy – a modern liberated woman who was able to make a mature, informed choice to marry William after ten years of dating and is able to successfully balance being a wife and mother while performing her royal duties. This discourse is used to simultaneously celebrate her as a standard worthy of aspiration *and* one which is reachable. Yet she is worthy of that celebration because she is successful at self-management – in Barr's (2014) language in a piece entitled *Should the real Kate show herself? She already has…,* "She is a lady [as] she shows people she cares, but we are not her confidantes," and "she doesn't let it all hang out."

Barr writes in response to an article which asks, "Will the real Duchess of Cambridge please stand up? While she reserves the right to have both a public and private persona, what complicates matters is the fact that so many young girls now see Kate as a role model" (Tominey, 2014). The massive crowds who turned out to see her and William on the royal tour of New Zealand and Australia were not aging royalists but a new generation of young girls wanting to be princesses. Camilla Tominey (2014) then reveals the same double movement – stating that Kate's "Unique Selling Proposition is her likeability…She has every reason to be a show-off and yet she isn't one; the perfect female role model in this self-obsessed celebrity era." This is definitely part of Kate's appeal for me and many Kate followers – after the same tour Miranda Devine (2014) wrote that Kate is a welcome relief after the "desperate self-loathing exhibitionism of most celebrity females." She continued that this is why Kate is "raising hackles among snarky feminists" who have been fooled into thinking that "dressing like a stripper and acting like a hooker equals emancipation" (Devine, 2014). She concludes that Kate is the "anti-slut, the antidote to everything wrong with Western culture. She has put class back into sexy, made modestly cool, and added cachet to marriage and motherhood" (Devine, 2014) and in the process become a role model to a generation of young women. Yet at the centre of this argument are two obfuscations – a generalisation and misunderstanding of feminism, and a failure to acknowledge that Kate the role model is functioning as a site for the normalisation of the ideological underpinnings of that same Western culture in the form of white bourgeois patriarchy.

Devine (2014) does not name her but some of the quotes from "snarky feminists" come from the feminist author Hilary Mantel (2013: 3) – calling Kate "painfully thin" and "a jointed doll on which certain rags are hung." However, Mantel's *Royal Bodies* is actually an attack on the way in which royal women – and women – are canonised by some in the media. She identifies how Kate seems perfect for the princess role because she is "irreproachable: as painfully thin as anyone could wish, without quirks, without oddities, without the risk of the emergence of character" (Mantel, 2013: 4) unlike Diana whose "human awkwardness and emotional incontinence" (Mantel, 2013: 4) was demonstrated with every gesture. This contrast of excess versus successful self-containment reveals itself again. Mantel (2014, 5) describes an encounter with Queen Elizabeth in which she could not but stare with "devouring curiosity" - when the Queen turned to look at her for a moment she looked hurt, like the "young woman she was, before monarchy froze her and made her a thing, a thing which only had meaning when it was exposed, a thing that existed only to be looked at."

There was outrage when Mantel published this piece to the extent that the British Prime Minister publicly commented that she was "completely wrong" (British Broadcasting Corporation, 2013). Yet the outrage ignored the fact that Mantel, as she states, was clearly describing the "perception of [Kate] which has been set up in the tabloid press" (BBC, 2013). Catherine Scott (2013) points out that it only confirms the obsession with the "visually appealing, uncontroversial Kate Middleton that no-one seems to have noticed that Mantel also describes the Queen as 'a thing that existed only to be looked at.'" The strong language with which Mantel describes her compulsion to stare at the Queen reveals the role of the gaze as an exercise of power. This is central to understanding the way in which royalty functions in the modern world, and the dangerous implications of Kate, who is the object of constant surveillance even as she is a subject produced by it, being a role model for young women as she is defined by the successful balance of self-containment. The narrowness of this cage and the complicated role of the public gaze is revealed when Barr (2014) states that while the "candid moments when they are interacting in 'private'" contribute to the massive popularity of Kate and William, were the "same situations knowingly played out for public consumption [they] would feel cheap and make them look like exhibitionists."

Michel Foucault (1975: 170) establishes that "the exercise of discipline presupposes a mechanism that coerces by means of observation." This question of surveillance is at the centre of news media which function as "technologies of power" (Foucault cited in Repo and Yrjölä, 2015: 3) and produce particular subjects by training individuals to self-regulate themselves. The instruments of disciplinary power that Foucault (1975: 170) identifies are "hierarchical observation, normalizing judgement...and the examination." In the modern world, the media is central to these mechanisms which establish what is normal – and perpetuate the modes of governance of post-feminism and neoliberalism. Such modes of governance function via a double movement - as they use the language of freedom to renew and reify systems of containment and entrenched power relations with regards to race, culture and gender. While Foucault, as stated by Sandra Bartky (cited in Deveaux, 1994: 225), does not account for the reality that disciplinary power produces a "modality of embodiment that is peculiarly feminine," his analysis of the "power of the Norm" (Foucault, 1975: 184) remains applicable even if he has not specified the norms experienced by women specifically. The Norm is disciplined into people via the double system of "gratification-punishment" (Foucault, 1975: 180), where non-conformity is punished and conformity is rewarded.

Repo and Yrjölä (2015: 2) analyse three major British newspapers, *The Daily Mail, The Daily Telegraph* and *The Guardian* with an intersectional lens that considers the way in which "the discourses of happiness surrounding contemporary middle-class princesses are constituted through and intersect with discourses of gender, class and race" from September 2010 to October 2012 that includes Kate's engagement and marriage to William. These clearly affect me in different ways both because of my location and my subjective identity. One of the South African magazines I have read since childhood *YOU*, features Kate or her children on the cover 33 times since her marriage to William. Princess Charlene of Monaco, who is a South African, has been featured on the cover 13 times in the same period (YOU, 2015). This is a single example that demonstrates the predominance of Kate in South African media. The global reach of reporting on Kate is also revealed in a post by Barr (2014) where she reveals that at the time of writing people from Ludhiana, India, Durban, South Africa; Clisson, France; and Virginia Beach were on the blog.

When I am following a royal engagement, I, like many others turn to the *Daily Mail* and *The Daily Telegraph* for the most rapid reporting. I am therefore influenced by the British media discourses that Repo and Yrjölä (2015: 2) identify in these newspapers regarding how "contemporary discourses of monarchy in the British press are tied to ideals of neoliberal active womanhood and its qualities" which also affect the global media subject of Kate that is reported in local press.

It is impossible to neatly disentangle the layers of causation and contestation that inform such global discourses. However, in order to avoid falling into the trap of rendering globalization as a "monolithic phenomenon, destructive and negative" (Davids and Van Driel, 2005: 8) and to deconstruct "hegemonic discourses on femininity and masculinity [while] leaving room for subjectivity and agency," Sandra Harding's understanding of the three intersecting dimensions of gender, identified as the symbolic, the practices of social institutions, and subjective identities, is useful in understanding how the symbolic production of Kate by two modes of governance affects young women's subjective identities.

Repo and Yrjölä (2015: 4) define post-feminism as a set of assumptions widely distributed in "popular media forms, having to do with the 'pastness' of feminism." The discourse of women as already liberated and the language of individual choice are used to reinforce "regressive forms of femininity" (Repo and Yrjölä, 2015: 4) such as Kate's body, weight and dress being the subject of "constant media surveillance," and the scripted roles available to her remaining bride, wife and mother. Angela McRobbie (cited in Repo and Yrjölä, 2015: 4) establishes that the post-feminist premise is that one's happiness and success as a woman is dependent on self-measurement and self-perfection, and to stray into excess, "to neglect to control one's body and mind is equated with a failure to control one's life and therefore a failure to embody modern, liberated womanhood." The celebration of Kate in much of the media as the modern woman is therefore an enactment of this double movement of post-feminism – reinforcing a definition of modern femininity as fundamentally contained.

Neoliberalism, like post-feminism, is a "mode of governing everyday life that 'produces subjects, forms of citizenship and behaviour, and a new organization of the social" (Brown cited in Repo and Yrjölä, 2015: 3). It is defined as the "extension of market values into everyday values and practices" (Repo and Yrjölä, 2015:

3) disciplining subjects to be their most "active, calculating, consuming and enterprising selves." It creates and confers freedoms in a manner that reifies class power such that "middle-class respectability is normalised and solidified as the standard to which to aspire" (Repo and Yrjölä, 2015: 3). According to Repo and Yrjölä (2015: 3) it is the convergence of these two rationalities that has made a discourse of middle-class monarchy possible, which functions as a mechanism to produce and regulate the possible identities of future citizens and the path to their happiness. The results of this are seen in Barr's (2014) statement that "she inspires emulation" - not only does Kate set a standard to which one would aspire, unlike Diana. Rather, Kate sets a standard to which one *can* aspire. The discourse created around her "simple and normal background" (Barr, 2014) means that the standard she sets is attainable. And yet Kate's background is anything but "simple and normal" (Barr, 2014). Her parents are self-made millionaires. She is naturally thin. Yet her 'commoner' status, 'middle-class' background and likeability allow for such proclamations as featured in the *Daily Mail* on Kate's marriage-; "We are all princesses now" (cited in Repo and Yrjölä, 2015: 2).

The British newspapers that Repo and Yrjölä (2015: 9) analyse depict Kate as a "middle-class neoliberal subject par excellence, whose skills, education, possessions and position were detached from class privilege and attributed instead to the hard work and commitment of her and her family." In line with Foucault's (1975: 180) reward-punishment, if one works hard enough, and self-manages enough, one will earn (white middle class) happiness. Kate is depicted as a modern woman who "rejected the extravagance of past royals and the excess of fashionistas for a respectable wardrobe that the average British woman could afford" (Repo and Yrjölä, 2015: 10). Just as Barr (2014) uses the discourse of Kate's self-containment in contrast to Diana's emotional excess, Repo and Yrjölä (2015: 8) identified a consensus in the three papers that

Kate's normality was conceived as restoring the public image of the British monarchy by compensating for the "affective imbalance left by Diana" who disrupted the white femininity script. This demonstrates how Kate is a mutually constituted subject by the modes of governance that are post-feminism and neoliberalism (Brown cited in Repo and Yrjölä, 2015: 3) both of which are centred on the double movement of the "celebration of freedoms of the self-managing individual" (Repo and Yrjölä, 2015: 3). Self-management is about training oneself to contain the excess which does not conform because the "domain of the non-conforming is punishable," (Foucault, 1975: 179) and earn happiness.

The role of surveillance in correcting excess and retaining the barriers of containment is revealed in the scandal in which the French magazine *Closer* published topless photographs of Kate while she was on tour with William (Repo and Yrjölä, 2015: 13). According to Repo and Yrjölä (2015: 13), this revealed the "disciplinary techniques that produce and maintain the careful discursive mix of emancipation, progress and respectability." It was possible to see the unhappiness of the couple because they were on tour as well as the release of a strongly worded press statement that stated that the incident "is reminiscent of the worst excesses of the press and paparazzi during the life of Diana," (cited in Repo and Yrjölä, 2015: 13) and a criminal case being filed. The happiness of the couple, which was touted as part of what Kate brought to the royal family via her 'normal' background, was compromised by Kate sunbathing topless, being an "irresponsible, overtly sexual, vulgar and even unthinking woman – the opposite of the respectable and self-controlling British female subject deserving of the pursuit of happiness" (Repo and Yrjölä, 2015: 14). This reveals the double movement at the centre of the celebration of Kate as the liberated woman – she is free to choose so long as her choices are modesty and marriage.

These processes of surveillance and discipline establish and perpetuate a model of self-management that in line with the three dimensions of gender narrows the symbolic structures that inform social structures which are experienced and contested by subjective individuals such as myself (Harding, 2008: 112). This is possible because celebrity figures are "intimately linked to everyday aspects of people's lives" (Shome, 2014: 23). Importantly, while there are hegemonic discourses in the media, it is not monolithic. *The Guardian* newspaper, in response to these photos, asked why these photos were any less invasive than the on-going speculation regarding whether she is pregnant. Rebecca Davis (2015) wrote a piece in the South African *Rand Daily Mail* about the "idiocy of the live TV" coverage of the birth of Kate's daughter, Charlotte – which was muted compared to the birth of George in 2013 when media vans set up outside days in advance and the BBC reported that the day of his birth was the "biggest global day and second biggest UK day ever for BBC News Online, with 19.4 million unique browsers globally and 10.8 million from the UK" (Philipson and Carter, 2013). Kate stepped out of St. Mary's Hospital in May, having given birth to Charlotte ten hours before. She looked the "picture of perfection" (Kozicka, 2015) – such that a Russian newspaper reported the conspiracy theory that the birth had been faked. The word that was deployed in the media was most commonly "perfect" (examiner.com; hollywoodlife.com; Us magazine; the *Mirror*). What is now known as the 'Kate effect' has been reported to have caused women to feel pressurized to meet this standard after labour (Diente, 2015). While getting a stylist into a hospital room is a single example of the 'Kate effect' that is economically available to very few, because of social media's accessibility, this does not stop other women encountering and being impacted by this standard of perfection – and the erasure of the corporeality of birth.

The narrowness of this self-containing white femininity, being propounded in the language of freedom, is revealed by the comparing of Kate and Princess Charlene in the same three British newspapers (Repo and Yrjölä, 2015: 7). Charlene is a South African born swimmer who married the Monaco monarch Prince Albert. Prior to her wedding which followed shortly after Kate's, she was rumoured to have attempted to flee Monaco and return to South Africa three times. This was contrasted to the *happiness* of Kate and William, the foundation of which was said to be her middle-class family. Charlene and Albert's wedding was seen as the latest example of the archaic and sexist traditions of arranged marriages long rejected by 'modern' Britain. She came to be represented as a "foreign repressed and domesticated femininity of the past far removed from the liberated consumerism of the British Kate, further consolidating the latter as an exemplary and empowered neoliberal and postfeminist subject" (Repo and Yrjölä, 2015: 7). This white, slender, blonde, coiffed and privileged princess is framed as an Other compared to Kate. This, better than anything else, reveals the danger of this neoliberal positioning of Kate as accessible – an ideal that can be emulated and attained. Charlene being unable to meet that standard demonstrates the impossibility of the standard of white femininity, functioning under the guise of possibility. As a universal standard in a racist world, it automatically and intentionally excludes people of colour. The totality of its dysfunctionality is however revealed by the fact that it cannot be attained, period. It excludes everyone to some extent encouraging a regime of self-surveillance and self-containment to attain female empowerment in the form of "conspicuous consumption and blissful monogamous domesticity" (Repo and Yrjölä, 2015: 13).

The media subject that is Kate is made possible by the two global modes of governance that are post-feminism and neoliberalism. Through this subject, the embodiment of contained white femininity and a model of self-discipline is exhibited and endorsed as the ideal to which young women should, and specifically via Kate, *can* aspire to be happy. The dissemination of this message, which reifies white femininity as defined by its relation to white patriarchy, via the media as a technology of power is particularly apt as its mechanism is both analogous for and constitutive of the gaze that women internalize. Even as Kate is celebrated as that most likeable and relatable of royals, the questions of what is being reinforced as normal – wealth, thinness, hetero-normative romantic love – and who 'deserves' happiness goes unasked. Better than anything else, the small space prescribed for this most privileged of women demonstrates and perpetuates the narrowness of white femininity and the impossibility of ever truly fitting within its constraints.

On Woman's Day this year, I was in the midst of writing this essay and feeling far away from home. Listening to the music of South African liberation struggle that I grew up with, and thinking about this year and my country's history, I was overwhelmed by the ideological underpinnings of the images on my walls. For the first time I did not see the images that had reassured me and papered over my excruciating awareness that I was not at home, images of a comfortable, secure and happy life. I saw the impossible confines of white femininity and the lie of its attainability - and tore them down.

Works Cited

Barr, J., 2014, *Should the real Kate show herself? She already has...*, http://fromberkshiretobuckingham.blogspot.co.za/2014/05/should-real-kate-show-herself-she.html, *Date of Access: 30 July 2015.*

Barr, J., 2014, *Why Is Kate such a Star? Diana's Legacy is a Factor*, http://fromberkshiretobuckingham.blogspot.co.za/2014/09/why-is-kate-such-star-dianas-legacy-is.html, *Date of Access: 30 July 2015.*

British Broadcasting Corporation, 2013, *Author Hilary Mantel defends Kate Middleton comments, 8 March,* http://www.bbc.com/news/entertainment-arts-21710158, *Date of Access: 03 October 2015.*

Brown, W., 1992, *Finding the Man in the State, Feminist Studies 18(1):7-34.*

Davids , T., and Van Driel, F, 2005, *Changing Perspectives, InT. Davids and F. Van Driel (Eds.), The Gender Question in Globalization: Changing Perspectives and Practices:93-21, London: Ashgate.*

Davis, R., 2015, 10 May, *Royal Baby coverage shows idiocy of live TV,* http://www.rdm.co.za/lifestyle/2015/05/10/royal-baby-coverage-shows-idiocy-of-live-tv, *Date of Access: 03 October 2015.*

Deveaux, M., 1994, *Feminism and Empowerment: A Critical Reading of Foucault, Feminist Studies 20(2):223-247.*

Devine, M., 2014, *26 April,* http://blogs.news.com.au/dailytelegraph/mirandadevine/index.php/dailyteleg raph/comments/kate_has_put_class_back_into_sexy/, *Date of Access: 03 October 2015.*

Diente, T., 2015, *Kate Middleton's glow, perfect tresses following Charlotte's birth pressures pregnant women 'to look perfect' after labour,* http://www.ibtimes.com.au/kate-middletons-glow-perfect-tresses-following-charlottes-birth-pressures-pregnant-women-look, *Date of Access: 19 August 2015.*

Foucault, M., 1975, *The means of correct training, Discipline and Punish:170-194,A.Sheridan (Trans.), Penguin Books: London.*

Gevisser, M., 2007, *The Dream Deferred, Johannesburg and Cape Town: Jonathan Ball Publishers.*

Harding, S., 2008, *What is Gender?,Sciences from Below. Feminisms, Postcolonialities and Modernities:110-114, Durham and London: Duke University Press.*

Kozicka, R., 2015, *How did Kate Middleton look so good after giving birth to Princess Charlotte?, 4 May 2015,* *http://globalnews.ca/news/1977604/how-did-kate-middleton-look-so-good-after-giving-birth-to-princess-charlotte/, Date of Access: 19 August 2015.*

Mantel, H., 2013, *Royal Bodies, London Review of Books 35(4):3-7.*

McRobbie, A., 2007, *Top Girls? Young Women and the Post-Feminist Sexual Contract, Cultural Studies 21(4-5):718-737.*

Philipson, A., and Carter, C., 2013, *Royal baby: as it happened, 24 July,* *http://www.telegraph.co.uk/news/uknews/kate-middleton/10155483/Kate-Middleton-birth-pregnancy-baby-live.html, Date of Access: 18 August 2015.*

Rayner, G., 2015, *Royal baby: How Kate Middleton looked so good leaving the Lindo Wing,* *http://www.telegraph.co.uk/news/uknews/kate-middleton/11580264/Royal-baby-How-Kate-Middleton-looked-so-good-leaving-the-Lindo-Wing.html, Date of Access: 19 August 2015.*

Repo, J. and Yrjölä, R., 2015, *'We're all princesses now': Sex, class, and neoliberal governmentality in the rise of the middle-class monarchy, European Journal of Cultural Studies:1-20.*

Scott, C., 2013, *Hilary Mantel wasn't attacking the Duchess of Cambridge,* *19 February,* http://www.telegraph.co.uk/culture/books/booknews/9879875/Hilary-Mantel-wasnt-attacking-the-Duchess-of-Cambridge.html, *Date of Access: 03* *October 2015.*

Shome, R., 2001, *White Femininity and the Discourse of the Nation:* *Re/membering Princess Diana, Feminist Media Studies 1(3):323-342.*

Shome, R., 2014, *Diana and Beyond: White Femininity, National Identity* *and Contemporary Media Culture, University of Illinois Press: Urbana,* *Chicago and Springfield.*

YOU, 2015, *YOU South Africa,* https://za.zinio.com/www/browse/back-issues.jsp?productId=500604906&offerId=500358059&subscription=true #/backissue, *Date of Access: 28 August 2015.*

Bibliography

Harris, N., 2011, *"Revealed: Royal Wedding TV Audience closer to 300m* *than 2bn (because sport, not royalty, reigns),"* *9 May 2011,* http://www.sportingintelligence.com/2011/05/08/revealed-royal-wedding%E2%80%99s-real-tv-audience-closer-to-300m-than-2bn-because-sport-not-royalty-reigns-080501/, *Date of Access: 18 August 2015.*

Indo-Asian News Service, 2015, *"Kate Middleton gets diving* *certification,"* www.india.com/showbiz/kate-middleton-gets-diving-certification-488036, *Date of Access: 18 August 2015.*

Weaving, D., 2015, *Facebook meme upload,* https://www.facebook.com/photo.php?fbid=10153532500254445&set=a. 10150289584654445.352630.752104444&type=1&mref=message_b ubble, *Date of Access: 19 August 2015.*

Williams, C., 2011, *"Royal wedding breaks online streaming records," 29 April 2011, http://www.telegraph.co.uk/news/uknews/royal-wedding/8483524/Royal-wedding-breaks-online-streaming-records.html,* Date *of Access: 18 August 2015.*

EDUCATION AND VOCATIONAL REHABILITATIVE ASPIRATIONS OF STREET BEGGARS IN BAUCHI STATE, NIGERIA

Amali, I.O.O (PhD), Saleh S, and *Amali S.E.*

Abstract

The presence of street beggars in many urban places has attracted public concern that requires urgent redress as the activities of the beggars appeared to have become a social ill that affects the environment, economic and civil life of Nigerian people. This study therefore explores the education and vocational rehabilitative aspirations of street beggars in Bauchi State, Nigeria. Descriptive survey design method was used in this study. The population for this study covered all street beggars in Bauchi State, Nigeria. A total number of four hundred (400) street beggars were sampled from most of the strategic places where beggars were present, using cluster sampling technique. Researchers' structured interview with a reliability coefficient 0.74 which was used for data collection. Data collected were analysed using frequency, percentage and bar-chart to answer the research questions raised in this study. Findings obtained from this study revealed that all categories of persons who engaged in street begging in Bauchi State had aspirations for education and vocational rehabilitations. This study concluded that people do not deliberately engage themselves in street begging but engaged in begging because they lacked support and opportunities to attain their aspirations. Therefore, if government and well-meaning individuals and organisations could come up with a kind of intervention programme which will go a long way in meeting the educational and vocational aspirations of these beggars, they could disengage themselves from this informal economic activity (begging).

Keywords: *Aspiration, Education, Vocation, Rehabilitation, Street Begging.*

Introduction

Begging for alms as an informal economic activity is not a new thing, but an ancient practice. As a practice, it is a means for survival by those who feel they cannot sustain themselves or their family due to age, bad health or poor economic condition. Begging involves a request directed to general public or individual in the society seeking for assistance or help. Gloria and Samuel (2012) reported that people who beg do so in order to solve their problems. Street beggars are people with physio and socio-economic challenges who approach other people on the street to ask for alms in the form of food or money (Bose & Hwang, 2002; Collins & Blomley, 2003).

Street begging is one of the age-long activities and perhaps occupations of the highly vulnerable, poverty-ridden individuals in the society. Street begging is seen as an act to simply ask people for money, food, clothes, favour or charity without an exchange of services in a public place (Tambawal, 2010). The presence of street beggars in many public places of urban areas of Nigeria has attracted public concern that requires urgent redress in most cities. In Nigeria, street begging has become a social ill that affects the environment, economic and social life of Nigerian people (Ogunkan & Fawole, 2009). Street begging is not peculiar to Nigeria; it is a global or universal phenomenon (Jellili, 2013). While a considerable number of cities are identified in Nigeria as having a significant number of street begging activities, cities in Northern Nigeria have been described as homes of different categories of beggars that include the abled poor, the disabled, the homeless and the praise singers (Smith, 2005).

Adedibu and Jelili (2011) classified street beggars into a number of categories which include the disguised beggars, the apparently disabled beggars e.g. lepers, blinds, crippled, etc, cultural beggars (which includes multiple child bearing begging mothers and praise singers) the young and the elderly usually refered to as the Almajiris in the Northern part of Nigeria. These beggars go about with unkempt hair, blistered lips, dirty fingers, bare footed, torn clothes, congregated into small groups, chanting or singing some line in order to win the heart of those that give them alms. These categories of beggars are mostly found at motor-parks, places of worship, markets, road junctions, and venues of ceremonies and in other public places soliciting for alms (Ojo, 2005).

Street begging is common in the Northern part of Nigeria particularly in Kaduna, Zaria, Maiduguri, Bauchi, Sokoto and the other major cities. The begging syndrome is not only restricted to the young school boys (Almajiris) going around in the evenings to get a plate of food for a meal but has included the adult destitute found in the major towns and cities across the country (Gloria & Samuel, 2012). Teenage beggars or Almajiris are very common in Kano state in spite of the efforts of Kano state government to check begging on the street. These teenage beggars attend school in the morning and take to the streets in the afternoon and evening for begging (The Guardian, 8, February, 2015).

The phenomenon of begging is as a result of a number of factors, such as: poverty, inadequate access to housing, poor income, weak health support services, religious belief, physical disability, cultural expectation, national disaster, civil war, bad habits due to drug, alcoholism, gambling dependencies, uncontrolled rural to urban migration, and psychiatric disabilities and disorders, etc (Kennedy & Fitzpatrick, 2001; Ogunkan & Fawole, 2009: Demewozu, 2005: Carter, 2007).Thus, in the absence of any viable means of livelihood, poor people who are unable to satisfy many of their basic needs due to poverty would take to begging to meet the needs for their living (Namwata and Mgabo, 2014).

Street begging according to Namwata, Mgabo & Dimiso (2010) is a social ill whose implications for city, economy and environment call for concern. This is obvious with the tendency of beggars to delay and obstruct free flow human and vehicular traffic and their high propensity to generate dirty environment due to materials waste or refuse disposal. It is also believed that street begging could be risky to life especially in areas where there is heavy traffic. Street beggars also expose themselves to harsh weather condition and unhealthy environment which create for them unhealthy conditions. According to Mortimer (2015), the danger of street begging includes sexual harassment of female beggars by the prospective male benefactor, exposure to harsh weather condition, vulnerability to human trafficking and exposure to road accidents. Anthony (2007) observed that most of the people who engage in street begging lacked formal education and training in various trades (vocational skills).

Education is widely recognised as a means of eradicating illiteracy, developing human capacity and human capital to improve economic potential and to enhance people's capabilities and choices. The policy of Federal Government of Nigeria, according to Jelili, (2013) saw education as an instrument for national development and social change in order to meet the needs of the citizenry. It is a key factor for liberating and engaging people to live a meaningful and self-sustaining life (Anthony & Idemudia, 2015). Educational aspiration has been defined as the need or desire to have intellectual knowledge_ the feeling of being able to read, write and do some simple and complex calculation in a formal setting (Abubakar 2010; Abubakar and Ahmed, 2012). Vocational Rehabilitation on the other hand is seen as a measure designed to help someone to live a healthy, useful or active life and making him or her to become a participatory member to the social and economic development of his or her society. It is an attempt service provided to vulnerable individuals in order to restore them to the fullest physical, mental, psychological, social, vocational and economic usefulness for which they are capable (Asokhia & Osumah 2013).

A number of vocational rehabilitation programmes have been put in place in Nigerian states like Lagos, Edo, Kaduna, Bauchi, Enugu etc. to curb poverty and street begging. According to the editor (The Guardian, 18, February, 2015), beggars are taken to rehabilitation homes not to take care of them but just to get rid of them from the street. Also the existing rehabilitation homes are a mockery and not fit for human habitation because they lacked basic facilities needed for human habitation. Abubakar (2010) explained that the former Federal Capital Territory (FCT) Minister, Malam Nasiru El-Rufai opened a vocational rehabilitation centre in Kuchiko, Bwari on the outskirt of Abuja. This centre was established to train the destitute such as beggars, physically challenged persons and the mentally disabled who invaded the Federal Capital City, Abuja in search of greener pasture for survival. The scheme succeeded in providing skills in various trades such as tailoring, shoemaking, leather making, bead making, computer appreciation and metal works to a significant number of disadvantaged individuals.

Bauchi State is noted to have a very high number of street beggars. The reason for this as observed by Balogun (2015) is because many of them are reported to migrate from neighbouring states such as Borno State, Yobe state, Kano state and other places due to insecurity and the conditions created by Boko-Haram insurgency. Legislations made in the neighbouring states has significantly influenced their influx to Bauchi State. Thus, Bauchi State appeared to be like a mere dumping ground or safe haven for every beggar (Abubakar and Ahmed, 2012). It is on the basis of this background that Bauchi State was chosen as crucial to this study.

Statement of the Problem

Some State Governments in Nigeria have enacted legislations to curb socio-environmental and economic challenges caused by street begging and aimed at keeping them from the streets yet the beggars tend to re-surface when the enforcement of the policy is relaxed a bit. Also, despite the setting up of rehabilitation centres in some states to take care of and keep beggars off the streets, reports still show increasing rate of people getting involved in begging activities in the Nigerian major urban streets. Also it appears that in Bauchi State there have not been serious commitments on the part of government to address the challenges of street begging officially. It thus becomes necessary to examine the educational and rehabilitative aspiration of street beggars in Bauchi State.

Purpose of the Study

The purpose of this study was to explore the education and vocational rehabilitative aspirations of street beggars in Bauchi State. Specifically, this study examined

1. Educational rehabilitative aspiration of street beggars in Bauchi State
2. Vocational rehabilitative aspirations of street beggars in Bauchi State

Research Questions

The following questions were raised to guide this study:

1. What are the educational aspirations of street beggars in Bauchi State?
2. What are the vocational rehabilitative aspirations of street beggars in Bauchi State?

Methodology

Descriptive survey design method was used in this study. The population for this study covered all street beggars in Bauchi State, Nigeria. However the target population consists of all beggars in

Bauchi South Senatorial District, Bauchi State, Nigeria. There are seven (7) Local Government Areas in Bauchi South Senatorial District and these are Alkaleri, Bauchi, Bogoro, Dass, Kirfi, Tafawa Balewa and Toro Local Government Areas. A total number of four hundred (400) street beggars were sampled from most of the strategic places where beggars were found to be present, using cluster sampling technique. Researchers' structured interview was used to collect data for this study. The interview was designated into Section A and B. Section A was used to obtain demographic data of the respondents and Section B part contained 20 items to obtain data on education and vocational rehabilitative aspirations of street beggars. Data collected were analysed using frequency, percentage and bar-chart were used to answer the research questions raised in this study

Data Analysis and Results

Out of 400 street beggars that were sampled for this study, 252(63%) of the respondents were male and 148 (37%) were female. Also, 92(23%) of the respondents were blind; 75(19%), were crippled; 41(10%) were lepers; 27(7%) were deaf/dump and 165(41%) were Almajiri/able-bodied.

Answers to Research Questions

Question One: *What are the educational aspirations of street beggars in Bauchi State, Nigeria?*

Table 1: Frequency and Percentage of Street Beggars with Respect to their Educational Aspirations in Bauchi State, Nigeria

S/n	items	Blind	Crip ple	Lepp ers	deaf / dum p	Almagiri / Able- bodied	Total %
A	**Western education**						
1	Primary education	(1%)	(7%)	(0%)	(0%)	(9%)	(17%)
2	Sec education	(2%)	2%)	(0%)	1%)	(4%)	(9%)
3	Tertiary education	(0%)	0%)	(0%)	0%)	(0%)	(0%)
4	Adult education	(3%)	1%)	(3%)	(5%)	(2%)	(14%)
B	**Islamic education**						
5	Ibtidaiyyah	(2%)	1%)	(0%)	1%)	(0%)	.7(4%)
6	Iddadiyyah	(3%)	(3%)	(4%)	0%)	(12%)	(22%)
7	Thannawiyyah	(6%)	(2%)	3(3%)	0%)	(5%)	(16%)
8	Madarasatul a'ala	(3%)	(1%)	(0%)	0%)	(3%)	9(7%)
C	Both Western and Islamic education	(3%)	3(2%)	(0%)	0%)	(6%)	(11%)
	Total %	(23%)	(19%)	(10%)	(7%)	5(41%)	0(100%)

Table 1 shows that out of 92(23%) blinds sampled for this study, 5(1%) aspired for Western primary education; 7(2%) aspired for Western secondary education; none (0%) aspired for Western tertiary education and 11(3%) aspired for Western adult education. Also, 9(2%) of the blinds aspired to attend Islamic Ibtidaiyyah (lower-basic schools); 13(3%) aspired to attend Islamic Iddadiyyah (upper-basic schools); 23(6%) aspired to go to Islamic Thannawiyyah (senior schools) and 13(3%) aspired for Islamic Madarasatul a'ala (Higher institutions) while 11(3%) of the blinds aspired for both Western and Islamic education.

Also, out of 75(19%) crippled sampled for this study, 27(7%) aspired for Western primary education; 9(2%) aspired for Western secondary education; none (0%) aspired for Western tertiary education and 5(1%) aspired for Western adult education. Also, 4(1%) of the crippled aspired to attend Islamic Ibtidaiyyah (lower-basic schools); 10(3%) aspired to attend Islamic Iddadiyyah (upper-basic schools); 7(2%) aspired to go to Islamic Thannawiyyah (senior schools) and 5(1%) aspired for Islamic Madarasatul a'ala (Higher institutions) while 8(2%) of the crippled aspired for both Western and Islamic education.

In addition, out of 41(10%) lepers sampled for this study, none 0(0%) aspired for Western primary, secondary and tertiary education while 11(3%) aspired for Western adult education. Also, none (0%) of the lepers aspired to attend Islamic Ibtidaiyyah (lower-basic schools); 17(4%) aspired to attend Islamic Iddadiyyah (upper-basic schools) and 13(3%) aspired to go to Islamic Thannawiyyah (senior schools) while none (0%) aspired to attend Islamic Madarasatul a'ala (Higher institutions). In addition, no (0%) leper aspired for both Western and Islamic education.

Further, out of 27 deaf/dump sampled for this study, none (0%) aspired for Western primary and tertiary education while 4(1%) and 19(5%) aspired for Western secondary education and adult education respectively while the remaining 4(1%) aspired to attend Islamic Ibtidaiyyah (lower-basic schools). No deaf/dump aspired to attend Islamic Iddadiyyah (upper-basic schools), Thannawiyyah (senior schools) and Madarasatul a'ala (Higher institutions) Also, none of deaf/dump aspired for both Western and Islamic education.

Moreover, out of 165(41%) Almagiri/able-bodied sampled for this study, 36(9%) aspired for Western primary education; 17(4%) aspired for Western secondary education; none 0(0%) aspired for Western tertiary education and 9(2%) aspired for Western adult education. Also, 0(0%) of the Almagiri/able-bodied aspired to attend Islamic Ibtidaiyyah (lower-basic schools); 48(12%) aspired to attend Islamic Iddadiyyah (upper-basic schools); 21(5%) aspired to go to Islamic Thannawiyyah (senior schools) and 11(3%) aspired for Islamic Madarasatul a'ala (Higher institutions) while 23(6%) of the Almagiri/able-bodied aspired for both Western and Islamic education. From table 1, it could be observed that no beggar aspired for Western tertiary education.

Figure 1 presents the summary statistics of educational aspirations of street beggars in Bauchi State, Nigeria.

Figure 1: Educational Aspirations of Street Beggars in Bauchi State, Nigeria

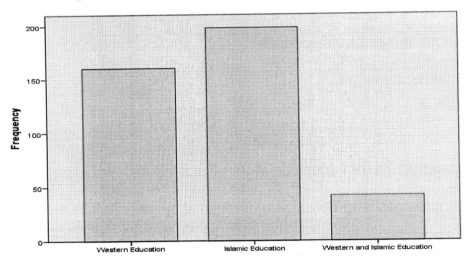

Source: Researcher's Field Work (2016)

As shown in figure 1, it is observed that out of 400 street beggars sampled, 198(49.5%) of the respondents aspired for Islamic education and 160(40%) aspired for Western education while 42(10.5%) of the respondents aspired for both Western and

Islamic education. This shows that majority of the street beggars aspired for Islamic type of education in Bauchi State, Nigeria.

Research Question Two: *What are the vocational rehabilitative aspirations of street beggars in Bauchi State, Nigeria?*

Table 2: Frequency and Percentage of Street Beggars with Respect to their Aspirations for Vocational Rehabilitation in Bauchi State, Nigeria

s/n	items	Blind	Cripple	Leppers	Deaf/dump	Almagiri /Able-bodied	Total %
1	Training in shoemaking	(0%)	(5%)	(0%)	(2%)	(6%)	(13%)
2	Training in welding	(0%)	(1%)	(0%)	(1%)	(3%)	(4%)
3	Training in Tailoring	0%)	(4%)	(0%)	(1%)	(5%)	(10%)
4	Training in plumbing	(0%)	(0%)	(0%)	(0%)	(2%)	(2%)
5	Training in Electrical-work	(0%)	(0%)	(0%)	(0%)	(1%)	(1%)
6	Training in Furniture-Carpentry	(0%)	(0%)	(0%)	(0%)	(3%)	(3%)
7	Training in weaving and bead making	(6%)	(2%)	(0%)	(0%)	(0%)	(8%)
8	Training in Agriculture	(0%)	(0%)	(0%)	(0%)	(6%)	(6%)
9	Training in Painting and Decorating	(0%)	(0%)	(0%)	(0%)	(0%)	(0%)
10	Training in blacksmithing	(0%)	(1%)	(0%)	(1%)	(2%)	(4%)
11	Training in Hairdressing and barbing	(0%)	(2%	(0%)	(2%)	(5%)	(10%)

12	Trading	(0%)	(2%)	(0%)	(0%)	(8%)	(10%)
	No aspiration	(17%)	(2%)	(10%)	(0%)	(0%)	7(29%)
	Total %	(23%)	(19%)	(10%)	(7%)	(41%)	(100%)

Table 2 shows that apart from the blinds with very few aspiring for just a vocation, other categories of beggars such as crippled, lepers, deaf/dump and Amagiri/able-bodied sampled aspired for one vocation or the other in Bauchi State. As revealed in table 2, 50(13%) of the respondents aspired for training in shoe-making; 17(4%) aspired for training in welding; 42(10) aspired for training in tailoring; 8(2%) aspired for training in plumbing; 5(1%) aspired for training in electrical work; 13(3%) aspired for training in carpentry/furniture; 32(6) aspired for training in weaving/bead-making; 23(6%) aspired for training in agriculture; none (0%) aspired for training in painting and decoration; 15(4%) aspired for training in blacksmithing; 38(10%) aspired for training in hair dressing/barbing and 40(10%) aspired for trading. This shows that vocation in shoe-making among others has the larger number of aspirants.

Figure 2 presents the summary statistics of vocational rehabilitative aspirations of street beggars in Bauchi State, Nigeria.

Figure 2: Vocational Rehabilitative Aspirations of Street Beggars in Bauchi State, Nigeria

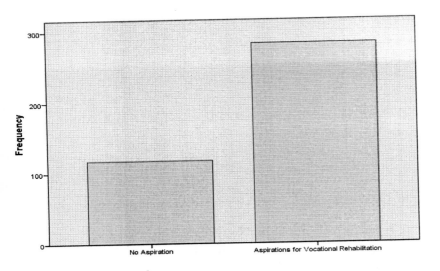

Source: Researcher's Field Work (2016)

Figure 2 shows that 117(29%) of the respondents had no aspiration for vocational rehabilitation while 283(71%) aspired for vocational rehabilitation. This implies that majority of the street beggars aspired for vocational rehabilitation in Bauchi State, Nigeria.

Discussion

Findings from this study revealed that all categories of persons who engaged in street begging in Bauchi State had aspirations for education. This finding corroborates the saying of some of the respondents that "we can leave begging and attend adult schools provided government and well-meaning individuals could cater for our basic needs". Some even asserted that "we were drop out, we wanted to pursue any of the educational opportunities around us but we lack support and encouragement from our parents, community and even government. If we can get financial support, we will certainly go back to secondary school or High Islamic school (thanawiyya)". This corroborates Adedibu and Jelili (2011) who stated that people who engage in street begging lacked assistance from families (either because of families' economic difficulties and disharmony) and financial support to attend school. However, none of the lepers sampled for this study aspired for Western primary, secondary and tertiary education as they asserted that "our physical condition would not permit us to attend any school". Also, it could be observed from table 1 that no beggar aspired for Western tertiary education.

Findings from this study revealed that majority of the street beggars aspired for vocational rehabilitation in Bauchi State, Nigeria. This outcome is in line with Yusuf, Bello, Ahmed, Ogungbede, Omotosho, AlHassan and Mustapha (2012) whose findings indicated that majority of street beggars in Ilorin Metropolis had high vocational aspirations. Also, Anthony and Idemudia (2015) revealed that most beggars had shown interest to have one vocational skill or the other. Namwata and Mgbo (2014) in a study conducted in Dodoma and Singida, Tanzania showed that majority of the beggars aspired for doing businesses. This implies that street beggars aspired for one vocation or the other in Bauchi State, Nigeria.

However, findings revealed significant number of the blinds had no aspiration as very few of them aspired for just one vocational training (i.e. training in bead-making/weaving) while other categories of beggars such as the crippled, lepers, deaf/dump, and Almagiri/able-bodied aspired for one vocation or the other in Bauchi State, Nigeria. This is not in agreement with study of Abubakar and Ahmed (2012) which showed that the only group of disadvantaged persons who did not participate in the skills acquisition was blind due to their physical condition. In contrary, CYDI (2008) revealed that blinds partook in skill acquisition programme.

Conclusions

Based on the finding from this study, it is therefore concluded that street beggars in Bauchi State aspire for education which is a fundamental human right and a tool through which they can be self-developed. It is also concluded that a significant number of people who engage in street begging in Bauchi State aspire to have one vocational skill or the other. However, those beggars who do not have aspiration for vocation were due to old age, nature of sickness and critical conditions.

The implication of this study is that people do not deliberately engage themselves in street begging as they also aspire to be educated and have some vocational skills to be self-reliant and to live better lives. Unfortunately, they lacked the supports and opportunities to attain these aspirations. Therefore, if government, organisations and well-meaning individuals could come up with a kind of intervention programme to assist them, this will go a long way in meeting the educational and vocational aspirations of these beggars as they could disengage themselves from this informal economic activity (begging).

Recommendations

Based on the findings obtained from this study, the following recommendaitons were drawn.

1. Government should make education available for street beggars and also establish vocational training centres in all the 20 local government areas of Bauchi state. This would provide opportunity for skill acquisition and entreprenuship for the street beggars.

2. Government should also ensure that provision of education to street beggars, especially the physically challenged among them. This would go a long way in meeting the Goals of Education

51

for All, as contained in the Millenium Development Goals (MDGs).

3. Non-Governmental Organisations in conjunction with government should offer scholarship to any street beggars who aspired to go to school at every tier.

4. There should be regular sensitization and awareness programme scheduled for street beggars on the importance of educaiton and skill acquisition, so that they become self-sustained and useful to themselves and the nation at large.

5. Government alongside cooporate bodies should complement the effort of Challenge Your Disablties Initiative (CYDI) in Bauch State through its vocational training, education and social intergration programmes geared towards empowering people living with disabilities and rehabilitation of street beggars in Bauchi State

References

Adedibu A. A.& Jelili M. O. (2011). *Package for Controlling Street Begging and Rehabilitating Beggars and the Physically Challenged in Nigeria: Paper for Policy Consideration. Global Categories of Street Beggars and Factors Influencing Street Begging. Journal of Human Social Science 11(1), 17–24.*

Abubakar U. & Ahmed A. (2012). *Poverty and Almajiri Issues in Northern Nigeria. Journal for International Institute for Policy reviewed and Development. 1(2), 69.*

Abubakar, U. (2010). *Factors Responsible for Almajiranci Phenomenon in Bauchi Metropolics. An unpublished BSC Project Bayero University Kano.*

Anthony T.(2007). *Almajiris Defy Governor Shekarau. Guardian Newspaper, Daily, Sunday July 29, 2007, P. 15.*

Anthony T.(2007). *Almajiris Defy Governor Shekarau. Guardian Newspaper, Daily, Sunday July 29, 2007, P. 15.*

Asokhia, M. O. and Osumah, O. A. (2013). *Assessment of Rehabilitation services in Nigeria prison in Edo State. American Journal of contemporary research. 3(1), 113 -121.*

Balogun, A. O. (2015) *Assessment of Intervention Programme for Meeting the Educational and Social Needs of Internally Displaced Persons in North-West, Nigeria. Unpublished Ph.d Thesis University of Ilorin.*

Bose, R. & Hwang, S.W. (2002). *Income and spending patterns among panhandlers. Canadian Medical Association Journal. 167(5), 477–479*

CYDI (2008). *Breaking All Barriers for Challenge your Disabilities Initiative: Improved Quality of Lives of Persons with Disabilities. Bauchi. Excellent Press Nig.*

Collins, D. & Blomley, N. (2003). *Private Needs and Public Space: Politics, Poverty and anti-panhandling by-laws in Canadian Cities. UBC Press.*

Carter T. (2007). *Panhandling in Winnipeg: Legislation Vs Support Services. A study for the Public Interest Law Centre, University of Winnipeg, 1-3*

Demewozu W. (2005). *Begging as a means of livelihood: conferring with the poor at the orthodox religious ceremonial days in Addis Ababa. African Study Monographs, Suppl. 29, 185-191.*

Gloria, O. & Samuel, A. (2012). *The prevalence of street begging in Nigeria and the counselling intervention strategies.Review of European studies-Vol. 4 (4), 24 – 30.*

Jelili, M. O. (2013). *Street begging in cities cultural political and socio-economic questions.Global Journal of human science sociology and culture.13(5) 142 - 153.*

Kennedy, C. & Fitzpatrick, S. (2001). *Begging, Rough Sleeping and Social Exclusion: Implications for Social Policy, Urban Studies* www.sagepublications.com

Mortimer, L. (2015). *Developing a strategy for street begging. Portsmouth: Community Safety Executive. Retrieved March 8, 2010 from* www.portsmonth.gov.uk/media/cs20051005m

Namwata B. M. L and Mgabo M. R. (2014). *Consequences of Begging and Future Aspirations of Beggars to Stop Begging Life in Central Tanzania. International Journal of Human Resources and Social Services 6(4), 61 - 69.*

Namwata, B.M.L., Mgabo, M.R., Dimoso, P.(2010). *Demographic dimensions and their implications on the incidence of street begging in urban areas of Central Tanzania: The case of Dodoma and Singida Municipalities. Global Journal of Human Social Science 11(4): 53–60.*

Ojo, Y. A. (2005). *Begging: 'A Lucrative, Booming Business' Nigerian Tribune, Tuesday, June 21 pp 15 – 16.1*

Ogunkan D.V.& Fawole O. A. (2009) *Incidence and Socio-Economic Dimensions of Begging in Nigerian Cities: The Case of Ogbomoso. International NGO Journal 4(12), 498-503*

Smith, P. (2005). *"The Economics of Anti-Begging Regulations". American Journal of Economics and Sociology, 64. (2), 549-561*

Tambawal, M. U. (2010). *The Effects of Street Begging on the National Development: Counselling Implications. A paper presented at the 1ˢᵗ National Conference of the Counselling Association of Nigeria (CASSON) Katsina State.*

The Gardian (2015 August 4). *The ugly spectacle of street begging.* Retrieved from <u>http://www.ngrguardian.com/2015/08/the</u> *ugly-spectacle-of street.*

Yusuf, A., Bello M. B., Ahmed S., Ogungbede, O. K., Omotosho, J. A. Al-Hassan, Y.S. &Mustapha, J. (2012). *Patterns of street begging, support services and vocational Aspiratory of people living with disabilities in Ilorin, Nigerian. Research on Humanities and social sciences. 2(5), 115 – 120.*

You have struck women! You have struck a rock! A South African Perspective on International Women's Day

Lynnda Wardle

On the 9th August 1956, 20,000 women marched to the Union Buildings in Pretoria—the official seat of the South African government, and symbol of white Afrikaner pride and political dominance. This demonstration was the biggest mass gathering of women ever seen in South Africa. It was organised to protest new legislation forcing black women carry a Pass—an identity document containing their personal and employment history. Pass Laws were designed by the apartheid state to control the movement of black people, and all men over the age of 16 had been required to carry a Pass since 1952. Failure to carry a Pass resulted in imprisonment. But in 1953, the apartheid government decided to include women in this legislation also, and there was a groundswell of resistance. Women knew that carrying a Pass would severely limit their ability to move around for work and make it impossible to look after their families if they were imprisoned.

When I was a small girl living in Pretoria in the 1970s, my father and I used to visit the Union Buildings on a Sunday. We'd walk up the green terraces and he would point out the statue of Louis Botha, the famous Afrikaans Boer General. 'A great General,' he would say, 'a true Afrikaner.' But the Boer War, to my seven-year-old self, was a faded black and white photo of men in ill-fitting suits and enormous beards next to women in long dresses and bonnets.

Having reached the first terrace, we surveyed the city below us. The sprinklers spritzed the bright flower beds. Of course, there were no black people up here, other than a few of the gardeners and cleaning staff. The higher we went, the less likely we were to see anyone other than people like us—white families—in their Sunday clothes, licking ice creams, playing hide and seek around the statues. In this memory, the space is empty of black faces, an omission that seems so obvious now, and yet on a shimmering summer's day in 1971 was not visible to me. The scene seems to belong to another world: white children, green grass, blond stone and the sun baking down on the folly. Certainly, these buildings were our civic church, a place that whites, especially Afrikaners like my father, were proud of. For him, the Union Buildings represented the triumph of their struggle for independence from Britain and colonial rule.

Four women: Lilian Ngoyi, Helen Joseph, Radima Moosa and Sophie de Bruyn, the organisers of the 1956 protest march, knew that this was a dangerous undertaking. As Sophie de Bruyn explained later in an interview, 'We entered the Holy Grail; it was like us being cheeky! We dared to enter their domain.'

They knew that this political gathering, like so many others in South Africa during the 1950s, could end in violence and bloodshed. However, all four women had years of experience working in the trade union movement and were veteran labour activists. Because black people were not allowed to gather publicly at this time, they put out a message through their networks that women attending the rally were to make their way to the Union Buildings in small groups, careful not to appear to be marching together. By late morning thousands of women had gathered, many dressed in the green and gold of the African National Congress or wrapped up against the cold in brightly coloured blankets, carrying on their backs their own babies or the white children they were looking after. Over and over they sang **Wathint'abafazi, wathint'imbokodo!** *You have struck women; you have struck a rock!*

The organisers stacked the petitions signed by thousands of women at Prime Minister Strijdom's door. He had not deigned to come out and meet them, and the rumour was that he was not even in the building. Lilian Ngoyi then led the women in half an hour of silence, symbolic of the silencing of women's voices for decades under white rule.

My father would have known about the women's march of 1956, but he never told me about it as we wandered up the same steps, climbed the same terraces, and sat in the same amphitheatre as the protestors would have sat. That was an event from another world which we did not incorporate into our own. It was the way that things were then— apartheid was made visible not only in the benches we sat on, or the areas where we could visit, or the parts of the city where we lived—it was also in the histories we called our own and shared with our children; both the stories and the silences. The campaign against Pass Laws for women continued for another seven years but increasing police intimidation, harassment and arrests eventually wore down resistance, and black women were finally forced to carry passes (nicknamed 'Dompas' or 'stupid pass') in 1960.

On the 9th August 1995, the first National Women's Day in South Africa was celebrated, a year after the Democratic elections. While South Africa has a democratic constitution and the rights of women are enshrined in this document, the reality is that life is still very difficult for the majority of South African women and girls today. Poverty, poorly paid domestic labour, low educational attainment, high unemployment, HIV Aids and domestic abuse are still issues that are not being properly addressed.

So the fight is not over. The need for women to be courageous and stand together in the face of poverty, sexual discrimination and oppression is greater than ever. The march in 1959 was one of unity and defiance in the face of injustice and has become a symbol for women who continue to fight for women's rights in South Africa today.

With them, on International Women's Day, we will continue to say: ***Wathint'abafazi, wathint'imbokodo!*** *You have struck women; you have struck a rock!*

Bibliography
An earlier version of this piece appeared as part of the *'Dangerous Women Project'* in 2016 for South Africa's National Women's Day *http://dangerouswomenproject.org/2016/09/11/south-african-national-womens-day/*

For more detail on this topic see
'Women in South Africa: *Walking Several Paces Behind (2010)* *http://www.economist.com/node/17204625 (Accessed 31/03/18)*

'History of Women's Struggle in South Africa' in South African History Online: *Towards a People's History* *http://www.sahistory.org.za/topic/1956-womens-march-pretoria-9-august(Accessed 31/03/18).*

'South Africa Celebrates the First National Women's Day' (1998) in South African History Online: *Towards a People's History* *http://www.sahistory.org.za/dated-event/south-africa-celebrates-first-national-womens-day(Accessed 31/03/18).*

History of the Union Buildings in South African History Online: *Towards a People's History* *http://www.sahistory.org.za/places/union-buildings (Accessed 31/03/18).*

Mulaudzi G., *South Africa: Celebrating South African National Women's Day Available at:*
http://allafrica.com/stories/201108091319.html(Accessed 31/03/18).

Randeree, Bilal. (2009) *'When you Strike a Woman you Strike a Rock' in* _http://thoughtleader.co.za/bilalranderee/2009/08/12/striking-rocks-women-fight-back/_ *(Accessed 31/03/18).*

Visual material for National Women's Day in South Africa at _http://www.saha.org.za/women/index.htm_ *(Accessed 31/03/18)*

International Defence & Aid Fund for Southern Africa: *You have Struck a Rock: Women and Political Repression in South Africa (1980)*

60

IT TAKES A VILLAGE
EDITH OSIRO ADHIAMBO

The curse of Babel is slowly lifting; many tongues have merged into one. Where we were once many and scattered, millennia have brought us together again. Are we back to Eden, Olorgesailie perhaps? Time will tell. For now, we are a global village. Borders have been traversed and seas sailed, history has taken its course. Now we stare at memories, legacies and graves. The global village is a reality that would make the visionary Kenyan chief Odera Akang'o tear up as Kenya takes her place in the global arena. Our neighbours know us for green tea, a trade seeded by colonialists at a bloody cost. The medal dais has honoured Kenyan athletes in a predictable fashion that many marvel at. Notably the sports events are held outside Kenya, including the United Kingdom as a host venue. As Kenya, Nigeria and other African countries battle terrorism and attempt to stabilize war-torn nations whilst addressing the refugee crisis, we can see the benefits of good neighbourliness.

A good neighbour looks out for the thief at his own door. A better neighbour looks out for both his and the neighbour's doors. You cannot argue with the wisdom of hospitable African ancestors who interacted with and welcomed Arabs, Asians and later Europeans. Moreso now as we are moving to a digital age that will probably see diverse interactions, uniformity in governance systems and a bigger population than previous historic ages. The dream of a free world clocking humanity's greatest potential is slowly becoming a dawning reality. Democracy appears to be the catapult to truly attain this, no wonder the fragile balance between peace and anarchy in every election.

Elections are an emotive affair, the world over. The campaigns, nomination, voting and tallying processes have been digitized to achieve optimality. Development partners under the African Union,

IrishAid, European Union, USAID and JICA have invested heavily to ensure strong civil societies, credible elections and a referendum. Yet even with all these advances, it is evident that the enemy within has tentacles stretched from without. In Kiswahili, a neighbor is cautioned to wet his head when he sees the barber working next door. The proverb could not be truer when one links the wave of globalism sweeping our planet. Coming closer to home, Kenyan elections ring competition at best and war drums at worst. The disastrous 2007 Kenyan post-election conflict left a country tittering on the brink of destruction.

2010 saw a Panel of Eminent Persons help Kenya reel back from the brink of civil war. The European Union, USAID and other development partners helped midwife the 2010 Kenyan Constitution as part of the rebuilding agenda. The Grand Coalition Government formed in 2009 was a model copied from Ireland's Belfast Agreement and has subsequently been mirrored in Zimbabwe, Iceland, Italy and Germany. The 2013 Kenyan election period was rocked by the fear of civil strife, International Criminal Court Trials and compromised government agencies. Kenyans were however congratulated for choosing peace and moving on despite deep suspicions of an impartial electoral process. Development projects continue to leverage on international partnerships such as IrishAid training specialist surgeons to be redeployed for public service in African hospitals.

The noisy arguments in the house can at times be quelled by a neighbour's knock on the door. It was the United Kingdom's Special Fraud Office (SFO) that broke the tense silence on Kenyan electoral fraud by unearthing the Chickengate scandal. SFO investigated Smith & Ouzman officials over codename "chicken" used to grease palms of Kenyan Government officials. The bribes were brokered by Kenyan officials and touched on sensitive contracts involving printing of ballot papers and school examination papers. So while the neighbours prosecuted their children for their misdemeanor, our Kenyan leaders back at home were more worried about how bad the legitimacy of their election was threatened. Needless to say, the Government agencies in charge of prosecution were the last to prosecute in a case involving their own affairs.

Corruption in Kenya is a serious menace, a national disaster that has crippled our growth and earned us a notorierity. Kenyans are obviously not the black sheep of the family, as Panama papers revealed. Yet it leaves a lot to be desired when mega scandals like Anglo-Leasing and Goldenberg are prosecuted abroad, with little or no co-operation from local agencies. The Kenyan public was accessing much needed truth and justice, the beautiful irony was that it was coming from United Kingdom's courts. As the dust on Chickengate settled, the British American Tobacco BAT, bribery and corporate espionage saga was unearthed. Cigargate as it was called was once more prosecuted in British courts. Foreign investors had previously demonized corruption as a necessary Kenyan problem with their involvement appearing to be sanitized. However the recent moves by UK Government agencies to freeze assets and pursue extradition charges have partly helped punish culprits that are deemed otherwise immune and powerful in their home countries.

International journalism, human rights activism, witness protection and asylum provision has protected democracy in countries where such efforts are stifled. Countless of journalists in the United Kingdom have put themselves in the line of danger to release exposes that have been shouldered by brave whistleblowers. Our conscience is becoming collectively pricked as we become our brothers' keepers. This collective responsibility is vital in a global economy that's masking the perpetrators who prey on countries with weak laws or wanton impunity so as to water down democracy to quasi-dictatorship.

We are now faced with psychological manipulation of the electorate through the data mining firms SCL and Cambridge Analytica. The network traces through White House, Brexit campaigns, Kenya and counting-from unfair campaign tactics, propaganda to foreign attack on sovereignty. The integrity of the vote in Kenya has been challenged twice, stalling the economic growth of the country. The foreign envoys and observer missions were challenged in Kenya for enabling an undemocratic atmosphere in Kenyan elections. "Accept and move on" was a mantra touted in the 2013 elections to avert reprisal protests of the election results. This move only delayed the protests that culminated in the removal of that electoral commission from office and death of sixty seven Kenyans after the elections of 2017. As the Kenyan Supreme Court made history by overruling the 2017 election of an incumbent president, the possibility of election tampering got a huge boost. Add the resignation of and infighting amongst electoral commissioners days to the election and the resurgence of ethnic violence by gangs; this was a recipe for disaster.

As the Cambridge Analytica scandal unfolds, we can only hope to learn key lessons on globalism. Whistleblowers and the British are helping people that might never meet, armed with a conscience and self-belief. The UK has also offered asylum to dissidents that flee their African homes to realize the true goal of independence. Some of these brave people have paid a price so high facing murder and deportation charges, for a country they need not call home. We are glad to have neighbours who form the village that raises healthy children. It has taken us an eternity to get here, talking with each other. More remains to be seen and done, in whatsoever fashion.

Transcription of a Conversation

Andrea Mbarushimana

A: So, I don't know what Post-Colonialism is really, I'm not an academic, but I wanted to ask you about the role that NGO's play in former colonies.

JP: To ensure permanence – the remote permanence of the colonisers.

A: Yeah, it's promoted under this kind of this International agenda, like Development Goals and stuff like that, but actually it comes down to those countries that those NGO's are based in and they're inevitably colonising countries, aren't they?

JP: Well, it's hard for me to speak about it and it could come across as hypocritical because I'm one of the many, many people who've benefitted from the actions of NGO's. I was an employee to start off with, for the International Red Cross, helping Burundian refugees. I can't deny that although my title was 'volunteer' I was paid a huge, well, relatively, a huge amount of money.

A: Relatively huge for a Rwandan.

JP: Yeah, at that time, compared to a civil servant for example. And then I became a refugee and in the camp, everything I knew was provided by different NGO's… I'll give you a quick overview of the camp. Healthcare was provided by International Red Cross and Red Crescent. Water was provided by Médecins Sans Frontières – the French one. Firewood was provided by GTZAid– a German agency – that's just firewood, nothing else…

A: Wow.

JP: Food distribution that was done by…World Food Programme? No, they did all the deliveries – but the distribution was done by someone else…I can't remember. There were at least ten NGOs. Some doing huge things, others doing small things. All in competition for responsibilities, for funding. Those services kept us alive for a long time. A huge number of people going through problems.

A: What numbers are we talking?

JP: Half a million in our camp? Half a million easily altogether.

A: There were other camps at that time?

JP: There were three camps, but there was only like, 100 metres between them. There were other camps in the North of Congo with thousands more. The one I was in was South Congo called Kashusha, but there were Adi Kivu and Inera and those were just metres apart, being run by different NGO's. Kashusha is where rich people ended up.

A: Really? Like...what?

JP: The way it happened – Inera was built on a mountain, on a hill. The plastic sheeting tents were on a hill. So if you fled with your vehicle there is no way you're gonna live there and if you fled with your vehicle then you are rich. Kashusha was on the flat. There were different people running the camps with different rules.

A: So how did the different rules in the different camps impact you as a refugee?

JP: If you knew somebody who lived in the other camps you went to see them, but most of them came to Kashusha because that's where the market was; it's where most of the business people who fled ended up. Also, a lorry would be driving up and down mountains bringing fresh water all the time.

A: It was brought by lorry? Wow. That must have felt really insecure. You must have felt as a refugee – you could see it, how reliant, how vulnerable you were.

JP: Exactly! We don't know where the firewood came from. Had the delivery stopped we would be doomed. Which actually happened in the end...Another thing that I noticed was that the presence of the representatives of different NGO's only happened in the day time. At night, they went back to the city. They drove off in their big 4x4's...

A: Oh yeah. I remember the dust they kicked up in my face in Rwanda. They never gave anyone a lift.

JP: It's against their rules. Lots of things happened in the night, people getting ill and stuff. We didn't have any vehicles or any way of contacting anybody.

A: Yeah, people give birth at night, for example.

JP: We had no way of contacting anybody. There were no mobile phones.

A: I'm sure they had their reasons, but it does leave you wondering whether the refugees are that important to them. It must create a real 'us and them' feeling…Did you come across that when you worked for the Red Cross?

JP: We had a Japanese American in charge. She was so clueless. She was the one coming in saying things in English, assuming that no-one could understand English, saying all sorts of things about us – telling her white colleagues we were selling off empty sacks from the food, instead of sending them back to HQ. It wasn't true! I did sell things that I wasn't supposed to…there are times we did distribution and there would be extra sacks left over. To send them back would maybe mean they gave us fewer than they were supposed to next time… to waste it would have been unthinkable. I sold maybe one or two for a beer or a favour, or sometimes gave them away if people needed more. I got told off for that.

A: She assumed you were criminals. Or less moral somehow. Whereas you were demonstrating different values, weren't you? Not a lack of values.

JP: Because you know that African people from birth are supposed to be corrupt. You get that idea from everyone in the West. David Cameron saying to the Queen that the Nigerian President was coming and that Nigeria was a state of corrupt people and the Arch-Bishop of Canterbury tried to fix the situation. There is that idea…

A: So basically, people bring their prejudices with them?

JP: Exactly, of course they do!

A: You can't expect people not to.

JP: But it's crazy. The boss in the field, what they're looking for is not that you're doing your work properly, but that you aren't selling things from right under their nose! I'll guard you from being corrupt rather than do my job, that's the attitude that they brought.

A: Going back to the Oxfam thing...People who work for NGO's in other countries have incredible power. They provide everything for you. They are the means of your survival when you are in that situation. So, you are bound to get people drawn to that position of power who want to abuse it.

JP: Of course. We were like religious people praying to God. I'm in difficulty, God will provide. There is that distance between the recipients and the providers.

A: The biggest power imbalance. Like a parent and an infant. You were in a position of huge vulnerability.

JP: Some of the Aid workers, at night they are in the city, drinking with city girls or prostitutes. There is still a power imbalance even though they aren't refugees. The girls know the guys have money. Why? Because they live in hotels. For a whole year. They are the bosses. I'm not saying that they were exploiting those girls.

A: But the situation is exploitative.

JP: (nods) In Congo, where there was a military contingent hired to protect the camps. Which was needed because the camps started to be run by Interahamwe militias. That official force, unfortunately...there was huge corruption. It was rife. They were supposed to get good salaries, but I'm horrified to tell you that every month, when they got paid, you would see refugee girls with them.

A: Of course, because those girls were starving. Because despite the fact you were getting food, it was never enough, was it?

JP: No. Those girls were feeding families and extended families. It's not this white man doing it, but UNHCR is supposed to keep an eye on them and they didn't, they went off to their hotels and didn't care. Black people are there. White people are in the City.

A: That was the difference that I felt profoundly as a white person in Rwanda, in the sticks, in a little town on the road with no other white people around. I was a focus for the huge amount of racism that everyone had suffered in that area. And it wasn't always anger. Some of it was...you know...being found attractive, being ushered to the front of a queue, being assumed to be an authority in all sorts of things when I'd done nothing to earn that respect...and I was shocked. I was deeply shocked by the amount of racism in Africa. I'd seen racism here in England, but I didn't expect to see it there. And again there was the money, the exchange rate... I got a normal teacher's salary and an additional salary.

JP: Hardship salary

A: Yeah. I used to buy teachers lots of beers and stuff. It was a source of embarrassment, but it was very useful when we got married!

JP: Of course!

A: There was just a huge gap between white people and black people and NGO's profoundly maintain that imbalance of power and intellectual...they maintain the fiction of Western superiority.

JP: Let me help you here. Because if you are not living with people you are in charge of. You are just seeing them in the day. You are wearing different clothes. You are not making any effort to learn that language. Of course they think you are...it's dehumanising. They pump in so many resources and withdraw without thinking, 'What's the long term impact of what we've just done'. They create dependencies, upset balances of distribution... What happens to people once they are not there?

A: And they did move on from the camp didn't they?

JP: When the war reached us, they didn't come and tell us. They just went saving themselves, leaving all those hundreds of thousands of people with no food or water or firewood and with

69

no idea of how to get any, being pincered between opposing
armies.

Fiction

One Man and His Axe

John Eppel

In the grounds of a derelict colonial hotel on the outskirts of Bulawayo, Comrade Ihloko ran his butchery. He used a baby scale to which he attached, with the aid of a large biltong hook, a sling seat redesigned to carry chunks of putrid meat. The queue, mainly grannies and diffident girls, with zinc buckets or enamel dishes to carry their purchases, was long and winding.

Comrade Ihloko worked alone. He had always worked alone. That's how his patrons had wanted it, demanded it: on his own, with a short-handled axe. That tool, over many years of service, had distorted his long, ropey body, tilted him sideways, left to right. His thick, grizzled beard and balding head reminded some of a Vapostori priest, but he had no interest in bizarre rituals, and no penchant for under-age girls.

Chunks of unidentifiable meat hung from a barbed-wire fence which enclosed Comrade Ihloko's garden. He fertilised his onions, tomatoes, and chomolia with bird droppings and compost made chiefly from amaranthus weeds, with their purplish coxcombs. They grew abundantly in the cracks and crevices of the brick and concrete ruins of the Torquay Inn.

His free-range poultry - chickens, turkeys, Muscovy ducks, guinea fowl, and peacocks - were plump and healthy thanks to the offal he removed from the carcasses after gutting and skinning them with a knife fashioned from an old hacksaw blade, its handle made of several layers of stretched and wound rubber tubing. He preserved the animal pelts with coarse salt and sold them to arts and crafts co-operatives where they were transformed into belts, headgear, and ornamental shields.

Comrade Ihloko was dressed in a ragged white shirt, untucked, with rolled down sleeves, and a pair of worn khaki trousers with one pocket flapping. His sandals, made from an old motor car tyre, were thick enough in the soles to withstand the stud thorns with their pretty yellow flowers that grew abundantly in desolate places.

In front of the queue was an ancient woman dressed in rags; they were all dressed in rags. He waited patiently for her to untie a few coins from a soiled handkerchief. 'Cela two bob nyama,' she croaked. He fetched a piece of meat from the fence, shook off the flies, flopped it on the scale, trimmed it down to 20 cents' worth, and exchanged it for the old woman's coins. This procedure went on for hours, until the queue had come to an end. He watched the last customer, a barefoot little girl about seven years old, struggle down the pathway with a load of buzzing meat in the dish she carried on her head.

It was late in the afternoon, and the butcher still had to replenish his stock. His source was quite a long way off, in the bush behind the premises of the SPCA. The animals had to be put down because their owners were leaving the country and because fewer and fewer remaining families could afford to keep pets. They were buried in shallow graves, and the earth and rubble above them was easy to excavate. He could leave his shambles unprotected since no one dared pilfer from a man whose name was whispered in the same strangled breath as names like Gayigusu, Gwesela, Thambolenyoka – so-called dissidents, so-called assassins, so-called contract workers. He gathered a large, woven plastic sack, and walked westward, away from the dwindling light.

Along the way he thought of his new assignment, strictly business, always strictly business. That's how the go-between put it. The instructions, he knew, always came from someone very high up in government circles. The pay was good, especially since it could not be taxed. It came in a brown envelope that Comrade Ihloko, once he had removed the contents, converted into cigarette papers.

At the point where the bush path joined the Khami Road he turned left and broadened his stride. There were no vehicles, no

73

cyclists, no pedestrians: signs of a depressed economy. He was about to return to a bush path when he felt a presence. The hairs on the back of his neck bristled. He stopped. Something behind him. He tightened his grip on the axe-handle, and turned. It was only the moon, beginning to rise through the silhouettes of stunted acacia trees. Briefly he stared back at it.

He reached the mass grave, retrieved the rusty shovel from a nearby ant bear hole and, bathed in moonlight, began to exhume: a golden Labrador, a Border collie, two Jack Russells, three mongrels, and a tortoise shell cat. There were too many for him to carry so he reburied the smaller animals, and stuffed the Labrador, the Border collie and one of the mongrels into his sack. The journey back would be hard work.

They wanted him to start as soon as possible. Time was running out. No longer can we abide the presence of these blue-eyed devils, these unrepentant imperialists, these white mischief-makers. No longer can we allow them to bear witness to the destruction of our country, our sovereign land, by the unlawful implementation of sanctions, the continued hegemony of racist minority capital, the ... er ... army worm. The last remaining settlers must go. Now.

The moon was high by the time he could finally relieve himself of his burden. He immediately set to work gutting and skinning the carcasses. The stench didn't seem to bother him beyond appetite control. It was an hour or so after the first cock crow that he rinsed his knife and his axe and set them aside to make preparations for sleep. His living quarters were underground, in the only remaining part of the Torquay Hotel that was more or less intact: the wine cellar.

Go for the innocents, they advised, the little children. Seek out the crèches, the pre-schools, the baby-groups. These are their last remaining sanctuaries. Strike there, once or twice will be enough, and they will leave in their droves, these... these boiled potatoes.

74

Comrade Ihloko reminded himself to sharpen his axe before the taxi ride to the suburbs of Bulawayo. He turned onto his side and fell into a deep, dreamless sleep.

Jo'burg

Valerie Southgate

When Mom told me about the lady and her boy moving into the Units, she said, "I hope to God they're not more blacks." I didn't care because whatever colour a new kid is, he's a chance for something better. Mom shouldn't have worried. Tim was white, white as the snow in the old Christmas cards from my dead English Granny.

I'd slipped a note under Tim's door the morning after he arrived, saying to visit if he liked because, even if our ringer's kaput, our front door's always open to let fresh air through. Strangers too, like the thief who took Mom's wedding ring, though I know she pawned it.

It was three days later when Tim came around. I was first to see him in the shadow of our kitchen door that opens onto our scrawny veranda that leads into our back yard. I saw him and I saw I'd made a mistake. The problem was the other kids visiting my place: Solomon and Thandi, the hotshots around here. Dear God almighty, I said in my head, don't let them see him.

Thandi and me were chilling on towels, catching the sun. Solomon was on the old trampoline pushed into the back corner of the yard, under the oak where the concrete's cracked up. That oak's the only glory in our grey, boxy place, but bounce too high on the trampoline and the branches whack your head. Two other guys were with Solomon, but they don't matter. They just follow orders, like me. The guys wobbled. Their beers fizzed. That trampoline, Dad's beer, and my famous legs are my only charms, but I knew they weren't enough to get me out of the trouble of a white boy stuck in my doorway.

Tim was studying the broken glass bits all over the veranda floor, like he was fascinated, like it was a puzzle with a big cash prize. I thought then that maybe he wasn't used to the business of

76

living somewhere like the Units. Anyone could be tricked by the name. Pinefields. Sounds plenty nice until you see there's no pine tree or field to be seen, only our places lined up along the driveway, like crappy beads on a necklace. Ten on each side, twenty overall. I'm in Unit One and Tim was in Two, putting us at the top or the bottom of the line, depending on your view. News was that he lived alone with his mom. No dad, not even one to mope around at home.

Thandi saw Tim when he stepped over the glass, into the sun. She stood and said kind of quiet, "Who does pink shorts? What fucker does that?"

She's not a fan of pink, or blue eyes or blond hair, not since she met mine. When Thandi laughed about the pink, I got up and laughed too. Tim's shorts were too short, and I could see the pinky-white stripe at the top of his leg. Tim smiled and I saw how sunlight in his eyes made him miss our meaning. Thandi asked me who'd asked him to visit, like she knew what I knew. I shrugged and said, "Hey, he just moved in next door."

"But how did he get in your house?" Thandi pinched me, to get my attention maybe, but more likely because she's my friend on the outside but not underneath. She hates me because I'm white, even though I'm covered with brown freckles like paint shook off someone's brush, a careless flick marking me different, like the lonely leopard who's almost extinct. I don't say anything because colour's not supposed to matter anymore, not since Mandela came along and made things right. I guess the problem is that he went off and died.

Anyway, Thandi had a point: Tim stood slap-bang in the middle of my veranda, where the steps lead down to the yard. Confusion was coming over his face, but I ignored his squinty eyes. I said, "Maybe my dad let him through. You know how he doesn't care."

When Thandi started in nippy to Tim, I stepped back, into the wall. "Ouch," I said when the raggedy bricks scraped me. Thandi didn't care. Or maybe she didn't hear. She rushed on and that made Tim step back quick. "Ouch," he said when the glass cut his foot. He stopped and hopped on one leg.

By then Solomon had woken up. "Watch out," he said, "It's a *tsotsi!*"

The other guys laughed because obviously a boy in pink shorts is no lay-about gangster.

Thandi was on Tim and she swung him around like a pit bull a cat. Her eyes on me had their regular sly look. After all my work being nice and stealing beer for Solomon, because he's underage sixteen, even after that, the question was still there. Do you belong? When Thandi called me over, it seemed her finger hooked me up and wound me in.

The guys screamed to pull down Tim's shorts. "Pull. Pull. Pull." Quick and regular as an AK-47.

Tim tried to get away, but Thandi had him strong. She's almost as big and fat as my mom, though she's only thirteen like me. Those two don't use their softness for goodness like giving hugs. They prefer to stamp on a person.

I knew Tim was done when Thandi said she hated white fairies. She kneed the back of his legs and put him off balance. His face was a fright under his scrappy, stand-up white hair. He looked young, tiny Tim, maybe eleven. Thandi twisted his arms behind his back. She said to shut up or she'd kill him. She was that hot for trouble, hot as the hottest Jo'burg day turning tarmac soft and tin huts into ovens. I suppose Tim believed her because he took to quiet crying in hiccups and burps, hot tears on his cheeks.

"Take his shorts," Thandi yelled, like I was her person to boss.

Then the guys came up and Solomon's friends grabbed Tim's ankles.

Solomon said, "My Wednesday Legs does it."

He looked over my legs, like I was the one, like there was no boy panicking. Wednesday Legs is my nickname, because my legs are so long and thin that the kids joke *wen's dey gonna break?* I thought they might break then, cracking like glass.

One girl, three guys, and their prey pulled flat as a plank. Tim was done with wriggling and kicking. His eyes were screwed shut, as if he'd given up, except for his snivelling. I knew the gang could do whatever they wanted all by themselves. I also knew that I had no choice. I took the top of the shorts in my hands. Tim screamed then, but I shut my heart against the wet gap of mouth. The rip put me off balance, but Solomon caught my arm. "Good girl," he said and quick-kissed me on the cheek. Then he yanked off the shorts.

I closed my eyes.

Maybe it was an ugly thing I did, but everyone needs friends. For once I was one of the ones left laughing behind. Solomon put his arm around me and called me an African babe. He asked me to go swimming later that evening. Pinefields is lucky that way, with a little pool at the back of the units, even if it's sometimes yuk with floating stuff, dead mice that get too close to the edge. The grown-ups say they must fill it in to save funds because the economy's rotten. Mom says we must keep it because the climate's shot and one day we'll be thirsting to death like Cape Town with no water.

Solomon's invite gave me a glow like a candle lit inside. Maybe he didn't finish school, but he's still king of the block. Even Thandi follows his orders. I said I'd go. That's when Thandi stepped on some broken glass fallen in the yard.

"Fuck!" she screamed. "You people are pigs."

"It's my dad's," I said. "I can explain."

She said to fuck off and that she was going home and that Solomon had better watch out mixing with poor whites. Solomon laughed and told his friends to clean up.

79

"Hell, no!" I said. I told how the glass came from the night before, from one minute after Mom, Dad and me were eating pizza from paper plates, sitting on our stools in the back-yard with the brick walls around and one tree lonely in the corner. The night had been cooler than the day, but hardly cool at all. Dad was cross. Who knows about what? He's always cross about something. Especially about crooked Zuma still in his house like a palace, and four fat wives coming and going. Dad threw his bottle at the wall. It gave me a *skrik* — the kind that sucks blood from a heart — because I didn't expect it that time. Carling Black Label, the beer that makes a real man. That's what Dad says, but he doesn't need it. See him and you'll know straightaway that he's a real man.

Mom jumped up and screamed, "Pick it up!" Like he cares what she says. He just chucked the crusts and whirled his plate through the air. When the second bottle hit the wall, it cracked and hissed a mighty spray. Mom turned on me when Dad started to laugh, her face burning red with her fireworks inside. "You leave this for him to tidy or you get a thrashing. You hear me?" She clapped the air in front of my face, so close I whiffed her sweaty smell. "I'm warning you, I know you." Her words were thunder and spit and I knew that she would. Dad hits Mom and Mom hits me. That's how it is.

Solomon smiled so big during my story that I thought his face must split and swallow me up. He said, "Problem is big daddy wasn't chief from the start." He pressed his thumb into my shoulder, ground it around. A big wink and he said tough love is what makes a lady happy.

I took some time thinking after the guys went home. It was sad to have my goodwill greeting ending in someone's disaster, like the butterfly who flaps his wings in England and sends a tidal wave to swallow Africa. I wondered whose fault it was — especially whose fault it was. In the end, I walked over the road to Pick 'n Pay and got some blue shorts with white stripes down the side, like Adidas but not so pricey. They still cost me everything I'd saved from the coins that Dad gives me here and there. "Get yourself some Chappies," he says, as if that bubblegum is all that exists in the sweet world. I got a ribbon to tie around the shorts. Orange. It looked friendly.

No-one answered when I knocked on Tim's front door, right there in view of the other Units. There was a green pot with a rose bush by the door. Pink roses, but there was no time to smell them. I nipped down the alley on the side of Tim's house to get to his Unit's back-yard. The alleys are skinny, no room for roses. But in Tim's back-yard, there were a million more: roses in pots along every wall. I thought his mom must be obsessed, planting roses on top of the hassle of moving in. Still, pink roses are better than concrete and glass.

Tim didn't answer my knocking, though a ghostly shadow behind the curtain showed he was surely there. I sat with the roses and counted to a hundred and then knocked again, and then another hundred and again, and all over again. Between times, I watched the shadows lengthen over my legs, and then my bare feet, because South African kids don't bother with shoes in summer. We prefer to run like Shaka Zulu warriors over thorns and hot stones without hesitating, until we grow up and put leather and plastic between us and the earth because we want to be civilized.

In the end, I got mad with Tim for keeping me in line like everyone does. I didn't have all day, and I really needed to do my business before his mom got home. Also, I needed to wash my hair and paint my toenails. I knocked and knocked. I bet there were maybe a hundred knocks when Tim cracked the door.

There I was waiting for just that, but still it gave me a *skrik* and I almost fell off the step. I said I was really sorry and that I never knew what was going to happen until it happened. I held up my gift. "Blue shorts," I said. I thought he'd be happy but, oh no, he started to shut the door. So, I said what I really think. I said, "I know how it feels to be white around here." He stopped then and looked at me with one misty green eye through the crack in the door.

I said, "Please, please, take it." Only, that gave me tears and so I put down the shorts and did some swirls in the yard, whirling round and round, my arms spread wide like a washing line in a wind, like when I was a kid and needed to put my crying away.

Tim's big eye was still there when I came back to the door. I thought he might prefer Afrikaans, so I said *jammer* instead of sorry. Then I tried the Zulu *ngiyaxolisa* and held out my gift like a real African would, with both hands and a little dip of my head. In the shadow of the door, I can't say if he really smiled, but he took the shorts.

He closed the door then, gently.

Knocking came on my own door at half past six. I opened up with a divine smile, but there was no Solomon, only Thandi and some girl come to march me off.

I asked Thandi, "How's your cut?"

She said, "Now for some fun."

"Hey, let me grab a key," I said, though it was in my pocket.

I popped my head into our lounge where everything's done, from TV to sleeping. I said, "Got to go into the night." I prayed Dad would say, "Oh, no, please watch this enjoyable rugby with me." He just grunted. Speaking is a bother for him. He rather keeps his words growing inside. When the load gets too much, he hits Mom. Nothing too bad. No breaks or blood.

Mom was her usual no-help as well. "Not a damn peep when you come in," she said, with lots of wagging finger.

Other kids were there when we got to the pool, maybe fifteen altogether. They were packed in, bouncing around purple balloons bobbing on the water. There was the usual Unit crowd and some big shots from school. They were all sorts: black, brown, white. Only the Chinese guy from Unit Ten was still on the edge. His black and red *cozi* made me think of a Coke. I could have done with the sweet fizz in my mouth right then. I saw the rush was on to pop the balloons. Plain old good fun, it seemed.

Solomon got out of the pool and came over with eyes drugged and airy. Water dew-dropped on his skin. I thought that's a boy wasted and wasting his chance, better be careful. Still, I wasn't too worried because he was relaxed with arms and legs woolly-like. He pulled me to the scrubby grass at the top of the pool. "Pleeease." He used a silly voice like my baby brother used to use, before he was run-over dead and left crumpled by the road, before Dad gave up words and Mom took up fury.

Solomon and I took a seat, and the sunshine caught up in the wall warmed my back. I liked the feeling, and I liked the look of our fingers mixing, the way my tan went back to white beside the chocolate of his skin. My legs stretched out from my bikini to point red toenails at the kids shouting and laughing and popping balloons. For a minute, I felt perfect.

The kissing was lovely, toasted marshmallow silky. I hoped the others would see that I was Solomon's girl and needed respect. I hoped someone would take a photo and put it on Facebook and Twitter it to the world, to show I was somebody. I should have known that things never work out right. When Solomon slipped his hand under my bikini top, my happiness went to ice. I rolled over and got up like it was a natural thing. Why, I do need a good stretch, or something like that. It was coming to me that sometimes you can be chosen by a person, but that doesn't make it a good choice. Solomon started off dreamy surprised, like, dear me, why not? But then he got up and yanked me in and said I was shaming him.

I don't suppose Thandi meant to save me when she came over and put her arms around Solomon. "Come here, Baby," she said, like in a movie. She kissed him and they swayed in a close dance. A hectic terror was growing in me for what would come next. I went casual to the pool's edge, dipped my feet in the water. By now it was darker, with everything gone grey.

"Cluck, cluck," Solomon said when he plopped down beside me. "Little chicken never been felt." He squawked and flapped his arms like the rooster Unit Twenty keeps in their back-yard. Everyone stopped their swimming to look and clap for him, star of the show.

I thought, Hell, now what have I done, but I said, "Let's go play toktokkie." Everyone likes that. A person leaves a horrible little something, then knocks and runs away. Nobody gets hurt, except the poor mice and frogs left bloody behind.

Thandi took a seat on the other side of Solomon. She said, "Better to burn down the fairy's house." She lit a cigarette and turned to the pool-load of people. "Well?" she said.

"I see firecrackers," Solomon said, and high-fived with Thandi.

Everybody cheered.

That's something else we do, put firecrackers in postboxes, but only at rich houses, not the Units, because Unit people are family, no matter what colour and even if you hate them. I thought I was being helpful when I told the kids that we'd better watch out not to burn down all our places one on top of the other.

Thandi stretched in front of Solomon and jabbed her cigarette at me. "Burn out your eyes, maybe," she said. "Gotta do this right, use my petrol for the fire."

It's how she gets cigarette money, siphoning for her dad's second-hand petrol business. It's very successful because South Africa's police don't have time to worry about bits stolen here and there and nobody shot. Problem is that only poor people's cars have open caps, not the Mercs and BMWs that can afford a full tank in one go.

"You coming, Darling?" Solomon asked, as if my past wrongs were forgotten.

I said, "Would love to, but Mom will go crazy if I'm late."

Thandi laughed. "The bitch doesn't give a fuck about you."

I smiled, though it was true. I knew no one was waiting to ask how my evening was. I couldn't blame Mom because of her lost son, which is the worst thing that can happen to a mother, which is why she takes Normison 20mg every night at eight.

Solomon said, "You go, Wednesday Legs, and you're on your own." The sweat on his chest made his muscles shine. He's a beautiful one, I thought, on the outside.

I pretended that I had no choice, and I pretended to be sad. It wasn't hard because my insides were cramping, and I thought I'd gone mad with the idea of choosing home.

"I warned you," Thandi said to Solomon — or to me, I wasn't sure who.

My place isn't exactly Heaven, but for once it was a break. I had my concerns, but still I took Dad's pay-as-you-go cell from the couch where he lives. Already he was snoring in his sleeping bag, bug in a cocoon, escaping the world.

I called 112. I told the lady, "Come quick, some kids are burning down a house." She wanted my name, but I only gave Pinefields' address and said to look for Unit Two with the pink rose at the door. When she asked if it was a prank, I got cross because I was taking a big, foolish risk, and that's no joke. I said, "Hey, when our places go up in smoke, you'll be the one who's sorry." Give lip like that to grown-ups around here and you get whacked. I quickly cut the call.

I replayed all the words after I put the phone back next to Dad, like remembering a fine film. It felt like Santa bringing peace to the world, without missing any house on the way. Maybe I should have gone next door to warn them, but I say that's the police's job. I'm only a girl. I got into my sleeping bag and pulled the top over my head. I wished out loud to be heard: "Please let tonight be a careless mistake and not a hellfire." I was a cold in my bikini. I couldn't sleep. I smelled burnt toast, but I supposed it was my imagination alive from too many horror movies. In the end, I got up and put on my PJs and looked out of the front door. Everything was fine, no smoke or anything. All's well that ends well, I thought. Still, I couldn't sleep.

Finally, after long enough for Jo'burg to burn down, the police came slinky as the night. There was shuffling and talking, gruff voices grumbling. No spinning lights and whoop-whoop sirens — I guess because Unit people aren't worth it. A deep freeze hit me when knocking arrived on our door. I opened my mouth to breath, and then I closed it to stop me from bawling for bringing trouble to our house again.

Knock, knock, so loud I knew these were big hands. I was scared, but I was more scared that Dad would wake up, and what he'd do a policeman, and so I went to the door.

The policeman was a giant with thick blobs for features. Washed-out eyes stared from under his cap, as if he expected everywhere to be a horrible place, and our place especially.

"You the white girl called us out for nothing?" he asked, as if he wasn't white himself and had better things to do, like stopping traffic for made-up wrongs and a bribe. He wrapped his hand around the open edge of the door. Behind him, the world was the fuzzy darkness of a big moon. Perfect for poaching rhinos, I once read in a mag.

I stepped back, he stepped in, and now the toes of his boots were over the entrance. I said, "There's also two Chinese girls at Unit Ten, and a Jew who lives at Eight. You'll find very white skin on them."

"You being funny?" the policeman asked, and then his hand was on my shoulder. He squeezed hard, so hard that his fingers made marks that I only saw later.

I jolted away and the useless old phone fell off the table that stands by the front door. Crash! Even the policeman *skriked* and let go of me.

"What the hell!" Mom's voice bawled through the air, with her a madwoman behind, rushing down the passage in her nightie, her flesh sloshing about. Metal curlers in her hair looked like a helmet, and her face was the wreck of all the wars she fights. I thought she'd charge right through us, but then she twigged the policeman and pulled to a stop.

"Get out!" she screamed, like she'd screamed when they brought news of my dead brother, and like she screamed when his little coffin floated behind the curtain into the fire, and like she screamed when they said the hit-and-run accident was closed with nobody caught. I'd thought those types of screams were used up.

I felt sure and strong when I put my hand on her arm. I said, "It's okay, my darling, they're just investigating an incident."

"And what incident is this?" the policeman asked me, though he kept his eyes on Mom.

Her breathing was wispy, and I saw how she worked to step out from the drugs and the pain of her life, into the now.

"I don't know." I said. I put an honest look on my face "But, Mister, it must be something because you are here."

He said, "I don't like your attitude."

Mom said, "I don't like *your* attitude." She put her hand on my shoulder. It felt meaty and warm and I loved the feeling.

That mighty lady was wider than the big *boer* policeman but not even as high as his chin, and I guess he would have won any fight, but still she pushed back her shoulders and pushed out her chest. I was proud to see her so terribly ruined but still brave. She listened to his story of the white girl who'd phoned in a false report. Arson, the man said.

Mom said, "What's her name, this so-called girl who so-called called?"

The policeman said he didn't have that information. He warned again about attitude.

Mom asked how he knew the girl was white, which made him confused, until he said all high and mighty, "These things are apparent in the sound of the voice." He squeezed his nose and his eyes flicked around our entrance, maybe looking for something to help his conversation.

"So, now colour has a sound?" Mom said.

I said, "I told him about the Jewish and Chinese girls."

"There's also that nicely spoken Muslim," Mom said. "And the new boy next door. White as a lily and probably still sounds like a girl."

The policeman said, "You think he set fire to his own house?"

"Is there a fire?" I was scared again. I wanted to look outside and smell the air for danger.

"No fire, lucky for you." The policeman wagged his fat finger.

That's when Dad came along bleary-eyed and scratching his stomach and asking what was going on.

Mom didn't take her eyes off the policeman when she said, "Seems they can't find who killed our boy, but now they want to take our girl because she sounds white."

I could almost hear the tick-tick of Dad's thinking as he looked at the policeman to Mom to me. You would have sworn the air was smoky, the way he rubbed his eyes, working out the people and their purpose, I guess. He sagged like a kick in the guts, but then he pulled up tall.

He said, "Show me your warrant." He switched on the light that's one bulb on a wire. The blaze came a shock. I shaded my eyes.

"I don't need a warrant." The policeman was plenty bold with his gun cozy on his hip.

"You need a warrant to enter my house." Dad stepped forward and his slippers faced the black boots standing on our brown tiles.

Two beer *boeps* like pregnant bellies almost touching and cheeks the same blotchy red, but it was the matched eyes that worried me: unblinking, unmoving. Behind them, heavy breathing and the smell of old booze. It came to me that this was another T-junction when you must decide left or right, forward or back, and though it isn't clear, doing or not doing are both doing something.

I said, "Please, Dad, I don't want you to go to jail." It was smashing the police over my brother's death that got Dad into jail and took away his job. Something else too. Mom says a king went in but never came out. I visited Dad once, took him biltong. Mom cried a lot.

"Please," I said, thinking how I wanted to hit the policeman hard in the face, see him the one on the ground bleeding and crying for time to stop and give him a chance.

It was the policeman who gave in and broke the eye-lock with Dad. He turned to me and there was something in his face that was sad.

"Sorry, Mister," I said, also feeling sad.

Clever Mom saw the chance. She bent to get the phone fallen on the floor. She rested on one knee, and then the other, until she was kneeling. Then she was on hands and knees, plugging back the line from where it was pulled from the wall. Her bum was thick as the pig's that lived at Unit Twenty, until it escaped and ate Nineteen's garden and became pork chops. Mom seemed to be saying kick me if you want, it's your choice.

With my hands on my mouth, I shoved back my cry.

Dad hooked his hands under Mom's armpits and helped her up. Her knees conked in and she sank into him, two bodies become one. Their heads leaned in and touched, and then they pulled back

89

and looked at each other with the old kind of look with caring inside. I hoped Dad might say, "Beautiful as the day I met you." Then Mom could blush and say, "Oh, you are too much."

Mom took the phone handle and offered it to the policeman. "Dead," she said. "You try."

The policeman didn't move a jot. He looked hard at the phone.

"Telkom SA," Mom said. "Bloody hopeless." She sniffed pissed off-like.

The policeman nodded and said, "Telkom SA." He touched his cap and lifted his eyebrows friendly-like.

"Just a rat at Number Two." A new voice arrived, and our policeman turned around, and I guess everyone saw the plastic packet that the second policeman held.

"Lots of rats around here," Mom said.

"And fight cocks at Nine," Dad said, and I was amazed to find that he'd been paying attention.

The new policeman was black and scrawny next to our big blobby white one. He turned the bag upside down and out fell a hamster, furry and brown. It lay dead on its side with a yellow pen stuck in it. No blood leaking. It looked like it was sleeping, its little feet curved in like commas.

Dad jumped. I jumped. Mum yelled, "Goddam!"

"Jesus H Christ!" our policeman said. "This voodoo, you think?"

"I don't know, Mister," I said. "We're also Christians in here."

"You playing with fire?" the black policeman asked and glared daggers at me.

Dad huffed and said, "You accusing my daughter?"

I grabbed Dad's big hand and held it tight. I said, "I'm sorry to hear about these troubles, Mister, but your friend said there's no fire and our phone is dead."

90

Everyone looked at me, and so I said, "Dead as a dodo and I can't call anybody." I showed them my hands empty and harmless, no nasty doings in them.

It was a surprise when Dad pulled me in, putting my back against his belly while he wound his arm around my shoulders.

"She's a good girl," he said.

Mom sniffed and said, "Friendly with them all." She put a hand on Dad's arm, and I wished for a photograph to snag the vision.

"Is this the girl?" the black policeman asked. His hand wandered to his belt with the gun.

"I don't think so," I said. "I love God's creatures."

Our policeman kind of smiled and said, "I don't think so." Then he said, "Do we need to wake them all up, find out who's playing silly buggers?"

"I don't think that's necessary," I said, and wrapped both my hands around Dad's arm around me.

Mom said, "Please take that rat away."

My policeman hesitated and then he said to me, "You call if there's trouble."

"Will do," I said.

"I thought there was no phone," he said, and the black policeman clicked his tongue and said something in his language.

"Hotline to God." I smiled to show my humour.

Little monster my policeman called me, half joking, half serious. His friend put his hand in the plastic packet and scooped up the hamster without touching it.

They went quickly then, leaving me and my folks like strangers woken up in a bed on a lost island. Dad grunted and looked around, like the policeman had, like for something to inspire him. He didn't find it. He said goodnight and went back to the lounge.

"Not a sound tomorrow morning," Mom said. Then she said a crazy thing. She said, "I'd like to go to the Rock of Gibraltar. If I could, I'd go there." She looked out of our door as if she saw the rock far away.

"It sounds very nice," I said.

After a while, she said, "Would you?"

"What?" I said.

"Like to go?"

"Definitely!" I wasn't sure whether I would, but I wanted to boost her dream. Also, I couldn't see anything outside, no black boy, no white boy, no green country, no roses, and so why not a rock?

"I won't get there," Mom said, "but you might." She lifted my chin and studied me hard. She smiled and looked younger, a sweet chubby lady with feet bare and innocent.

Her eyes travelled over the walls, over the patchy paint and the picture of a fine house by the sea. She came to the calendar stuck at January, though it was March. She unpegged it from its nail, flipped the pages, and put it back a cheetah chasing springbok through the veld.

Mom said, "You must keep hope alive." She wrapped her arms around herself and looked outside. I guess I knew then that she thought for her it was hopeless.

A MODERN RWANDAN FOLK TALE

Ashby McGowan

(In Kinyarwanda and) English

When God finished working on Rwanda, he stopped for a rest and handed out jobs to all the spirits of the world. He cared very much for the small pretty flowers that he had planted in all the hills and valleys of Rwanda. These tiny white flowers made Rwanda the prettiest country in all the world. And so, he asked the Sun and the Rain to look after these flowers. They were told that this was very important and they must ensure that the flowers prosper and grow.

Well the Sun wasn't very pleased with this and he said to the Rain, "I think that I would be far better doing this job on my own. You are too different to me. You are not hot. You are not bright. I will look after the flowers on my own. I am warmth. I am the brightness of the day. Nothing personal, but I am the giver of life."

Rain was so angry that she blurted out, "You proud conceited bag of fire. I am water. I am the quencher of thirst. I will look after the flowers on my own. It is me that is the giver of life."

They argued like this for some time. Some very strong words were said, that I shouldn't really repeat. Anyway, they decided that the Sun would go to the Virungu mountains and look after the flowers on the hilltops. The rain would go to Kivu and look after the flowers in the valley. That way, they could see who was the best at giving life. And, more importantly, they would be able to keep out of each other's way. As you may guess the Sun and the Rain were enemies. God had more than once intervened to stop them fighting.

The sun worked hard on the tall mountains of Virunga. He shone all day and made sure his bright rays reached every flower. But the flowers began to wilt. As the flowers started to wilt, so the sun became angrier. He did not want to be beaten by that awful spirit, the Rain. He shone brighter and brighter. And hotter and hotter. The flowers all died. And when they died, the sun shone even brighter. He scorched the Mountains of Virunga and turned all that land into burning Volcanoes.

In the lands of Kivu, the Rain was making sure that every flower had lots of water. The land became quite muddy and the flowers all began to wilt. The Rain sent down more and more water. It had to succeed. It had to beat the Sun and show that it was the true giver of life. But all it did was to drown the flowers. As the flowers all died, so the Rain lost its temper and threw down torrents of water from the sky, day after day. Eventually, Kivu was turned in to a Lake. And dead petals floated on its still surface.

The next day, the Sun and Rain met. They apologised to each other and said that neither of them was the giver of life. After some time the Rain said, "Look, there must be another way. We will do what God asked; we will work together and look after the flowers together."

The Sun replied, "Yes, I am willing to work with you. But I think that all the flowers are dead. We must first find a flower that we can look after. I do not think that God will be pleased with us if we have killed all the flowers in his favourite land of Rwanda."

It took them many days, but eventually the Sun found one tiny flower growing in stony ground in the North of Rwanda. Each morning the Sun and Rain met and worked out what they must do to keep this little flower alive. They would often disagree at the start, but eventually they always agreed on the right thing to do. The Rain shook down some soft drizzle on the flower and the Sun shone just enough to keep the flower growing. Not too little, and not too much.

At the end of the summer, the little flower was covered in seeds. The Sun and the Rain asked the Wind, very politely, if it would please blow the seeds from this flower all over Rwanda. And this it did.

And so to this day, if you ever visit God's favourite land, you will see these lovely white flowers growing everywhere. Please remember when you see them, how much trouble they inadvertently caused.

The Eyesore

Christopher Kudyahakudadirwe

His eyes are red like someone who smokes dagga every day. They are frightening and glowing like embers that have been stirred to ignite an almost dead fire. His nostrils flare out like those of a donkey that has mistakenly eaten a pod of hot pepper and, from them, two jets of foul breath are spoiling my air. There is a thick smouldering cigar clamped between his yellowing teeth. It smells like the cigarette I once found our neighbour sharing with his friend behind his shack the other day. I clearly remember that after smoking that cigarette, they coughed like motorcycles running out of petrol. Now, in this man's hands is a large pair of scissors – the kind that is used by the caretakers to trim the hedge at my school. I see him now coming to me opening and closing the scissors, snapping the foul air in-between us in a scary way.

I look into his red eyes trying to read what his intention is but it is difficult because of the smoke that is curling around his head and his heavily bearded face. One thing that I am sure of is that he is up to no good and as such I am moving backwards trying to get as far away from him as possible. But his stride is longer than mine. He is gaining on me quickly. My right heel kicks a stone half embedded in the dusty road and I fall on my back. Now I am looking at him from where I am lying down on my back. He yanks off my khaki shorts in one swift move, grabs my small balls with his left hand the way one would squeeze a 2kg sugar plastic bag half-full of water. Then with his right hand he brings his scissors slowly towards my groin. My skin is crawling all over.

"Maiwe-e!"

"What is it, Tammy?" Mother's voice pierces the morning silence from the kitchen-room of our shack.

I wake up. Sweat is streaming down my forehead like water flowing down the rocky summit of a mountain after a thundery afternoon shower. My sleepy eyes are stung by the morning sunlight beaming through the un-curtained rectangular hole which functions as the window. I have to squint them to get them used to the light. To speed up their adjustment, I also knead them with my balled hands like a cat waking up from an afternoon nap. At that moment, the door flies open and Mother comes in, water dripping from her wet fingers.

"Why are you screaming like that, Tamai?"

I do not answer immediately. My heart is still drumming from the fright that I had gone through a few moments ago. I scan the room trying to find out if the man with the pair of scissors was really there in the room.

"H– he wa-wanted t-t-to cut me with a pair of scissors." I stammer. Unseen ants still crawl over my skin.

"Who is he?" Mother's face is worried. She has never wanted anyone to hurt me. She loves me. I am her only child. She has often fought my battles against bigger boys who bullied me. Father left us four years ago when he went to another country because he had lost his job on the farms when the 'children of the soil' claimed their land from the white farmers. Since then he has not come back and we have not heard anything about or from him.

"A big bad man, mama. He wanted to cut me here." I point at my groin shy to tell her that the man wanted to remove my testicles with the pair of scissors.

"Dreaming again? Was it a dream?"

I am not sure yet if it was a dream. I'm still looking everywhere: at the floor, at the roof and behind our clothes hung on a wire line because we do not have a wardrobe and behind the door. The man is not there. So, he surely was in my dreaming head.

"Don't worry, my child. You're not cut at all." She takes me into her arms and brings me close to her warm body. I crush into

97

her abundant bosom and do not want to separate from her for a while.

"Now, go to the bathroom or you'll be late for school." She pushes me away gently but firmly.

Mother releases me from her comforting embrace. From a nail on the other side of our bedroom I unhook a small towel and pick a slab of green soap from the upturned box that serves as our dressing table. There is a cracked mirror that stands on this table. I look at myself in it. Mother has often told me that I look like Father. On many occasions, I have taken out his photograph that Mother keeps in the big suitcase under the wooden bed and tried to look for these similarities but I have found none at all.

The bathroom is a makeshift one. It is an enclosure next to this shack that we call 'house'. It is made of hessian sacks tied to a frame of poles. It is mainly for bathing but when it is night time we can go in there to urinate because the communal toilets are far from this part of the informal settlement. It is such that when it is a hot October day, the whole suburb is engulfed in a strong stench of urine rising from these establishments.

When I get in there, I find a Chinese-made plastic dish full of steaming water. Mother always boils bath water for me in winter. She does not want me to bath in cold water. She wakes up around 4 o'clock and makes the fire to boil the water before she takes a kombi to the big market near the city centre to bring back tomatoes, onions, cucumbers, *rugare* and fruits that she sells at the roadside market in the settlement. This is how we have survived all these years since Father left us.

I take off my vest and hang it on the wire that has been put there for the purpose. My shorts follow it there. I have no underwear -an underwear is a luxury that I never dream of. After a long spate of urination, which is quite enjoyable, I start the ritual of taking the bath. I throw water over my head and then lather the short hair that is stunted there with the green soap. I hate this part

98

of my bath because sometimes water gets into my eyes and the stinging soap is not welcome in them. I scrub my head with my fingers to remove the dirt that maybe stuck there. My teacher actually runs her fingers through out hair daily at assembly to check whether we wash our hair regularly or not. If found with dirt, she pours a whole bucket of freezing water on you and you will spend the whole day in class shivering like a mangy dog.

My eyes are closed. I am engrossed in the business of washing my head when I hear a drone coming from the direction of the only 'road' that serves our settlement. This road comes out of the main road that leads to the international airport. Generally, there are no cars that come to our settlement because we are all poor people. Very few people have jobs and those who work earn very little to have the luxury of buying a car. The only cars that visit us are police vans when there is someone to be arrested or an ambulance when someone is terribly sick. Rarely do cars come to this place in the morning but, there, I hear the sound of an engine approaching us. The sound is growing louder and louder by the minute. I am wondering what this sound could be. As time slowly crawls by, I get the feeling that the sound is not of one vehicle. It sounds as if there are two or three vehicles approaching. Now I can hear residents shouting to each other as if passing a message. I cannot hear properly what they are saying because of the pitch of the vehicle noises. I stop scrubbing my head to listen.

"Tamai, come out quickly." Mother's voice anxiously loud calls out.

I take the dry towel and wipe my face. "What is it, Mother?"

I am struggling to get into my shorts at the same time walking out of the makeshift bathroom. Some soapy water from my hair has streamed into my eyes and it stings irritatingly.

"They have come with bulldozers this time."

"Mother!" I have to call her three times. She can hardly hear me in the increasing noise. "Who is coming with bulldozers?"

"The government."

I can see wells of tears in Mother's anxious eyes. I do not understand. Why would Mother want to cry because the government was coming with bulldozers? I have heard government people on radio saying that their government is by the people and for the people. It had been chosen by the people and was there to do the wishes of the people, the speakers on the radio had gone on to explain. I look around at the neighbouring shacks. Everyone is out and looking in the direction where the yellow bulldozers are approaching from. Some are busy bringing out their possessions — rickety tables, chairs, suitcases bursting with clothes and kitchen things. These people could have had a similar experience from the year 2005 when Operation Murambatsvina was carried out on illegally built houses. I was not born yet but Mother has often told me about it.

The big noise of the approaching bulldozers is now threateningly loud. I can feel my insides jarring due to the sound. Their bucket-size exhaust pipes belch dark smoke that is added to that from our own wood fires. This cloud of smoke hangs over our shanty-town like a cloud of locusts which is about to descend on the ground for an overnight rest. Following behind the bulldozers are three trucks full of policemen wielding glass shields and batons. A few of these men have guns — probably teargas-canister launchers.

We stand there and watch them approach. I must be looking like I have been dragged in dirty water because soapy water still drips from my head. I am wearing shorts only. The bulldozers have disrupted everything. I could have finished my ablutions by now and would be tucking in my breakfast, but as I see it, I am considering school as having been cancelled. And speaking of school, there is no school in our plastic and cardboard shanty-town. We have to walk about four kilometres to attend school in a proper suburb which is to the east of the airport.

Mother is confused. I am confused. Everyone around us is confused.

"Why are the bulldozers coming here? Do they want to do roads for us? And look, they are being escorted by policemen." I point to the security personnel carriers full of policemen following slowly behind the loud-mouthed monsters. Mother follows where I am pointing with her teary eyes.

The monsters are now at the edge of our suburb. They have already moved out of the road that leads to the international airport. We no longer hear the humming of traffic to and from there. These monsters are moaning and droning like hungry monstrous creatures ready to maul everything in their way. Everyone is standing outside their dwelling gaping at the machines, not knowing what is going to happen. I can smell the spent diesel fumes from those chimney-like exhaust pipes. They stop as they enter our stadium where we play soccer with plastic balls at the end of each day. The police personnel carriers drive past them and stop. A smaller police van (which I had not seen yet) comes away from the back of the fleet and proceeds into our shanty town.

"Residents of Garikai," the booming loudspeakers on top of the small van blast our ears with a loud male voice. "The government has given you a very long time to move away from here and it seems you have not bothered to do so. Therefore, today you're to be forcibly removed. You have been warned several times to go back where you came from but you are obstinate. Today we will see who is stronger: you or the government. If you don't remove your things from those shacks, the bulldozers will destroy them together with the shacks. Any resistance will be met with teargas and batons."

Mother looks down on hearing these words. Is she going to cry again? I am trying to read her face but she does not look at me or up. By now all the flurry about going to school has been suspended. I am gripped by the mystery of the presence of the bulldozers and the police. I am thinking of the picture I am going to draw when I go to school next time. It would show the bulldozers raving up into our shanty town and the police standing stupid behind their glass shields in the lorries wielding the black batons. In my Grade R class I am well known for drawing pictures of what happens in my neighbourhood. I once drew a picture of the opposition party leader shouting a slogan, his hand open in their symbolic party salute, when he came to address us at the beginning of this year. My teacher refused to put it on the display board. She said it could get her into trouble with the police if they were to see it. I was confused.

"We are giving you thirty minutes to take out your things from those shacks." The loudspeaker fills every corner of the settlement with the deep voice again. I am sure even the rats that are our unwelcome housemates could hear and understand this. I could see one or two of them coming out of their hiding places, whiskers twitching and trying to make sense of the situation.

The waiting is not long. Soon the half hour is up and the bulldozers are revved up. A long thick chain is fixed to the two bulldozers. Then they move away from each other to stretch out the chain and are approaching one section of our 'suburb' with the chain in-between them. I am not sure of what they are up to. As they sidle towards the shacks I see behind them another machine which I learnt later that it is called a digger. It has a long arm in front that is similar to the front legs of a praying mantis. It can swing this one arm in whatever direction the driver of the machine wishes it to swing. Next time I am going to get my hands on some wires I will be making a resemblance of this funny machine. All in all, it is fascinating watching the three machines as they swing into action.

The bulldozers, with the one-hundred-metre-long thick chain in-between them, slowly approach our shacks. Some of the people have finished removing their meagre belongings and are standing away from the path of the two bulldozers as if they are would-be sojourners waiting for a bus at a roadside bus stop. I can see rickety tables swinging in the morning breeze, backless chairs with torn seat pads, old sofas picked from dumpsites, old mattresses stained with the urine of delinquent babies or drunken fathers, some black handles of pots poking out of hessian sack-bundles like cow horns; there are suitcases dating back from the 60s and the 70s almost bursting with old clothes and blankets.

Some of our neighbours are not at home. Their shacks are still locked with everything that belongs to them inside.

My age-mates are near the bulldozers now, curiously following them as the machines approach the houses. They are having fun seeing those monstrosities at close quarters. Mother has forbidden me from joining them. She is afraid that I might get lost in the confusion that she thinks is going to follow. I hate Mother for doing this to me. I need to see these machines at close quarters for the benefit of drawing them accurately when I go to school the next day.

The chained-linked bulldozers are now near the dwellings. The heavy chain, having brought down a few small trees at the edge of the settlement, scythes one of the shacks and the roof comes down on top of the remains of what had been the walls. From how my friends are shrieking and running around I can see that they are chasing after rats which are fleeing the destroyed shack. More structures are coming crushing down as the bulldozers move along. Behind them the digger is busy knocking down whatever the chain was unable to level down. Red dust is rising up into the morning air as if a dusty-devil is passing through the settlement.

Now the bulldozers are approaching the shack of Chimumumu, the Silent One. I cannot remember the owner of this shack speaking to anyone in the shanty-town. Perhaps that is the reason why people called him the Silent One. No one knows his name. No one knows where he came from so as to be here living with us.

Most of us know where we came from. We came from the white people's farms after the people had taken 'their soil'. Our lives had been tied to the farms but when the 'children of the soil' had come to wrestle it from the settlers, Father and Mother and others lost their jobs. Therefore, the only places where we were welcome were the outskirts of cities and towns. Mother says we are from a country to the east. Our ancestors came to this country many, many years ago when people were shading skin clothes and putting on cotton-cloth clothes. We had no rural-areas-of-origin as default home areas to go to. This is how Garikai had sprung up right here on the red soils east of the big city.

Chimumumu bothers no one and no one, in turn, bothers him. But recently he had not been seen in Garikai. His cabin has been locked for a week now. Since he bothers no one, no one cared about his coming and going. But now the machines were going to flatten his shack. So as the chain between the machines scrapped the ground towards the Silent One's shack we all stood there wondering if people should have broken his door to save his belongings like they had done with the others who were not around.

As we watch the bulldozers flattening the shacks, no one has anticipated what would happen before the chain hits the Silent One's cabin. Without warning, a swarm of bees buzzes angrily out of a hole in the door of the shack. The bees are so many that we can see them flying out like a small grey cloud from where we are standing. They attack the drivers of the bulldozers who jump down from the bulldozers leaving them standing there punting and puffing like elephants bogged in mud. They attack the policemen in their eggheads behind their glass shields. The drivers run wildly towards the police personnel carriers. Their hands are flailing above their heads in a frantic bid to drive away the mad bees. The policemen who have been walking besides the bulldozers as they flattened the shacks have thrown their glass shields away and are running around like ants whose nest has been unintentionally disturbed by a herd of cattle.

Everyone is surprised by what is happening. Children, like me and the others, find it a lot comical to see the policemen running around like mad men chasing shadows, leaving their lorries behind, running wildly, beating the air besides their heads with their open hands, their boots thudding on the ground raising puffs of red dust with each thud. Some of them remove their egg-heads and throw them away because the bees are getting inside. We laugh and roll ourselves in the red dust. Our parents are not amused by all this. I don't know why. Could it be because the red dust that we are rolling in would stick to our khaki clothes and be a problem on a wash day and they are worried about that? They look at us with talking eyes, but we don't want to understand that kind of language now. Instead we choose to crack our ribs with laughter as we watch the police run for their lives.

*

After four days, the bulldozer crew and the police are back. They are accompanied by the people from the wildlife department who specialise in capturing bees. It is a Saturday. We have not gone to school. So, we have the ample opportunity to watch what is happening without the worry of going to school. The police help the bulldozer drivers to refuel their machines while the bee-catchers go to the Silent One's shack. The bulldozers were left running by the drivers for four days and the fuel in their tanks ran out. We are standing at the safety of our mothers' shacks looking at the unfolding scene with interest. The bee-catchers, looking like space travellers in their plastic suits and visors, advance towards the shack shaking from the fear of the mysterious bees they have heard of and had come to remove so that the demolition of our settlement can go ahead. Government is really determined to uproot us from where we have been staying since 2011 when the 'children of the soil' had taken our boss's farm.

The bee-catchers approach the shack cautiously. Not a bee has come out to investigate them. They look around the shack trying to locate the entrance through which the bees go in and out of the shack. They have gone around the shack several times the way goats do when they are scratching themselves on the walls of a hut. This tells us that they haven't found the entrance-cum-exit for the bees. One of them produces a pair of cutters and breaks the chain that secured the door of the shack. When the door of the shack is flung open, we all expect a swarm of bees to burst out and start to sting the intruders, but nothing like that happens. Cautiously, the man who has cut the wire securing the door enters the one-roomed structure and we hear him rummaging inside like someone looking for something. Shortly he comes out. From where we stand we cannot hear what their verbal exchange is but from the men's gestures, Mother can tell that the man did not find any bees inside the shack. The man does not bother to close the door of the shack, instead the two of them walk towards the drivers of the bulldozers who have just finished refuelling the machines and have successfully brought them back to life again.

One of the policeman takes out a megaphone. He climbs on top of the police van before he speaks into it: "Residents of Garikai, we would like to advise you to take out your belongings from your shacks. We would like to finish off what we left unfinished four days ago. Be quick about it. We've no time to waste here today."

Mother looks at me as if she is seeing me for the first time. Her eyes are misting with tears. I know she cries easily. She must be thinking of where we will go from here. Perhaps she is not the only one going through such thoughts. However, the revving sounds of the bulldozers spur her into action. She goes inside our shack to remove our property. I am also going to help with that.

106

"I don't know what to do, my child. I wish your father was here for us. He is the one who brought us here in the first place." She says as she wipes her cheeks with the end of the green apron tied around her waist.

I look at her in the face. I want to tell her that everything is going to be alright but I do not know how. I am only a child; I have not yet read a manual about how adults work. Perhaps if I act like a man she would know, so, without hesitation I shoulder butt the door and start bringing our belongings out of the shack and handing them to her. Mother is piling them a few metres away. We do not have much though. Soon we are standing beside our property: a wooden bed with a mattress with maps of the countries of the world from my urine when I was much younger, two pots and several plates, an old garden chair which my father had been given by his boss at the farm, a canvas bag in which are our blankets and clothes – that was that! We watch the bulldozers as they raze down the rest of Garikai. Everything is flattened and the rats are running here and there trying to find some hiding places among the rubble and plastics.

Then, from the big city direction, we see a cloud of red dust rising in the air. Soon a fleet of seven lorries has arrived at our ruins. The same policeman who spoke through the megaphone previously climbs on top of the van again.

"Former residents of Garikai, your government has sent these seven lorries that you see here for your transport. I'm advising you to load your belongings into any one of them and you will be taken to your new settlement."

On hearing this people pick up their beds, their bundles of blankets, their pots and pans, their chairs and tables and throw them into the nearest lorry. A few rats and some cockroaches, some hidden in the old sagging sofas and others in cupboards with doors hanging on their hinges, are loaded into the lorries. There is a frenzy of excitement that galvanises the people of Garikai into action. They run around like ants on a summer afternoon trying to plug their holes just before a rain shower. When everything is safely in the lorries we climb on top of broken property, bags of clothes and blankets, cardboard boxes of plates and pots and wait to be driven to this new place which has been described as being better than Garikai.

When everyone is on board, the lorry drivers jump into their cabins and our journey to the unknown new settlement begins. Later on, we were to learn that we had been removed from there because we were an eyesore. People arriving in the country were first greeted by our desperate situation so we had to be hidden away from foreign visitors.

Life Can Make You Cry

Kiarie Nyambura

Alem Neh sat in his study, which was arranged so that his big mahogany work desk faced the big window through which the sun streamed in unabashed but slightly reined in by the window netting. Through this window he had a spectacular view of his garden. He was immensely proud of his garden, skilfully landscaped so that stone and garden merged in one un-interrupted conversation and without the awkward joints of ineptitude to distract the eye from the beauty upon which it feasted. He sighed thinking how like his daughters this garden was. Abeba his youngest child was aptly named. She was prettier even than the white and purple Iris on whose fragrant countenance his eye rested. She was the flower of his life. He wished sorely that his eldest daughter would live up to her name. Desta meant happiness in Amharic, his native tongue. His daughter was neither happy nor inclined to bring happiness into the lives of those she called family. He sighed again, albeit impatiently. Ever since Elisabeth his wife had convinced him to change their daughter from the Convent all girls school she had previously attended, his daughter had grown horns and turned into a little monster. "Little, my foot" he muttered aloud, "that girl was looking more like a grown woman each day!" His lips made a moue of disapproval. He felt so cheated by life trying to snatch his girl away before he was ready to see her as anything more than the little imp he used to bounce on his knee. And Elisabeth was of no help whatsoever, his thoughts ran un-forgivingly. As if by some evil kind of magic the object of his thoughts flew into his study without even knocking. "Father!", she began at once without even so much as a greeting, her face flushed with exertion, her blossoming chest heaving with the burden of a pent up fury just seeking a target to release itself upon, "Wedu and Abeba are not allowed into my room and to touch my things." She paused to collect herself for a powerful vitriol. Alem Neh was barely paying attention to the words of the irate girl standing hands akimbo before him. 'My God!' he thought in spite of himself, 'she looks magnificent, like the Queen of Sheba and Jezebel all rolled into one.' Having gained sufficient breath Desta proceeded to berate her father in high octaves.

Elisabeth was a worried woman. In the kitchen where she was busy preparing wot and injera, her hands stilled momentarily as she focused on her thoughts. 'Desta was going to bring trouble to her little paradise', she thought sadly, the clothes that child had taken to wearing, made her cheeks burn. 'One would think she was raised loose and scattered all over', she fumed inwardly. Just then she heard raised voices coming from the study. She left her tasks and hurried to find out what was going on.

Elisabeth was just in time too, she found just when Alem Neh, unable to bear his daughters breach of etiquette had risen up from behind his desk head lowered, seeming ready to charge like a bull. His face was flushed with anger and a fine film of perspiration dotting his brow. "Desta", she exclaimed in a sharp voice, "you will leave the room this instant and go to your room. Stay there and wait for me." Not waiting for the daughter to respond, she grabbed her by the shoulders and pushed her towards the open door. Alone with her husband she drew in a deep breath. "Husband", she began, adopting a correctly soft and pleading tone, "she is your daughter, our happiness; we must try to be a little patient." Alem Neh was done with patience at that particular instant, turning roundly on his wife he shouted, "Ba.leu.be.te (wife), I am tired of this nonsense. You stand there talking nonsense instead of busying yourself with the raising of your daughter. Don't stand there and yap, go raise me a daughter that a man of my stature, a successful

110

me.geb.seu.ri (Businessman) like myself can be proud of," he finished with a look so fierce it brooked no argument.

Stung to the depth of her heart, Elisabeth left the study blindly and slowly mounted the stairs to her daughter's room. 'My God she', she thought, 'what did I do to deserve this. I have raised my children myself, dedicating my life to making a comfortable home and just look at the thanks I get.' She sniffed loudly. She reached the top landing, branched right and made a beeline to her daughter's room into which she proceeded to open unceremoniously. Desta was sprawled artlessly across the bed weeping copiously. 'Spoiled brat', Elisabeth thought uncharitably, 'if she would only stop for a moment to think about what her behavior is doing to this household.' "Get up", she snapped at her daughter, "go to the bathroom and wash your face." Desta who was shocked at the sharpness of her mother's tone, her Mum, who was usually so sweet and pliable, thought better than to argue. She went and did as she was told. "Sit", her mother instructed tersely, pointing to a chair. Hands akimbo in an uncanny replication of her daughters exact pose minutes earlier at the study, she addressed her daughter sternly. "Desta, I am seriously beginning to doubt the wisdom of removing you from the convent school." She paused dramatically, "When you told me how unhappy you were there, I did what any kind mother does, I looked for a better option for you. I convinced your father to put you in a mixed, multicultural school so you could experience more of the world. Is this the thanks you then give to me?" Elisabeth's eyes opened and closed dramatically, her hands fluttering gracefully in the air as she spoke. "Look at you", she pointed an accusing finger at her daughter's apparel, "you dress as though you want to shame me before the entire world." She eyed the skin tights Desta wore with a wary eye and her gaze travelled upward to the equally clinging dress top with a plunging neckline revealing an inviting cleavage and the outline of two mounds of blossoming breasts 'My child is too beautiful for her own good', She thought fearfully, after completing a dispassionate inspection with the eye of a mature woman. Then without warning she sat down on the rumpled bed and started to weep. Desta was dismayed. "Mum", she whispered through trembling lips at once devastated and equally resentful. 'Everyone seemed intent on their own dramas', Desta thought, 'but who is listening to me?' She tried to gather and merge her feelings into the house of order, rage and remorse competed. 'Now, does she expect me to be the mother?' Desta fumed inwardly. 'Look at her, she's old, no wonder she weeps like the spineless woman she is', her thoughts continued spitefully. In the very next instant Desta shocked and ashamed that such a thought could form in her mind, jumped from her chair and knelt down by her mother, hugging her mother's knee, so fearful of the tumult raging within that made her wonder if she knew herself anymore. "Oh, Mommy, I am sorry. Please don't cry. I promise I will be so good, only stop Mommy!" She pleaded unconsciously reverting to the name she used to address Elisabeth as a child.

Elisabeth hearing herself so addressed, wrapped her arms around her child and held her close, kissing the midnight black tresses, her heart melting with maternal love. After a while she held her daughter slightly away from her and gazed upon her face, looking deep in the dark pupils that set off the smooth, glowing skin. She squeezed Desta's shoulders gently and spoke to her in that tone she used when Desta was a fractious tot. "We will go to the kitchen and you will help me to prepare your fathers favorite dish, doro wat, but first you will change and dress like the good Ethiopian Orthodox girl that you are eh?" Not waiting for assent, Elisabeth made her way quickly to the kitchen where she had left her preparations midway.

Desda watched her mother go with mixed feelings. She felt compressed, so tired of their conservative household. 'If only I was born somewhere else where people know how to relax and live',

112

she thought cynically. She walked slowly to her dressing table and surveyed herself critically in the full length mirror. What her parents found so offensive about her dressing escaped her notice entirely. "I look hot", she whispered softly to herself, "if only Mum and Dad could catch up to the real world, that this is how people my age dress like!" With a loud sigh she went to her closet and searched with savage fingers for a prudish frock that would kill her to wear but would definitely mollify her father. Her fingers caught a white spurn cotton dress with classic Ethiopian embroidery and she tugged it off the hanger and disconsolately removed her hot garments for what she considered to be a sexless, drab dress devoid of all personality. Nonetheless she put it on and hurried after her mother.

They worked in silence, mother and daughter, each lost in their own thoughts. Making wot was a task requiring concentration, roasting the onions on a hot skillet free from oil required vigilance or else burnt onions would be the result and one could not use these as the entire taste of the end product was achieving the right balance of flavor. Soon however a feeling of closeness engulfed the two and Desda, forgetting for the moment that she hated being a conservative Ethiopian girl was caught up in the joy of good cooking. Elisabeth sighed; she was glad that her Taita background had prepared her well in the art of home making and an innate love of good cooking. She was proud of her kitchen and her ability to master even difficult Ethiopian dishes. Alem Neh was a suave businessman outside his home but within the walls of his fortress he was most traditional and conservative. He liked things done in the way of his motherland. Soon the two had put together a delectable meal, Layered the injera (National Ethiopian bread) one on top of the other in a round woven basket and wot, arranged on a large tray like platter.

Mealtime traditions were strictly observed. The basket of injera was placed upon the table and the wot servings placed beside it in an eye catching manner. When all were seated, Alem Neh said Grace in low sonorous tones. After this he broke off a piece of injera and ate it thus signalling that the meal could begin and all could eat...

After clearing up at the end of the meal Desda escaped to her bedroom. She was glad that though so conservative her father had furnished her with a slick, pretty cell phone. Used to quality in material things, Alem Neh only bought the best for his family. Now Desda fished out her phone from under her pillow and scrolled to most frequently called number and selected Terry and proceeded to call. Terry picked up instantly as though she had been hanging on just waiting to grab the very next call. "Hey", she quipped, "waz up girlfriend?" "You are so lame, Tee", Desda chortled, immensely pleased to hear Terry's vibrant voice. 'Terry was so alive', Desda thought in an instant of uncontrollable envy, the blasting music in the background seemed a true testimony to this. "Tee, don't your parents make a fuss when you blast away like that?" "My parents have their own space and I have mine", Terry replied nonchalantly," we try not to get into each other's hair", she continued smartly. "Anyway, parents are booooooring", she yawned tellingly in Desda's ear, "I hope that's not what you called me for?" she asked, with ill concealed impatience. "Oh no!" Desda exclaimed, eager to please and desperate in case Terry thought she was infantile or worse dry and dull. "I was calling about Nigel", she continued hurriedly, "he wanted to come and practice some music at our house but the old man's around and hell bent on staying put. Can you just conceive the thought? Ooooh, I wish I could fly far, far away and never see that Ethiopian man again", she finished melodramatically. "Hey", said Terry, "your Dad's kind of cute, a hunk sort of. I think he is cool. My old man has a belly that gets stuck in doors. Sometimes I feel like taking a gun and going 'pop' straight at that bellee. Yeesh, he so makes me mad!" Having uttered such convincing drama Terry felt like she was hosting a talk show, she arranged herself so that she could see her reflection in the full length mirror on her bedroom wall. She made a moue with her lips, checked out her lip gloss, and twirled her manicured fingers with nails painted a shiny black. "He is just too old, I wish he would do gym or something, even Mom thinks so", she continued. Desda giggled, delighted by such irreverence, though if she was honest the thought of her Dad being described as 'a sort of hunk', did not make her feel so good. She brushed the feeling quickly aside, mesmerized by Terry's capacity to say the most brazen things. She puffed herself up a little wanting to feel a little older, more sophisticated, and capable of saying that her Daddy was droll.

"Terry, could you get Nigel to come to your house at 4 pm tomorrow? I will ask Mom to drop me off. That's if you are okay with that." Desda added quickly. "Oh that's fine by me," Terry replied. "Ok see you then Tee", Desda concluded. Desda bit her bottom lip and her mind began to work on a convincing story to get her Mom to take her to Terry's house. Finally she arrived at a plot that pleased her and her face brightened up at once. She would be so good that her mom would have no reason to say no to a polite request from an agreeable daughter. Elisabeth was not difficult to please and when she saw her daughter trying so hard to be the daughter Alem Neh desired, she was very agreeable to allowing her daughter a visit to her friend's house the next day. Desda could barely contain her excitement, wishing the hours would gallop away fast and painlessly.

At the agreed time Elisabeth dropped off her Daughter at the Ndetu's House in Lavington. Desda and Terry fell into each other's arms giggling in that high pitched mindless way that girls at their school thought was so hip, traipsing through the huge villa that was the Ndetu's home, the two girls made a beeline for the kitchen and the fridge. They took out a 5 litre ice cream container and scooped generous helpings into two big bowls. They grated an Orange Seville Chocolate on top of the ice cream in the bowl, stuck a plastic spoon into each bowl and went on up to Terry's room. Terry's bedroom was large and en suite, complete with a pink bath tub and matching set, and a spacious dressing room. Desda came from a well to do family but she was still awed by such opulence so openly displayed. The bedroom itself was a vision in white and pale pink and there was still another full length gilt mirror hung on the wall facing the bed. French doors opened out to a pretty balcony. In the balcony were two white iron-wrought garden chairs and a little table. The girls flopped on the chairs and slurped their ice cream noisily, chatting nonstop all the while like two little monkeys. Desda opened her almond eyes wide as she listened to her friend. "Tee is Nigel coming?" She asked. "He should be arriving any time now," Terry said nonchalantly slurping ice cream and tapping her toe to some music in her head.

"Terry, Nigel is waiting downstairs, what should I tell him", asked Karimi, the house help, appearing suddenly at the open French door. "Send him up", Terry replied without batting an eyelash. Desda gaped. At her house it was unheard of to entertain visitors or friends in the bedroom let alone boys in the girl's room. 'Wow, Terry is so lucky', she thought rather enviously. In a minute Nigel sauntered into the balcony slinging a jacket carelessly from his middle finger over his shoulder. He did a dramatic pose, smiled winningly and said, "Waz up, you guys are having a ball I see. Hey can I have some that?" Without waiting for assent he grabbed Desda's bowl and attacked the ice cream with relish. Desda suddenly didn't know what to do with her hands and she lowered her eyes bashfully. When she recovered some poise, she glanced at Nigel from the corner of her eye. 'He is so good to look at,' her eye lingered on the broad athletic shoulders which tapered to a slender dancer's waist, 'My, he's hot', Desda's thoughts made her cheeks burn and suddenly she felt out of breathe like she had run a marathon or something. Perspiration suddenly stung her under arms, she squirmed uncomfortably. 'Oh Lord just what I need, to

116

have a sweating fit!' Desda thought frantically. Nigel was of a dark chocolate complexion. He had a flashing white smile and a hint of a dimple in his left cheek. He knew he looked good and he worked it, secretly enjoying the effect he was having on the two girls. Even Terry who was normally not one to let others hog the spotlight when she was around was quiet. She had a stupid dreamy look on her face. Nigel walked over to Desda and sat on the thin iron arm of the garden chair. It must have hurt something but you wouldn't know it for the charm he turned on. He draped a careless arm on Desda's shoulder and looked down into her eyes. He felt the slight trembling of her shoulders. 'Yes!' he thought excitement racing through his veins. "Hey Des, you signed up for music club but you never picked up the music. I wanted everyone to check out the video clips before our next club meeting." He gushed. He gave her shoulders a light gentle squeeze, leaning forward to catch a waft of the light fragrance she wore. He definitely liked this girl and he thought she was hot too, an Ethiopian or something. 'Maybe she would be his girl. He could just imagine the other dudes drooling with envy when he announced that the hottest girl in the school was his,' he thought smugly. Meanwhile Desda barely heard a word. She thought she would get a heart attack or something from the heat of his closeness. He turned his attention to Terry who was beginning to frown; one thing Terry could not stand was being ignored. "Terry I almost forgot. I wanted to invite you to my house next Saturday. I'm having a bash and you can't guess who will be performing live." "Who? Ebu tell just now!" Terry exclaimed forgetting her irritation. "Gilbert Mwadilo!" Nigel exclaimed unable to stop himself. "Waaat, oh man. How did you manage that Nigel? Of course I am appearing!" Terry shrilled. She got up and did a dance aping Mwadilo's hit song Mpenzi, very convincingly. Nigel jumped up and joined her singing some of the lines and dancing provocatively. Desda forgot her shyness and dissolved into a fit of laughter. Nigel came to the chair took her hand and pulled her up.

117

Wrapping his hands on her slender waist he sung to her as though the song was written for her. Desda threw her head back enjoying the moment and danced with Nigel, matching him move for move. Then panting and breathless the three flopped down on the floor. Nigel stretched his tall frame on the floor and gazed up at the blue sky. They talked about Mwadilo's music and time flew. It was getting late and promptly at 7 pm, Desda knew that her Mom would be there to pick her up. "I best be getting downstairs guys, my mom will be here anytime now." She stood up. Nigel stood up too, took her hand and said, "Des promise me you will be there. It will be my birthday you know and I so want you there." "I will try", Desda replied. "I want you to promise me", Nigel said earnestly squeezing her hand tight. "Okay Nigel, I promise", Desda said unable to think of an excuse.

Back home Desda was in a daze going over the afternoon time she had spent with Nigel and Terry. She needed to ask her Mom for permission to go to Nigel's party just this minute. 'Where was Mommy dearest now?' she wondered. She went to her parent's bedroom and knocked confidently knowing her Dad was out somewhere. "Come in", her mother called. She bounced down on her parent's huge bed. "Mom, Nigel has a birthday on Saturday, please say I can go. Pleeeaase!" she begged shamelessly. Elisabeth smiled at her daughter. "The child looked so radiant", she thought to herself. "I will have to speak to your Father about it and then I will let you know", she told her daughter. Desda hugged her Mom impulsively. Sometimes her Mom was the best. She leaned forward and smacked a sloppy kiss on her Mum's cheek. Then she jumped up twirled around for her Mommy dearest and blew her another kiss, said Good Night and went back to her room. She thought of herself at Nigel's bash and her heart raced. She could barely sleep. Eventually after tossing and twisting the sheets into a tangled mass, she dropped off to sleep.

Breakfast next morning was business as usual. Then Alem Neh fixed a sharp eye on his daughter Desda and said, "What is this your Mother tells me that a boy has invited you to a party?" Desda almost choked on the scalding hot tea. Confusion reigned in her mind. Her father did not give her time to answer but continued in a tone Desda knew so well and hated. "Well, my answer is no! No party, no boys! I don't want my daughter running wild like some of those girls I see in Nairobi these days. No, that is the end of that matter!" Desda trembled like a leaf caught in a storm. She looked askance at her mother, her eyes pleading. Her Mother avoided her gaze. Abeba looked at her big sister with sudden interest sensing a mystery but wisely she said nothing. Wedu never liked to get caught between his father and his sister so he concentrated on his eggs and pretended no one else existed. He hoped his sister was not going to make a scene and ruin the whole day for the lot for them. Desda, her throat constricting painfully mumbled an excuse and fled from the table as far away as she could from her father. In her room she stood by the window gazing blankly outside. She decided to call Terry at once for she felt a desperate need to connect to someone outside the household she called home. When Terry answered she jumped right into the subject of her consternation. "Terry, you have no idea how lucky you are to have such grown up parents who don't try to run your life through a microscope." Desda said forcefully. "Hey, calm down girlfriend! What's your beef?" Terry inquired rather taken aback. "It is my stupid father with all his Orthodox nonsense. I have had it! I won't stay in this house a moment longer. Say you'll help me Terry, Pleaaase." Desda finished dramatically. "What do you want to do" Terry asked with interest, sensing something to distract her from perennial boredom. "You know, I am always there for you girlfriend." She assured Desda immediately. Desda thought quickly. "Terry get a taxi and come to no 1687 Grevilla Grove, once you get there give me a call and I will come to you." Desda said with the conviction of thwarted fury. "I

119

will come at once," said Terry, who loved drama. Desda then looked around her room, ran to the closet and got a duffel bag into which she stuffed some tights, shirts, under wear and her toiletries. She opened the draw of her dressing table, took her wallet and threw that in too. She threw the duffel bag into a laundry basket covered it with some used towels and made her way downstairs, forcing herself to appear calm and collected. She made her way to the kitchen then on to the laundry room praying she wouldn't run into her Mum or any of her siblings. As luck would have it the coast was clear. Dumping the basket on the floor she retrieved her duffel bag and slipped outside. She saw the gardener. She beckoned him to her and when he came wearing a puzzled expression on his face she pressed a two hundred note in his hand and whispered, "Muka, let me stay in your house for a few minutes. Don't tell anyone that you have seen me. I want to go somewhere and you must help me get past the gate watchman and you carry the bag." She said handing it to him unceremoniously. Muka started to shake his head in the negative and Desda quickly added a shiny new 500 hundred bob note. Muka swallowed noisily. "Basi njoo haraka sana, twende", he said pushing Desda conspiratorially in the direction of the SQ. He opened his door with shaking hands and pushed Desda inside. "Wait there for me", he commanded and went out closing the door behind him. He walked to the gate whistling nonchalantly. "Sasa Chief" he greeted the gate Askari. "Eh, you would like some tea for drinking", he asked. "The Madam, she brought me a big kibuyu there in the garden kaseebo (gazebo). Man, I cannot drink all thata one. Eishh it will make me sleep in my job then the Mzee will become a lion on me." He laughed. "Just go there fast and drink quick, I will hold the gate for you" he continued generously. "Kweli jamaa ya kwetu! Aki kiu cha niumiza. Asante Muka." The Askari made his way to quench his thirst quickly in case the offer was rescinded. Muka watched him turn the corner and disappear from sight then he went back speedily to his house and told Desda

120

to follow him to the gate. "Hide there, down there," he said pointing to the gatehouse. Desda meekly obeyed. Within a few minutes her phone rang. It was Terry, the taxi had arrived and they were waiting at the gate of 1687. "Fungua gate and give me my bag," she told Muka who was just as eager to be done with her. She sped down the lane and sighed with relief when she saw the white taxi cab with a yellow line. She got in the back and without a greeting to the occupants within. "Let's get out of here" she urged the taxi cab driver. Once on Waiyaki Way, caught up in the rest of indifferent traffic, Desda began to relax. "Can you put me up at your house", she demanded of Terry. Terry did not even waste a second pretending to give it a thought, she had already made up her mind and had even started plotting the scenario way before while they had waited for Desda outside that place. She wanted to be in on this drama from beginning to end. She turned to her friend and said sweetly, "My house is your house girlfriend!" then she dissolved into excited giggles. "Turudishe nyumbani", she told the cab driver.

Safe at last in Terry's bedroom, Desda proceeded to give the low down on her parents. "Uhuh", nodded Terry sympathetically suddenly grateful for her pot bellied father who was too busy with his life to find the time to meddle in her own. "Of course you are so going to that party!" she exclaimed indignantly. "Don't worry your pretty head about anything. My parents rarely bother with me. We talk only when we must and for me that's to recharge my credit card. They won't even notice you live here trust me. I have lived with them my whole life and they barely notice me." Terry finished serenely. Desda though overcome with her drama was momentarily taken aback by that little speech but she was too concerned with her own agenda to ponder over it. Things it seemed were going to be smooth sailing, and then Terry proceeded to swear all the household staff to secrecy. They were more of her family than her parents who employed them. She did not encounter any difficulties

121

as it seemed she ran the ship in this house as far as staff relations went.

The two conspirators could barely get themselves to sleep that night so busy were they chatting about this and that and so infused by the adrenaline of a drama in the making that sleep was nigh impossible. They did manage their secret life in the sprawling Ndetu Lavington Villa.

Desda had never been so happy in her entire life. The freedom Terry presented was beyond telling. They had fashion shows and Terry's wardrobe seemed limitless. They went for ice cream at the Lavington shopping Centre, draped in Terry's fiery designs. There seemed to be no limit to what Terry could conjure up. Terry even bought her a clinging dress top and the hottest tights she ever laid eyes on, plus six inch heels that just screamed Hey, I am not you regular Jo! Desda decided that this outfit she would wear for Nigel's birthday party. She could hardly wait for Saturday and it came sooner than she thought.

Nigel lived with his parents in Old Runda. Their home was set in a spacious garden, immaculately maintained and screened off from prying eyes by a high stone wall with coiled wire barbs stuck to the top. The severity of this security measure was softened by the creeping ivy that adorned the wall, the huge gate was also handsomely carved and painted a soft shiny brown with cream borders. There was a high arch over this that was roofed in dark red bricks, that somehow concealed its imposing size. Nigel's party was set in the garden and there were picaresque tents artfully arranged, which housed the buffet, the band and provided shaded sitting for those not inclined to dance away in the sun. Desda regretted her heels at once which kept denting the smooth immaculate lawn and leaving foot indents that made herself conscious. She need not have worried for when Nigel spotted them he made a beeline in their direction, scooped her up in his arms and twirled her round and round and in an exuberant display of affection the wretched shoes came off and stayed off. Nigel was a dream host, charming and vibrant, his energy was amazing and Desda wondered that he seemed to appear to be everywhere at once pampering his guests. She was caught up with exuberance and all her Orthodox modesty disappeared somewhere over the high walls. She laughed and chatted, met so many people she could barely place names and faces. The music was superb and Gilbert Mwadilo seemed hell bent on outdoing everyone of his previous sterling performances. The party just took a life of its own and Desda felt like she had *finally found wings with which to fly, high, high above.*

She caught the eye of many of the young party blazers, Gilbert included and he turned on her the full force of his electric performance, singing to her like she was the only one who existed for him. Desda flattered by so much attention flashed him her brilliant smile and her eyes sparkled like someone high on Belle Donna. She threw back her heavy shimmering black Ethiopian tresses and her long neck made Terry think jealously that she looked like some of those ancient Egyptian princesses that they encountered in their History classes.

The band took a break and Gilbert found his way at once to the gorgeous girl who had captivated him since he laid eyes on her. He felt such a powerful attraction to this girl that were he capable of blushing, his face would have been a mottled red, thankfully his black skin hid a lot of his discomfort, even the fine film of sweat on his nose, chin and brow. Standing right behind Desda, he drawled in her ear, passion making his voice husky with an odd break that was very attractive even to Desda's untutored ear. "Hell Gorgeous," his smile flashed, his voice controlled and very compelling, "and who might you be? Heaven may have just opened up and dropped upon us one of its angels." He looked up at the bountiful heavens with obvious pleasure, clearly very pleased with their choice of angel. Desda was a new creature this day drunk with the sweet wine of a mountain of admiring glances and compliments that had been her fare since she stepped on the green lawn and subsequently brimming with a self confidence she had never known herself capable of displaying. She felt all grown up, powerful woman and she loved it. She turned gracefully to her latest admirer and dimpled prettily at him. "Who would you like me to be?" she teased, instinctively tapping into an innate coquetry that women seem to have coded into their DNA. Gilbert stepped slightly away from her and surveyed her with slow deliberation; his eyes it seemed could undress her and did. He cocked his head sideways, a lopsided mile forming his lips and pretended to be engaged in the most critical consideration. "Uh, Isis, NO!!! Venus and Aphrodite rolled into one and even more lovely!" he offered at last. Gilbert it seemed was more than a talker, his eyes looked at her in ways she had not been looked at before, if she was made of butter she would surely have melted, as it was, her heart was beating so fast and loud she thought he could hear it. He made no effort to touch her but he stood so close, it was a touch in itself. Nothing in Desda's short life had prepared her for anyone like Gilbert. He did not need any more word to tell her what he was thinking, and they were hot, hot thoughts, they burned her like a flame but it seemed she was drawn and she wanted more of this strange exciting places that his eyes promised her. She felt a need to touch him perhaps to make sure she was herself and she was awake and with trembling, awkward fingers she placed a splayed right hand square on his chest. Shocked by her waywardness, she snatched her hand back as though stung.

Gilbert whispered again in her ear, "Come with me gorgeous and I will show where we can talk without so much noise and the possibility of rude interruptions. I can't wait to unravel the mystery of such perfection!" Not waiting for her answer he turned and strode towards what appeared to be a guest house tucked neatly in the garden so that unless you had an eye for detail it was easy to miss. Desda hurried after him almost running and she caught up with him at the door to the guest house. The house was simply and tastefully furnished and a small porch shrouded a big mahogany door with a shiny heavy door knob. Gilbert who seemed to know his way around threw open the door and stepped aside to let her through. He closed the door softly behind him. Desda's mind was so filled up with the thrill of this man who was so unlike the boys in her class or her father and the friends he brought home. Once inside he drew her to a comfortable richly cushioned settee and his hands touched her for the first time. His hands were cool, and his was oddly economical in the way he used them, with a light touch his finger traced an outline of Desda's lovely face and wide eyed like a deer caught in the spot light she submitted to his touch, her mind seemed micro waved, she could not think, she could only feel and she was shocked at how much more she wanted to feel. Her body just took over her senses and it did not strike her as strange that there were no words between them or any need for them. He leaned forward and kissed her lips, she trembled slightly, and his hands seemed to have their own special magic as they moved slowly over her body touching her in places she could never have imagined could bring such a deluge of pleasurable sensations. His kisses become more passionate and his breathing became rapid, without any warning, he bit the tender inner part of her lip and the shocking pain jolted her out of whatever seemed to have possessed her. She instantly recoiled from him, gasping and tried to pull away from him. His hand changed, the fingers seemed to harden and he held her in a painful grip, with one hand he caught a bunch of her heavy tresses in a punishing grip and yanked her head into an awkward angle. Desda now began to struggle in real earnest and opened her mouth to scream. He locked his mouth savagely upon her open mouth drooling saliva, and pressed down so hard his teeth grated against the flesh of her lips in a pain so exquisitely sharp, her nose started running. She sobbed deep in her throat.

125

Wild with pain and confusion she racked her nails at his offending face feeling his saliva dripping down her chin. Her nails raked deep into his face and drew blood. He cursed, shifted and pinned her down with his weight choking her so she had to fight to find space to breathe. He ripped her clingy dress top off and grunted like a pig with the effort, drops of his blood spattered on Desda's eyes forcing her to blink in rapid succession. Holding her down by the neck, he lifted himself slightly away from her exposed flesh and gazed at her with a glint in his eye. Like a rabid dog he bit one pink nipple so hard he felt the blood spurt in his mouth. Desda thrashed around frantically, the pain was like nothing she had ever experienced in her life. Her eyes opened wide with the terror of the nightmare unfolding. "Daddy, Daddy," her mind screamed, for the hand pressing down on her throat made it impossible for her to make the cry. Tears rolled from her eyes, mucus streamed from her nose. So intense was her agony that she was not aware that Gilbert had ripped her tights off as well and her silky little undie, until, she felt him working her legs apart. With a savage strength he splayed her until she felt her hip bone socket crackle like a dry bone and suddenly he was thrusting himself into the deepest most hidden parts of her body. Her whole body went rigid and spasms gripped her wretched frame in agony and the bile rose up in her throat and the vomit came up with such force it hit him in the face. He cursed, "You B---h, he let go her neck and back handed her across the face so hard, her nose started to bleed. Desperately she turned on her side struggling not to choke on her own blood and vomit, making horrible gurgling sounds from some place deep inside her chest. Her vision blurred, the mad man atop her slapped her again. He grabbed her by the legs, raised her hips and hideously and assaulted her with a part of his body she had thought of as being only capable of bringing love and joyful tidings. Brutally he raped her, murdering her dreams, one by one as he ravaged her body. Like an enraged bull, he tore repeatedly into her until finally he was spent.

126

The smell of blood and sweat and other bodily fluids mixed to form a choking scent that hung over Desda's fevered mind like a thick umbrella of volcanic ash and sulphur, which follows a volcanic eruption. She floated on a red hot cloud of pain as she faded in and out of consciousness.

Gilbert done with his dirty deed looked upon the bloody heap that was once gorgeous, slippery now with sweat, blood, saliva and semen, mumbling incoherently and writhing like a demented thing and all at once he was overcome with revulsion. He jumped from the bed, hastily found a bathroom stripped and showered then rummaged through the closets and found a track suit which he wore. In the mirror he surveyed the long scratches the thing on the bed had made and he felt like going back to slap her some more. He cursed virulently. Then he slipped from the house into what was now the twilight of evening and disappeared in the noisy party going on outside. It was easy to slip away before anyone recognized him and he hurriedly left the House and its occupants still avidly and busily pursuing the distractions lavishly presented.

Terry was aware at the back of her mind that she had not seen Desda for a while but she was a bit miffed at all the attention her friend had gotten and she ignored the thought. However as the party progressed, Nigel came to her side and asked her if she had seen Desda. He was also irritated because his star performer Gilbert Mwadilo seemed to have disappeared into thin air. "Thank God", it was getting late and the party was almost winding up as his parents had clearly stipulated everything should end at 10.00 pm. It was now 9.02 pm. Terry had no idea either it seemed as to where Des could be. Joe his cousin who happened to be standing next to Terry heard Mwadilo's name mentioned. "Hey Cuz", he said to Nigel, "I saw Mwadilo heading to the guest house with that hot babe you were kookos for." Nigel did not speak but turned and headed to the guest house. He came to the porch and was surprised to see the door open wide. He quickly entered a strange sense of foreboding settling at the pit of his stomach. There was a heavy smell in the room and his eyes widened in shock as they settled on the writhing figure on the floor. The settee was bloody and bloody smears marked the track where the writhing girl had fallen off to the floor. He seemed rooted to the spot. He saw the ugly scene before him but his brain refused to comprehend it. The girl moaned and turned unseeingly in his direction. Nigel took a shocked breath, almost choking on his tongue. He could barely recognize the angel he had twirled in his arms earlier that day. Her face was swollen, bruised and tinted a livid purplish red. Her lips were like two sausages, torn and caked with spittle, dried blood and vomit. His unwilling gaze went further down and saw what appeared to be a nipple hanging on a piece of skin, with rivulets of blood running down her stomach where they smudged together to form a red blotch. He could look no further. He backed away blindly ran out and threw up on the porch, doubled over and wretched painfully feeling as though his heart was torn violently from his chest. "Oh God!" He whispered, "Oh God, no, no, no." He wanted to weep but his eyes remained painfully dry. Then he got a hold of himself and went back inside. He ran to a closet and found a bed sheet. By sheer will power he forced himself to kneel before the girl and covered her pathetic body with the sheet as best he could. Then sitting on his haunches he rocked himself back and forth, knowing he must do more but not knowing how or exactly what. With trembling hands he reached into his pocket for his phone and called Terry. She took time to answer. When she finally did and Nigel heard her voice, he just burst into tears."Terry you come at once to the guest house," he said in a tear roughened voice. "Nigel is something wrong?" asked Terry. He hung up. Terry stood still for a moment then rushed to the guest house.

Terry was not a girl who easily lost her composure but the pathetic scene that confronted her disbelieving eyes sent her mind reeling and she gasped for breath. She knelt down next to Nigel and with a fierce protectiveness gathered up Desda in her arms and held her tight. In a muffled voice she said to Nigel, "Get your Mum here at once and shut the door behind you, don't you dare say a word to anyone else." Nigel sprung to action as though he had been hit by a strong electric voltage. In a few Minutes he arrived with his Mum in tow. Mrs. Koya was a woman who was used to managing situations at home and in business. "Wrap her in a blanket, quick and Nigel get her to my car immediately, we can talk on the way to the hospital." "Shouldn't we get to a police station first?" asked Terry. "No, No police", croaked Desda weakly, "please promise no police." She begged pathetically. "Calm down dear, we will take very good care of you". The trio rushed their secret burden into Mrs. Koya's car and they sped to Aga Khan Hospital which was nearest from Runda. "Nigel, Call Dr Shamallia and ask him to meet us there as soon as he can." They arrived at The Aga Khan University Hospital casualty and since Dr Shamalia had not arrived they were seen by the Doctor at the casualty, who gave Desda the standard post traumatic rape treatment and decided to keep her overnight at the hospital. Desda was admitted and the three huddled outside the Female Surgical Ward and discussed the issue. "We have to get in touch with her parents at once", Mrs. Koya decided. Terry nodded dumbly and dutifully called Desda's mother. Elisabeth picked up at once, "Terry, thank God you called. Is Desda with you?" "Yes", answered Terry miserably. "Oh, thank the Lord!" Said her friend's mother in such obvious relief that Terry burst into tears and blindly handed the phone to Mrs. Koya. "Hello", she said, "my name is Mrs. Koya and I am Nigel's mother and I am afraid I have some bad news for you. Desda is here with us at The Aga Khan University Hospital. She is being attended to and is not critical but you need to come at once."

Elisabeth got the call in her living room where the family had gathered together trying to compare notes on how to find Desda who had gone missing almost two days previously. Now she grabbed her husband's arm telling him about the call as she marched him out to the car. They drove to the hospital in silence. They met Mrs. koya and the forlorn twosome at the lobby. Mrs. Koya haltingly explained what they had managed to gather from poor Desda. Elisabeth wailed and collapsed on the seat and Alem Neh stood frozen unable to comprehend what he had just heard. "I am sure your first priority is to see the child, then we can see how to proceed further with this", she said sympathetically. Alem Neh fixed her with a cold eye. "How dare you stand there and speak nonsense when you have no sense of responsibility whatsoever, throwing wild parties for your brood," he pause to stare at Nigel and Terry venomously, "harboring violent criminal rapists in God knows where you live!" He finished choking with such rage his fist balled threateningly. Elisabeth stood up and stepped in front of her husband. "I am sorry, Mrs. Koya. Please excuse my husband. He is obviously beside himself with the horror of this news." Alem Neh moved with lightening speed. He grabbed Elisabeth roughly by the upper arm pushed her away from him and slapped her hard across the face. "How dare you speak for me," he thundered, "all this is your fault. Have I not warned you about that stupid daughter of yours? Do you see the fruits of your laxity? You have shamed me before the entire world," he bubbled almost incoherent with rage. There was a stunned silence, and then the Askari at the entrance hurried forward to intervene in what threatened to get out of hand. Alem Neh shrugged him off furiously. Pointing a shaking finger at his wife he hissed, "I am going home and don't you or that ignorant, no good daughter of yours dare show up at my house." He stomped off in a huff. Elisabeth was dazed, both from the slap and the violent anger her husband had just directed at her in front of everyone present.

Mrs. Koya did not waste words, she hugged the distraught woman tightly and said, "You are among friends and we will give you all the support you need. Now wipe your tears and let us go and see that beautiful girl of yours. She will be alright. We will all see to that!" she declared, her glance encompassing Terry and Nigel and nodding at them encouragingly. The two women went up to the ward. They got there to find Desda heavily sedated and asleep. Elisabeth gazed at her daughter with unseeing eyes. Her heart clenched painfully in her chest and she bit back a cry. Mrs. Koya squeezed her arm and Elisabeth was so glad to have her with her. They went to the Sisters desk and consulted about Desda's condition. The Sister at the desk smiled warmly at them. "We have given your daughter the best medical attention for now but she will require counseling and a lot of support from family and friends. We have hospital counselors and we will have one to see her as soon as she wakes up. I also recommend that you speak to the counselor too. She will sleep through the night so you best get home and come back in the morning."

They went out of the ward. Elisabeth suddenly stopped in her tracks and in a wavering voice said, "I have nowhere to go, so I will go and sit in the lobby until day break." "Nonsense, you will come home with us!" Exclaimed Mrs. Koya. "Thank you, but I could not go to the place where this horrible thing happened to my poor child." Elisabeth answered forlornly. "Then I will find you a place. Would you want a hotel or can I put you up with friends." "We are Orthodox. A married woman does not sleep in a hotel. I know my husband has behaved like a boar but he is my husband and the father of my children, though right now I can't stand him!" "Don't worry I will arrange with some friends to put you up as we sort out this mess. Meanwhile we should be thinking of a police report." "Oh no, please no police. I don't want anyone else to know what has happened to my poor girl. I don't want to deal with policemen or put my daughter through more shame than is already hers to bear." Elisabeth sobbed.

***

Desta lay on a sofa, surrounded by her family and the errant Terry. She had just arrived home from the hospital where she had spent three days. Alem Neh could not bear the sight of his daughter and he looked at a spot somewhere above her head as Terry recounted the details of what had led to this sorry state of affairs. His face grew darker with each passing word and his stance became threatening, he could barely manage to bring himself under the rigid self control of the suave businessman that he was outside his home.

Terry finished telling her gruesome tale with relief, keeping a wary eye on Desta's Dad. Alem Neh shook his immaculately groomed head like a lion trying to rid itself of fleas. With great force he brought his large hands down together on a coffee table nearby and the glass shattered. He barely noticed it but the sound of shattering glass made the others jump and Desta quaked, wishing the ground would open up and swallow her whole. Alem Neh was beside himself with rage, and he did not seem to notice that Patrick, a stranger and employee was witnessing what was a private family affair. "Look at your daughter Elisabeth! See the miserable wretch that has returned to this house and tell me why I should not take her and physically throw her back to that terrorist that she was consorting with." He roared. "Elisabeth, did I not warn you countless times? This," he said pointing a disparaging finger at the offending Desta, "is no daughter of mine! She is your own Elisabeth. Damaged goods, unclean and unchristian and you better know what to do with her Elisabeth, because between the two of you, you caused this!" He finished with brutal finality. He shoved his wife aside and walked out of the room. There was a stunned silence

132

Patrick could not take his eyes off the battered face that had once so entranced him, nor could he get over the fact that Desta was dressed in an oversized man's track suit which made her look pathetically small. He listened to Alem Neh's outburst with an almost dismay, though his reasons were far less noble. Patrick who had witnessed some unsavory scenes while working with Michael was frightened at the rage he had just witnessed from his CEO, a man he knew at work as cool, polished and always civil. Terry started to cry, a fact that Patrick found very irritating, given that she was not the injured party here. He glowered at her from his geeky, close set eyes.

Elisabeth was almost numb with shock, but greater than her personal feelings at the moment, was a mother's instinct. Her child was hurt, her marriage was on fire but she knew that she had to concentrate very hard in order to help her daughter. From a well of strength, she did not know she possessed she took charge. "Patrick I need your help. Can you drive?" She asked, and not waiting for his answer she continued, "Carry her out to my car, the white one and Terry stop that sniffling and come with me." Patrick did not need telling twice, he picked up the girl and carried her out of the house and put her at the back seat. He took the keys from Elisabeth and got into the driver's seat. Elisabeth got into the back with her daughter and Terry got in beside Patrick, who ignored her. "Find us a good hotel Patrick," she instructed. Her mind immediately started to churn over the events that had happened. At the hospital casualty, Desta had gotten the standard post traumatic rape procedure however Desta had not wanted the police involved and no forensic evidence was obtained at the hospital. Elisabeth was finally thinking clearly and her brow furrowed in consternation as her thoughts ran on in utter consternation. "Oh my God!" She exclaimed close to tears, "that man will get away with doing this hideous thing to my daughter and there is nothing I can do about it." "Calm down Mrs. Mengistu," Patrick entreated her, "I can help. I know some people who can give this guy the justice he deserves." Elisabeth looked at him blankly for a moment. "What do you mean you know some people?" "Yes, I do. They do not operate in an orthodox manner exactly but they can come in handy." Patrick explained. "I am a Christian," Elisabeth replied coldly, "I do not want anything that will compromise my faith and make a bad situation worse." "Leave it to me Madam, what I will do even your God will see that it is Just, after all, are you going to just sit and allow that criminal to go desecrating other peoples sister's and daughter's and girlfriend's? Leave the details to me. All I will require from you is some money to facilitate the cause of justice." He said with such a force of conviction that even he was surprised at himself. He knew exactly what he had to do.

Patrick made a discreet call.

Elisabeth watched Patrick with something akin to hope as he whispered intently to someone on his phone. Patrick finished with his call and told her, "I need 100,000 Kshs and you can rest be assured that Gilbert Mwadilo will make restitution for the crime he committed." "100,000 Kshs, are you planning an assassination?" Elisabeth asked incredulously. "Look at it this way, if you went to the police, you would probably end up paying more and not getting any help at all." "Okay," Elisabeth sighed, "can I give you a check?" "Sorry, it is a cash only business." He replied.

***

Gilbert Mwadilo was convinced that the naïve Nigel had bought his story, hook, line and sinker. The fool had even paid him a bonus for his performance. 'Rich kids in Nairobi pretended to be so smart and yet they were quite daft', he thought smugly. He was in a good mood. He had just gotten a call to give a private performance for some rich lady at The Regency Hotel; he would be getting a cool 50,000Kshs for just an hour's performance. He hummed in the shower and then he dressed to kill. A dash of cologne and he was good to go…money beckoned.

Mwadilo was ushered to a private suite of the 5th floor. He would sing with play back so he did not need the Band, which pleased him as that meant pure profit. A rich lady wanted a serenade, he would play, and he knew he was good at those games. When he entered the room he was smothered with a cloud of perfume that reminded him vaguely of someone. Then a girl rose from a sofa like a shadowy wraith. Her eyes were darkly outlined with Kohl and her dark tresses were held up in an alluring design and she was beautiful. She came closer and he gasped, it was that girl, the nameless Nefertiti. 'What could she want with him', he thought in a moment of panic. After what he had done to her, he was amazed at her audacity to face him, to challenge him for this was obviously a challenge.

She faced him, no longer a broken doll but with fire in her eyes. She returned his stare, measure for measure and she stood her ground. He was amazed and in spite of himself, excitement coursed through his veins and his heart accelerated. He smiled mockingly. "Nefertiti returns for the second round, eh?" He laughed. "Sit down Mwadilo, the show is mine today. Make yourself comfortable. I would offer you a drink but who needs a drink with someone like you around," she mocked him back, ever so subtly. He sat down and then two men emerged from the bedroom swiftly and before he could say Mwadilo, he found himself stripped and trussed up like a chicken. The men bodily manhandled him into the bedroom and flung him upon the bed, then tied him up to the bed post, splayed like an X. One of them addressed him roughly. "Today is Judgment Day Mwadilo, and we have prepared for you a royal tribute," he said with a deadly menace. "An eye for an eye and a tooth for a tooth!" He exclaimed, obviously enjoying himself. "Unfortunately, you have no hymen to pay for the one you stole so brutally, but we will find a suitable substitute believe me", the geeky looking man continued with a sly smile. "But first the little angel whose face you marred with your fists has a little gift for you and as they say, 'Ladies first'," he bowed dramatically.

Desta walked in and in her hand she held a kiboko (whip). "You will see my face and you will remember me Gilbert Mwadilo," she said softly. Then she struck, with lightening speed and with the pent up rage of all the humiliation she had endured, since the day he murdered her soul, her spirit, her sense of self and then insolently thrown her soiled garments at her face, smelling of her blood and his semen...she had prayed for this day. The first cut of the kiboko split his lips and he yelped in shocked agony spraying blood with his breath. The second caught him across his chest, and then his stomach and his thighs and he screamed like a woman. She flailed him until her hand ached and her breath came in short gasps. Then abruptly she laid the Kiboko down, straightened her clothes and walked out of the room regally.

"Ah look at the great Gilbert Mwadilo, sniffling like a woman, whipped by a girl," the geeky looking man mocked and his companion laughed. "Now the brothers have a gift for you my friend, so that you know that you made us look bad. You will remember this day, when you feel like biting a defenseless girl and raping her!" He held up a crude looking pair of pliers and waved them in the air. "Our little angel lost a hymen, violently to you and now you will lose a testicle violently to her." Patrick did not waste any more time with words but did as he had promised, he crushed Mwadilo's testicle as the other man held him down. Mwadilo screamed a high pitched scream that was somehow unearthly and the whites of his eyes showed wider as his eyes bulged. His chest heaved spastically and he vomited. The man holding him down cursed and jumped back, screwing up his nose in disgust. Patrick, then untied the bloody, trussed up man. Then between them they dunked him in the tub and roughly toweled him dry, and then they dressed him up in his clothed and took him back to the sitting

136

room and sat him in a chair. Patrick's companion mixed a concoction in a glass and then he made Mwadilo drink every bit of it. After a few seconds, Mwadilo felt himself floating somewhere and he felt no pain.

"Listen carefully Mwadilo, if you want to keep your other testicle healthy and you want to live to a peaceful old age, you will forget our faces and you will read this as dues paid that you owed. No one will remember that this night ever happened. We will take you to your house and remember, I mean every word I have said and believe me it will better for you if we never meet again."

Later that night Patrick escorted Desta back to her mother. It had been no mean feat convincing Elisabeth to agree to his game plan, but Desda had been able to tip the scales. She had agreed to the plan the moment she heard it and eventually, against her better judgment, Elisabeth has capitulated. "We will not talk of this thing again," she said to no one in particular. She took her daughter and they made their way silently back to their mansion on Grevilla rd, to pick up the threads of their life and to face another man, who was to them, husband and father... but that is a story for another day.

Haven Hunters

Yugo Gabriel Egboluche

The morning was very chilly and I prayed the hands of time stood still, just so I could lie longer and cuddle in bed not having to get up for work. I missed waking up by 9am, especially now I was compelled to get up very early for work no matter how I despised it because my life and subsistence depended on it. I felt I was sapped of freewill, even in the absence of chains.

It was 5.30am in the morning and still dark when I braced the cold and rushed over my morning routine. It was over five years now and I had become used to the early British mornings. Out from the bath, I hurried into the bedroom with hair and body still dripping and headed towards the wardrobe. I had sectioned my clothes in three; the first of which were worn on rare occasions, the second worn on hangouts and the third section, specifically for work. I frequented the third section more than any other since I became a workaholic, by reason of circumstance. I hurriedly picked one of the black bleached jeans from the lot, a white polo shirt and briskly put them on before hurling the knapsack containing my work uniform over my shoulders. I headed to the kitchen section of my studio apartment, grabbed a signature mug, poured out the boiled water and emptied two sachets of cappuccino into the mug. The croissants from the fridge were almost soggy. I cared less; after all, I was having it with a brew. I munched and swallowed while standing. I had dialogues within to call in sick, and slump back to bed. I relished the last sip, dropped the mug into the messy sink and dashed off to work.

My boots looked best in motion, cherished with every sprint. I was running late again. No matter how brisk I walked, I would still be late. Before long, I was in Madison Street panting towards the large office complex. Rob was already standing outside to let me in fully clothed and ready for work.

"Morning Rob... " I said, "... hope I'm not too late?"

"Naa, that's alright..." he replied, his eyes scanning the ends of the street. It was my second year working with him and I could pass him for the best supervisor I have had throughout my work in the industry. In my books, he was a very good lad. It was typical for him to engage in conversations before the start of work so it wasn't a surprise when he continued. "...No worries Akin, It's good you told me about African time. Since then, I have always expected you five minutes after normal." He spoke with a smile on his face. At twenty-something, he appeared more mature for his age with a bulky frame that betrayed his calm and accommodating demeanour. It wasn't the best of jobs but he made me find joy doing it.

I quickly threw my knapsack by the corner and brought out my uniform as he walked to the storehouse to bring out the vacuum cleaners, buckets and mops. I could hear the echo of his voice from the distance resonating within the massive apartment block housing the call centre. He was at it again. It was either he talked, sang or filled my ear with football talk every single work day. Who knows what he was on about this time? I knew I heard him say something about a Nigerian, but I preferred he repeated himself while I put on my uniform.

"Sorry, I didn't get you, Rob..." I shouted.

"Oh, I was talking about how I met this Nigerian in my other workshift and guess what..."

"What..."

"...he had just been on time twice since the week I started" I could hear him giggle as he went on "I told him I knew about African time and that I knew one of his brothers."

"I see," I retorted, a bit disturbed by my shortcoming, "...what a good way to introduce me Rob."

"Come on buddy, I was only teasing…" he apologised, sensing the pitch in my tone. He came closer, patted me on the shoulder wearing a casual smile, "…but truly, she had been late thrice and I mean, really late."

I knew at that moment he wanted to hear my defence, but I was caught-up in my own guilt. I picked up the bucket and mop from the corner where he left them and hoped his football team will lose tonight's game so I could get back at him. We worked non-stop for two hours- thirty minutes, vacuuming, cleaning and disinfecting the desks of the massive one storey building housing Argos call centre, easing the workload with intermittent jibes and whistling.

"See you tomorrow, mate," he smiled and zoomed off in his Renault two-seater car at a few minutes to nine before the Staff of the firm started congregating. I waved at him, longing to see him the next day when I would have dug out a shortcoming with which to get back at him. Unknowing what the day had in stock. All I longed for was to go back home, sleep and get ready for my main job in the evening with the Timbuktu fast food chain.

I looked on as the traffic blossomed into the peak of rush hour while I walked home. Everyone was rushing to work. It reminded me of those glorious days in Nigeria's commercial capital, Lagos. Ebutte-Metta was the market and all I did was go to the shop when it was right to be there. When there were big business transactions that the bond servants couldn't handle or when Niyi, my partner and I had to take stock. Those days my belly began taking a rotund shape from soft work. I felt that aura of status sweep through my face again. It didn't last long anyway, as I only had the afternoon before continuing my evening shift as an employee. The cold breeze breathed heavily, sipping through my head warmer and caressing my retreating front hairline. I walked energetically, every stride taking me closer to my residence. How time flew in the afternoons was beyond me; a little nap, a few hours on the internet and soon I would be getting set for another six hour shift- standing!

I couldn't believe it was already four in the evening when my alarm went off. I felt myself struggling once more to get up with an aching back which my muscular frame couldn't shield. I stood 6ft 2" tall, with cupped chests, bulky biceps and trimmed abs. I dragged myself through a vegan lunch and gulped down some pain relievers. Then I took a glimpse into the vintage mirror that hung close to the door, just to be sure I wasn't frayed. My boss, Hameed demanded we look good for the smiles.

'Good Evening,' I greeted, walking into the eating area of Timbuktu fast food. It was still quiet. The spicy Pakistani aromas from the kitchen filled the air. I lifted the wooden demarcation and went into the counter. Hameed was busy with some documents. Then I went into the convenience to change my uniforms. I came out and observed he wore an unusual countenance. I greeted again. And still did not get his response.

"Good Evening Hameed!"

"Yes brother, I heard you..." he replied harshly without removing his gaze from the papers spread out in front of him. I looked from the crown of his traditionally knitted white cap to the sole of his sandals. Nothing seemed unusual. He still wore his robes; the only difference was his trimmed beard. Through all the years I had worked for him, it was rare to see him put on his spectacles behind the counter or respond to anyone with such a tone. Although he might be tough and pushy at times, he never did so without mild humour. I had a hunch something was wrong.

"Is everything okay, Boss?" I asked. He looked at me rather compassionately, "...everything is okay except for you." I did not understand what he meant. I went numb as my thoughts raced. I never imagined a sack, not after giving my all to his business. No! Not after all the labour I had put in. I knew how hard it took me to get him to accept me for work because of my inadequate

141

immigration documents and how hard I have worked to maintain his trust. I was still wondering what the cold remark meant when he walked towards me and gave me a pat on the shoulder, "....I hope you will be okay brother." He walked past me, out from the counter and into the eating area where he sat down morosely in one of the eating tables.

"Good evening," came an unrecognizable voice from the kitchen area, "...are you Mr Akin?" I turned towards the direction of the voice only to behold an Immigration Officer. My breath went riotous, out of control. I tried to control it, but the more I tried, the more it ascended into chaotic spasms till I lost hold of myself. I reached for the counter to support my numb limbs, panting and shivering. I felt sweat trickle out from the pores of my skin to form steam on its surface. I was boiling in the cold. I felt someone hold me up around my shoulders, another by the waistline.

"Are you okay?" the female officer asked, fully clothed with bullet proof vests and mobile gadgets, "...don't worry we are not here to harm you." I slightly regained consciousness, lifted my head and beheld three Immigration Officers standing around me in the small enclosure that served as the fast food counter. I towered above them, though it made no sense now I was in their grasp. "We just wanted to confirm if you are Mr Akin..." the officer continued.

I felt the need to lie but knowing they must have drilled Hameed before getting to me, I resolved to tell the truth. "Yes I am."

"Good," said one of the male officers. I watched him reach out to his side to unlock the handcuffs. "Your hands please," he demanded. I didn't know what to make out of the ensuing episode. I watched Hameed sulk in regret. My hands shook tremendously, just as my thoughts paced in recalcitrant limbo.

"We are arresting you for immigration offences and a breach of contract", he proclaimed. There was no use saying it. I knew my sins were always before me. My thoughts quickly raced back to Nigeria. I began seeing flashes of me, trading our goods, everything we had laboured for in Ebutte-Metta market in the hope of gaining them in double folds once I set my foot in the United Kingdom. It's been five years now, and I have barely saved enough to payback Niyi, talk less of Kunle, my half-brother who I sold portions of his landed inheritance without consent. No! I can't go back this way, I breathed. What am I going to tell them back home? I grew aggressive. I held unto the counter and unto everything I could lunge my hands on, resisting an arrest.

"Mr Akin," the female officer chided, joining in the struggle that ensued "...it would be nice if you corporate with us and avoid actions or statements that could be used against you in the court of law." She said, gasping for breath after every word.

I had no statements to make if Mr Hameed had none. I wouldn't give in to their arrest without some form of masculine resistance either. Untiring, I somehow succumbed to the joint efforts of the three officers who overpowered me using cuffs and Taser guns. I bowed aimlessly; recovering from the Taser shocks. I looked on as the handcuffs greased my wrists. I could not believe Chief Adedamola's son was on handcuffs, the apparent heir of the Agbobi kingdom. How did the mighty fall? My kinsmen would never hear this, I breathed. The Officers held unto my shoulders like the convict I was and led me out from the counter. The same counter which I had laboured in, for more than three years. We continued into the eating area where I served customers from various nationalities. I fixed my gaze on Mr Hameed. He sat helpless and dumbfounded, scratching his hair laden with grey shoots. His feet tapped uncontrollably. I have never seen him like this, pensive and terribly shaken. I doubted if it was pity he felt for me. Perhaps, he pondered what would become of his business.

"Mr Hameed..." one of the officers called his attention, as they led me out unto the waiting van collecting the documents from him

"...we shall make proper arrangements for you to pay the fines as soon as possible." He didn't utter a word. No one would in that circumstance. Not when you are paying a fine running into thousands for another's misdemeanour. It was then I realised the subject of his disposition. I felt sorry for him but couldn't figure out what to feel for myself.

"In the meantime, Mr Hameed..." the officer continued, "...thank you for your corporation."

Then they whisked me swiftly into their waiting van, avoiding a scene. I was made comfortable in the trunk of the van guarded by two male officers. Two of whom were positioned outside with a waiting driver. The other rode in a smaller car behind us. It passed for a stealth operation, the type I watched on TV. Asides the two air openings on both sides of the van, it was pitch-black immediately the doors came to a close. I remembered myself watching the criminals from Kirikiri Prison, Lagos being taken to court without feeling a thing for them. I wondered if passers-by, did feel a thing for me. I thought of Lagos, I thought of Agbobi Kingdom. Then the car came to a halt and it was in front of my Rochester Street, London apartment. How they got to know my house address, was a mystery that my house changing tactics could not hide. I heard footsteps pacing up and down the staircase as I was led to the house. A loud bang came from our back door. I suspected Kola and Nirandeer, our Indian housemate escaping my ordeal. Only the two of them could have been at home by that time, out of the five of us that shared the apartment. I felt a scapegoat but consoled myself in the fact that it was only a matter of time; the law would catch up on them like it did those before us.

"Not to worry Akin," one of the officers whispered in my ear, "...they can run all they want. When the time is right, we will get them too." He scoffed.

'"Mr Akin," the female officer called out unwrapping a piece of paper "...we have the warrant to search through your apartment.

Any further resistance will be deemed an obstruction to lawful duty." She gestured me to open the door and lead the way. I stood by the side watching as they conscientiously ransacked my room. I prayed they don't find my passport. So I buy some time to figure out a solution to avert an imminent deportation.

"There we go..." the blonde haired officer spoke for the first time, unearthing my passport from a travel bag overlay.

I was led into the fortified walls of the removal camp by two officers. I saw only but pensive faces, no one seemed to care that it was winter. Their faces reflected the white walls and titanium bars of the camp. I bowed my head in shame.

"You have a good night Mr Akin, we shall begin work on your deportation arrangements tomorrow" echoed one of the officers in my sub consciousness. I remembered Rob, my jolly good friend. I remembered friends, I reminisced the times, I remembered my relatives. Never would they want me back empty handed. Then I thought about my little savings which would be confiscated once my plea fails. I sensed every ounce of hope drop as I slumped into the camp bed.

My body temperature blazed in the cold winter morning. I felt this unusual tremor in my legs, sweating and shaking uncontrollably underneath the duvet. I could hardly lie still in the single bed. There was an internal war waging in my mind; a war too strong that the small rectangular walls of the detention room couldn't contain. I was wary of my future, afraid of the weights from my past closing in on me. I heard someone in the room next to mine sob uncontrollably, his own fate awaited him. I could no longer cry. All of my tears, I had traded in sweat. I alone knew when I cried. I cry in times tears drench my clothes and dribbled down my torso as sweat. I had suffered to get to where I am, even though uninspiring. I have had my fair share under the sun and in the rain; in the summer and under the winter.

I dreaded the sight of the food pack and water bottle. There was no strength left in me for chewing and no saliva to swallow. My fate hung in the air and the weight of the world seemed to have fallen upon me. I needed strength to figure out an escape or to fight back. I watched the metal doors open and a gentleman walked in. And again I remembered Agbobi, Kingdom, I remembered Lagos. The mere thought of going back to Nigeria scared me.

"Good morning Mr Akin," the young officer said with a sincere smile "... how was your night?" It was no use answering him. There was nothing good about the night, which was undoubtedly the longest in my thirty four years on earth.

"What have I done to deserve this?" I spoke to myself looking up hoping I could see God. My eyes caught the light bulb on the hallway. And it immediately went off. Was it a sign that heaven had abandoned me? Or that God had nothing to do with this. Not after I willingly sold all I was blessed with, including family lands and inheritance for the sole purpose of achieving it in the United Kingdom. The land of dreams I called it.

"It's almost nine O'clock, Sir" the dark haired officer hinted as he walked me down the hallway, "...you are meant to be at the hearing at exactly nine." His voice wasn't British. I really couldn't place it, neither did I bother. His words reminded me of my predicament. Punctuality didn't matter anymore.

"Do you have a family?" I asked him, without a thought.

"Yes, I do sir. Two kids, a boy and a girl," he replied without hesitation. I rested in shock, brooding over his achievements at a very young age. I presumed he was only in his late twenties. I saw myself drowning once again in regret and self-pity, striding behind him like a convict sentenced by his own culpability. I entered the room, joining three uniformed men and two ladies seated evenly. The smiles they gave me looked every bit like the last I would receive. I likened it to a hangman giving a convict the chance to say his last prayer for a shot at heaven or hell. I strode in quietly and sat

146

on the empty seat opposite the man who appeared to be the Chief Interrogator. They had all my details; information of my dropping out from post-graduate study, six months into enrolment, to the details of my extensive work hours using a student visa.

It didn't take long for me to lose my cool, my voice; encumbered with the many facts of my misdeed. I feared my emotions. I felt guilt, I felt unappreciated for the hard work, the contributions and service to community. I watched them ridicule me with facts, leaving me at the mercy of the adjudicator. But how could I remain silent, when I had been robbed all these years from tax that could have come off as illegal. I found an unwavering courage to plead my case, rise within me, even if it came out as unreasonable.

I heard myself scream in their face, "For five years, I have paid my taxes and remained a loyal citizen..." standing on my feet, I waved my handcuffed hands vigorously "...why weren't the taxes rejected if you label me an illegal resident? If you had all these details and knew all the while, why did you delay the ordeal?" I fumed.

"Mr Akin" I went deaf on them, blabbing while the highest ranking officer tried to shut me up, "...Mr Akin," he went on, "do you want to shut up and listen to me or not?" He demanded, taking off his spectacles, "First of all, you are not yet a British citizen and based on your current details, you can't be," his voice pitched with a bout of ire, "... yes for five years; four of which you hid from the authorities, after dropping out from school, you had paid your taxes, which as a matter of fact are legal based on employment laws!" He calmed down a bit, holding himself back from losing his cool and went on, "I wonder why you could do this to yourself, being the loyal citizen you claim to be. You haven't even visited your own country since then, who knows what your family thinks of you..."

I couldn't control my eyes as it kept twitching, I longed for tears. I needed to tell a story; a story that could convince them. I felt sweat pour out from my sides, my head ached and I gradually went hysterical with no control of what I was saying.

"I have to be frank with you," I said turning to the ladies, hoping to appeal to their conscience, "I stepped on many toes to enable me get here ... if I go back, they'll kill me. I have nowhere to go. No house, no friends. The people I call my family would not accept me..."

"Mr Ah... kin, you have to tell yourself the truth." The blonde lady interrupted with a droll pronunciation of my name. She looked me straight in the eyes "...we are not here to judge you by your emotions; we are here to uphold the dictates of the law..."

"...Would your law allow one to be subjected to avoidable danger? Was the law not made to protect?" I cut in.

"I haven't finished Mr Ah... Kin. As the law dictates, you have been found wanting in many areas and therefore considered a law breaker. Disrespecting Her Majesty's Immigration laws is a heinous offence." She persisted, showing no emotions whatsoever.

"I am telling the truth Ma, my life is in danger..." I wailed and lost control of my manliness. I hit my hands on the table and on my head. I felt a cloud of despair and frustration envelope me, like a caravan swaying me through snow-capped mountains unto sun baked pebbles. Sweat streamed down my underwear. Never in my life have I felt this humiliated, dejected and forbidden. I started screaming, "they will kill me...they will kill me." That was all I could say, not because it would change the verdict but because it might delay the verdict.

My parents wouldn't want to see me. I left at the prime of my success, denying them the rewards of painstakingly bringing me up. My half-brothers would jail me for selling off our fathers landed properties to achieve my aim and leaving the family prone to lack. Niyi could kill me for betraying the trust he had in me and selling

148

off what we had laboured for over the years, leaving him with a note I could clearly remember its wordings that read: *'I am sorry Niyi. By the time you are reading this, I will be in the United Kingdom. Accept my apologies, though I strongly believe there is light at the end of the tunnel. I did it for our good and the good of our business. It wouldn't be long, till I pay you back in British pounds. Then we will be smiling daily to our favourite bars and do all the things we like. I hope you would find a place in your heart to forgive me for betraying the trust you have in me, leaving the business in my hands while you pursued your political ambition. I strongly believe you'll win. That alone, will alleviate every disappointment my forward thinking action might cause you. Truly yours, Adedamola Akin.'*

Niyi never won the local council elections. And I haven't spoken to him in ages. Truly, I had no one to turn to. I deserted many of my friends and relatives when I saw the success of my visa application and never kept in touch with them while I strayed to fulfil my London dreams. Now my people won't accept me and the immigration won't let me be. I have become a haven hunter, caught up in his own trap.

"I am finished. I am lost." I muttered, "why is this happening to me. Why now?"

"Mr Ah...kin, is there anything else you would want to tell us?" inquired the blonde haired officer.

What to say! I drowned in my sweat as I slumped back into the chair. My eyes still not letting out the tears I so desired. I no longer had control of my emotions. The room got smaller and swallowed me up. I was squeezed up in my world. I had become like a bat with no home. Not here in the United Kingdom. Not back in Nigeria. No one was willing to accept me. It also appeared no tree would allow me make a nest on it. No dock in sight, to anchor my sinking ship. My bags were all packed up with the little remains from my room, ready for deportation. It was all I had, nothing more to show from my five years sojourn. Nothing but my work credentials - requisite experience in a fast food retailing and food processing industry, nothing tangible for a second class upper graduate of political science. This wasn't what I bargained for. No evidence of my ultimate mission - the British pounds. I felt I wasn't done yet. I needed more time.

"You have to help me; my life is in danger..." I re-iterated, leaping forward to grab the burly officer seated beside me. She looked quiet and indifferent all through the interrogation. "You know I am a good man. I have done no harm to anyone...," the words kept coming. I sold the wisdom and confidence my age could garner in desperation. I thought her reticence could pay me in return but she quickly retreated from my grasp.

"Mr Akin," I was called again by the Chief Interrogator. I turned his way. He looked unperturbed and my disposition didn't seem to mean much to him. His spectacles were firmly put back sitting loosely on his nose.

"...It's no use putting up a show in here. The circumstances have been proved beyond reasonable doubt. It's clear you had no cogent reason for breaching our Immigration laws."

I watched as he put his face down and scribbled his signature on some documents placed in front of him and slid them towards me.

"I'm afraid," he continued, "...you have to sign the papers, or you will be forced to do so. The sooner we get them ready, the easier it would be for us to expedite actions for your removal."

I stretched out my hands to the table and pushed back the documents. I could feel my heart stop. My head fell, hitting hard on the table. I couldn't fathom the silence that followed. I shut my eyes hoping the angels would beckon me in the quiet; but none was in sight. It was all dark and scary. I heard voices humming mysterious medleys, swirling like incantations from the shrine of a Yoruba voodoo priest. I knew the voices. It was that of Niyi, my dad and that of Kunle - his first born son of whom the legal right to the land's I sold belonged. The voices grew loud in discordant rhythm and soon began fading. I heard again, a faint British accent. It grew loud, audible till I felt a gentle tap on my shoulder. My eyes opened to a brown surface. I smelt wood. I smelt coffee.

"Are you okay, Mr Akin?" One of the female officers asked now standing beside me. I regained consciousness, lifted my head from the table, to face my fate resting on the hands of the Immigration officers.

"We can understand how you feel...," I looked at her name tag as she spoke.

"I don't think you do, Mrs Perkins" I cut in knowing she was only trying to be nice. My story didn't seem new to them. They looked at me dispassionately all the while.

"...yes we do Akin. We have been on this job for years, and yes we clearly understand. But as it appears, we can't help you on this." She concluded and headed back to her seat.

"It is true the law permits one to seek asylum in another country in situations where his or her life is in danger," the Chief Interrogator stated. My eyes popped. "...But I doubt how that could be of help to you."

"I ...would definitely use that Sir. I really can't go back. Not now. Nobody wants me. They will kill me." I kept rattling without sparing a thought. Any option would do for me at the moment. This could be it, that last shot that might turn the pages for me. They took me through the asylum procedures. I signed a few papers. I watched them leave the room one after the other. The young officer came back for me. Held me up and escorted me out of the hearing room, back to my detention cell.

"Why don't you want to go back home?" he asked as we strode through the hallway.

"You won't understand," I replied.

"Don't you have a family; I mean a wife or kids back home?" In what appeared to be my darkest hour, it was the last question I had expected. How would I tell him that at my age I wasn't even

151

married, not to talk of having kids? He was bent on consoling me not knowing he was doing the opposite.

"Why don't you go back home and save yourself this boring life," he continued, "I really don't like it here either." His words confused me. I turned and looked sternly at him, with eyes blazing in perplexity. He withdrew and apologized in all modesty.

"Why don't you like it here," I asked him.

"I preferred it back in Russia," he said, "but can't go back..."

"Why?" I cut in rather curiously.

"I eloped from a covert conscription for espionage, so I could get married."

I couldn't believe my ears. I somehow smiled at the mere thought of success with the application since the warden attached to me, was himself a haven hunter. My mood lightened as I walked into my detention cell.

"One more thing," he added, "...about your asylum application, forget it. You won't be granted." At that, he closed the door behind him and my smile was short lived.

Beasts in the Farmstead

NURENI Ibrahim

There were Mole and his aides who penetrated every lane of the farmstead with an arsenal of ammunitions. This frightens all the beasts on the farm.

I was in the hut when a boom frightened me. *Boom! Boom!! Boom!!!* It sounded heavily like a sledge hammer thrashing a hard-hitting nail.

Could it be Mole and his aides again? I hummed.
As I peeped through the window of the hut, I sighted crowded legs mourning the unjust path of fate. Albeit, their unnervingly dirges were unknown to me yet; I felt a grip on my hand and opened eyes in an attempt to scream.

After the wild frightening booms, I moved out and eagle-eyed Squirrel, Gecko and Spider howling awfully beside Owl.

What happened...? I bellowed.

"Mole and his aides abducted over 200 beasts in the dawn"; replied Squirrel.

I sobbed profusely and wondered where the termites were ... when the aides abducted those beasts. Weren't they conscripted to secure the farmstead? I mused to myself.

That evening, countless rumored tunes flooded the walls of our farmstead. "See Dragon dancing over our plague of agony...." All the beasts echoed.

Dragon had once proclaimed that Mole and his aides were also beasts. "No beast should slay another." This was his anthem. Alas! Mole and his aides had killed a million or more beasts in this farmstead. Perhaps, he had forgotten too soon.

"How could 200 beasts be missing in this farmstead ..." I soliloquized.

As we sobbed upon the news of the missing beasts, Squirrel rushed to us hastily:

We all yelled out cacophonously: "What happened again?"
"They have bombed the windmill again"; he exclaimed.
"Which windmill?"
"The only one left behind"
"Who…"
"They are anonymous …but I suspect Mole and his aides"

Poetry

I'm honest
Asekho Toto

I'm in fear of touching you
Kissing your lips
Not knowing
If they are soft or not
Most of my life
I have lied
You can call me a liar
But now
I'm not lying
I'm being honest with you
I don't know nothing about love
The only sex
I know is the one
I see on the television
We all know what it means
I'm a saint
But a saint that's full of lies
I'm not expecting God to judge me
I'm expecting the community of men to judge me
I'm just being honest
Come to me
And teach me how to kiss
Those strawberry lips.

Let this world burn into ashes

Asekho Toto

have seen poverty
I have seen depression
But I haven't seen unity
Where people live together
Peacefully
Pride has captured our humanity
We never lived un harmony
This world
And it's money has been cruel to us
It's time to burn this world down
And rebuild a new one
Hatred has chased out love
Women are being abused
Children are being molested
Look at what we have became
We became monsters
In a sheepskin
We as men should stand up for women
Create movements alongside women
Women were alongside men
When Jim Crow's law still existed
When Apartheid still existed
Let's support each other
And bring this world to its knees.

Anagnorisis
Tomas Sanchez Hildago

Lastnight, whilereadingTheMetamorphosis, by Kafka (or Die Verwandlung), I realizedthat, actually, the real metamorphosisisundergonebyGrete, Gregor'ssister, and thatthetitle has itslet'scallit-ironic-burden.

Gregorundergoesaninitialmetamorphosis, theobviousone, thehigh-profileone (also off stage, orbeforethestage): histransformationinto ...a beetle? But (rock n' roll)?,as the novel progressesthere'sanothermetamorphosis, of theonlycharacterwhoempathizeswiththesickman: Grete.

And in theverylastparagraph, whenthe bug isalreadydead, herparentsnoticeher: she'smetamorphosedinto a beautifulwoman.

The novel isnotabout, shallwesay, fatalist horror (the-worst-is-already-over, like in a workby Francis Bacon), ortheimpossibility of communication in a masssociety;

itistheabovementionedmetamorphosis of a younggirlinto a woman, as herbrother, a travelingsalesman and seriouslyill, undergoeshisdegenerativeprocess.

Itisshewho, whenthelightswentout, takesover, and who in theendsurrenderswhenshesenseshow inevitable destinyis. "As theytalked-saysthesecond to lastparagraph-, Mr. and Mrs. Samsa (...) realizedthattheirdaughter (...) haddeveloped, and transformedinto a lovelyyoungwoman full of life."

Ifthetranslatorhadusedmetamorphised (instead of transformed), wewouldhave a closedcircle of metamorphosis.

158

Caballos en Möenchengladbach

Tomas Sanchez Hildago

Amongtelephonelistenings, and hidden cameras,
on a terrace in Germany, and infiltrators:
aswaiters, at noon and at three,
—and at nineo'clock and at six—,
adeliveryman,
andcustomers of every creed:
twolesbians, a Bateman and a mysticalmarriage.
<<Waitfor me to giveyoutheorder>>, in a racecourse,
andinfiltrators:
whiteslavetraffic in thenexttable.
I pretend to be betting,
amongtopics of conversation of poorquality:
these are concernsthatyou do notyoutake to a desertisland.
And theyserveus a couple of Martinis —theman at noon—,
and a couple of misfortunes —thetelevision—,
andmixedmessages: Interpol´sbackgroundnoise.
<<Notyet!>>, —I orderedthem—,
andfloods in Australia and droughts,
andindebtedstates,
andtheresurgence of theFascists,
and<<Notyet!>>.
And while At last !, Itwas time !, theyplaythecards
—passports, lives: girls in exchangefor euros— those of
thenexttable,
the Stock Marketis red orgreen,
earthquakes, typhoons, tsunamis,
andblackmenlosing a war,
andI'mstillworkingonthisfortherest of theafternoon,
althoughdisastersqueuing to eliminateus,
all of these are coming to my<<Now!>>.

And whiletheworldfallsapart,
tell me whatthehell I do
(forced voyeur)
on a daylikethis,
speaking of horses in Moenchengladbach.

Goree Place
Helen Harrison

Underneath pavements, the earth is unsettled
as though death can be shaken and rattled.
Aroused, the humus alerts mineral metals
who shudder in muscle memoriam from soil
the deep tissue flex, bulges piazzas.

The sun falls behind one side of the river,
cinnabar orange glows in chrome and glass
offices. The air changes to uncomfortable
and monolithic shadows of building-blocks
appear on cement covering the trade of souls.

Overspill
Helen Harrison

A city's summer night is ignited and we're wild,
stalking behind a stockade of torched Nissans.

We cover half our faces with the neck of Tacchini
tracksuits. Use forearms to shield eyes from tear gas.

In the surge of Upper Parliament, the incandescent
light of the Rialto dome burns for days.

The police's black Maria's are flipped with doors
stripped off them. Their wheels spin frustration.

Milk remnants are curdled in soap bombs,
flying skittles swung at by blood-starved batons.

Our looting arms overflow with stocked aspirations
and we hijack babies' prams to ram past them.

Siff Silver-Cross hoods cover Bird televisions
as bricks sleep-tight underneath navy covers.

'Am I not a man and brother?
Ought I not, then, to be free?
Sell me not to one another,
Take not thus my liberty.'

'Am I not a man and Brother,'
William W. Brown (1848).

Bread and Butter
Helen Harrison

Rancid butter from the city's bread
spread thickly to South Staffordshire,

the slave trade had churned its cream
to turbulence by the riches of its merchants,

who prospered and fed off the unfree.
Abolition inlaid by Potters on hair pins,

snuff-boxes; 'Am I not a man and brother,'
women wrapped it around wrists as bracelets.

Wedgewood's symbol you wouldn't find on
profiteer's dinner plates or soup terrines,

he glazed and fired a reminder of the bloodied
wealth the city was built on;

an African man festooned in chains,
pleading not to board Britannia.

This is why the colonial sea does not glitter
(for the Dutch poet Joop Bersee)
Abigail George

There's nothing as beautiful as the newspaper

   man eating fresh plums. The woods, mushrooms,
potatoes. The vibrations of foliage. Daylight.
   Glory. A tender swarm. The triumph of an athlete.
   The redemption of a sinner. Spring found in the
   desert. A Saturday morning. Leaf! Oh, sacred
leaf! Universal winter. Cat. The action of rope
   found in blood. The shadow of a woman found
in the venerable wild. There's nothing as beautiful
as deep-blue love. The echo of a bird. An icy
   wind that freezes everything green but the gap of
time. A page in a book. Golden people. Fire.
Bright places. Novel places. Iron faces. The out-
   lines of a lonely season and hills. There's nothing
   as beautiful as the woman in the photograph.
The bride of high summer days. The confession of a

sinner. The perfumed juice of a pear. Bird. Field.

A lovesick climate. The blessing of an emerald
day. Kite-flying. The fabric of a stream. The hidden wings
of a child. The swell of a rosebud's mute-bloom.
Thread of an owl through the air. The lengthened
passage north. Sinking-gathering-maturing cells of
sunburnt flesh and bone. The Mediterranean-
blue sky. The tarnished transaction of vital star
meeting black hole. No, there's nothing as beautiful.
I come to life in my sister's Cape Town flat. It

is raining men and women and when the radiant
sun comes out it rains golden. I think of people
    that only say things to be polite or diplomatic.
    I think of how before I do things now, I have to
wait for the tiredness to lift. I think of my flesh
and blood. And how everything around me is
    fragile and connected to God. Sometime I think

of the hospital room I found myself in when I was barely 20-

    years old at Tara, then at Golden City Clinic, then at
    Hunterscraig Private Clinic. That was before the renal unit at
the hospital where I was born. Now, I eat for three and

four and five. I have to find my own way to be cheerful,
    and it feels like the day after Christmas in my hands.

WE LET THEM
Thamsanqa Wuna

We ululated and praised them,
They who broke the shackles of colonialism,
The heroes of the struggle for freedom,
We sang songs of praise,
Grateful for a new era,
The beacon of hope ever so bright,
A new dawn, a new Zimbabwe,
We let them lie to us.

We let them taste the power,
We idolised them in return,
When they were challenged they began to panic,
Ethnic cleansing was the solution,
Gukurahundi they called it,
"The rain that washed away the chaff"
Genocide was their response,
We let them get away with it.
Our own "Moment of madness".

We let them rule despite their greed,
Despite their purely evil misdeeds,
We let them empty the breadbasket,
We let them kill our motherland
We let them kill her year by year
We let them abuse her, rape her, kill her,
We let them kill our Zimbabwe.

We let them violently grab the farms,
We let them inflict further harm,
We let them impose draconian laws,

We let them kill all those who oppose,
We let them destroy all those homes,
We let them rule us from their thrones,
One thing we let them do of note,
We let them rig and steal our vote.

We let them maim us in 2008,
Their apologies are decades late,
We let them steal our moment of victory,
And now we feel our torment and misery,
We're letting them lie to calm our fears,
Knowing that crocodiles have no tears,
Let's vote for change, a new era,
They're still the same, make no error.

Let's not let them rule us again,
Let's not let them cause more pain.

ASANTE SANA – (THANK YOU VERY MUCH)

Thamsanqa Wuna

The shock, the sheer nerve,
Defying the dawn of a new season,
A people united for what we deserve,
While the entire world sat and observed,
"Asante sana" he said, against all reason.

The horror, the overwhelming dismay,
Poisoning us with all that sorrow,
All we wanted was to end the decay,
A new beginning, a new day.
A hope for a better tomorrow.

The arrogance, a stubborn president,
A fiend, one we had to dispose,
The epitome of corruption and moral decadence,
The unity and purpose of every resident,
Asante sana, the incompetence exposed.

With the world waiting for his resignation,
He decided to act so tough,
He had no idea he faced rejection,
He wouldn't make it to the next election,
Because the nation had suffered enough.

Asante Sana, it wasn't a coup,
He's gone and it hardly seems real,
He's gone, he's gone; the news is true,
Now there's hope for me and for you,
Let's celebrate to express how we feel.

Asante sana, our new dispensation,
Asante sana, our new start,
Let the people dance in jubilation,
Let us have a free and fair election,
Asante sana, there is joy in our hearts.

(On the day) Robert Mugabe resigns
(a series of twelve haiku)
Abigail George

Bleak companions.
(little) (angel) you're with home-coming her.
Decaying beings.

Full throated horses.
The ploughman's evening-sky has fallen.
Cold stars in heaven.

As slow as baked bread.
Lonely crestfallen birds bloomed-out-of-nothing.
The tears that I've cried.

Those wise monsters.
Slow tongues of honey's northern skies-of-flame-and-snow.
Wake in hollow tree.

Calm. Selfless. Composed.
Through starving grass and tree falls-the-night.
Chirping birds. Warm earth.

Reminds me of you.
Sunless   nation   ending   in-mighty-once-there-was-beauty-here-
winter.
Bleak companions.

Sunburnt empty house.
Teams-of-horses and men designed by God.
A wind. Dust leaps up.

170

Autumn's roof shall pass.
Nothing belongs to burning-you in-any-way.
And snaps up the air.

Faded twirling leaf.
The beauty of the night branch-to-branch.
Abandoned to flirt-with-the-wind.

This compared to love.
The wide-eyed-dying-fearful vision of a hunt.
A scentless rosebud.

Mouth. A smile. A frown.
As white and numbing as melting snow's-glorious-wreck-of-cloudlet.
Wedding of grass against-life.

Sparse lissom river.
Each move like a woman's column-of-vertebrae.
Vows of the river.

LET MY POEM SETS ME FREE

Adewusi Raodat Abimbola

O Aseda!
Let my poem sets me free
From the garlands of corruption
Which grows within the
Throats of my country.
Let my metaphors blend into the vein
Of truths
Screamed for the fortune of this state.
Let my paradox grows
Like SOWETO,
In the midst of grief:
Shaking the hands of my clans
Into the rime of war.
O Aseda!
Let this poem set me free
From the freedom of distress.

A Prophetic History
Diane Pacitti

There is a space
Beyond the defended borders, where the visionaries
Of the English Civil War can meet Lumumba
To claim back the land.

   There is a song
Whispered through prison bars, rising in Soweto,
In Dublin, Glasgow, which will not be drowned
By the drumbeat of imperial histories,
Sung by the Suffragettes, danced by the crowds
Who greeted the freed Mandela.

 And just sometimes
We glimpse this space around us. Deep in Soho
The outcast William Blake pours out his rage
At the one white-haired God. He sees the rod
Of this false deity reach out from London
To wither and enslave. In grief he hears
His 'Jerusalem' roared by white football louts
As a crude battle-cry.

He turns his eyes
To the sprawl of London. In that city now
The god has Rasta dreadlocks, or perhaps she
Is many, and dark-skinned. Now Blake's true heir
Is a black rap performer who gives voice
To those who live on the edge. And now in Carnival
The weaving, dancing crowds of many cultures
Restore the capital's joy.

                              History brings
Undeserved blessings: those we enslaved
Are liberating us; those we oppressed
Restore to us Britain's long song of freedom.
Blake looks, and sees Jerusalem being built
By those who once were strangers.

SEASON OF CRIMSON DAGGERS
Adewusi Raodat Abimbola

in this season of crimson daggers, there
were baleful calamities that savaged
silence for the weeping waifs after storms
rained heavily in our marketplaces;
after the night fed our laughters with marauding
mourning; and the days with insuperable flames;
after the leech whacked away our wailing skins
by those goatish hearts—
who hide behind the facades of our tragedies
celebrating solely on our labeled-maps of agony.
in this season of crimson, the destiny of the missing
ones were chiboked in the famished-soil while the daggers
triumphed in massacring their daughters;
in this season of wailing tones; there were abattoirs
performing surgical operation, but never on
—animals.

THE ILLOGICALITY OF THE ETHEREAL
Colin James

Escaping heroes have always
depended on resourceful barterers
to camouflage the trapdoors
seamlessly beneath lectern oaks.
Immigrants need not affect
a drink of something bolder.
The truck in idle awaits.
Its long neck extending past
confrontational apocalyptic borders.
Advertisements have been burned off.
One letter only is left to scramble
as all oaths are coughed and exposed.

CAPTURE OF A CONCEPTUALIST
Colin James

The Procean Tabular walked sideways at birth.
She recovered enough to blend in,
for many years it was not empathized
then later in life she again began to list.
Harrangers, as they do, noticed
the signs of feigned noncompliance.
The lopsided desks
pant legs that didn't quite mesh,
and a looping shouldering gait
that seemingly preceded her arrival
by as much as a month, opportunistically
condescending enough to lead to her death.
Her funeral was attended by pointy hats
as well as lemurs, satyrs and asterisk printers.
They formed an unabated procession
walked the river path calmly
chanting as they picked up the litter.

SUNDAY LUNCH IN EXILE

Enesa Mahmić

We didn't talk about our suffering
We taught our children patience
Mastering the silent endurance
Our masters said:
Unnecessary sorrows hijack the glory of God
So, we ate the crumbs from their table
Without any complaint
We comforted our self: I'm fine. It's ok.
Tomorrow will be the same,
The concept of discrimination repeats itself.
Gentleman from social institution will remind me again
That I'm just a number in the system.
I will be thinking again
How I should leave everything.
Maybe move to another city, another country.
I comforted myself with the illusion of love,
Understanding and forgetfulness
But I couldn't escape from my black skin.
Deep in my heart I knew
There is no country for immigrants.

You
Gugulethu Radebe

I write notes in dreams
To dare to meet you,
To swallow my pride
And dare to need you,
To follow this heart
And dare to seek you,
Despite my constant groping
And reaching in the darkness
I know I'll still miss you.

To be you,
To be brave enough to love
You.
To allow myself to
Hold you
Without feeling like
I'll Lose you.

They hate you,
You were bolder than I was
So they fight you,
Break you,
Curse you,
Violate you,
Torment you,
And in the silence of
The night I dare to love
You,
When I know they don't see
That I'm just like you.

Packages

Gugulethu Radebe

In neat piles we stack them,
Careful not to wreck them,
Gently carry them in the packing,
Keep them safe in the chaos of moving.
Our boxes,
In beautiful piles of nothing.

In nice rows we place them,
Carefully wrap them,
In tidy little boxes we've
Packaged them,
In beautiful bundles of nothing.

We polish them,
Careful not to dent them,
With meticulous care we paint them,
Adore them,
Dare to love them,
Our beautiful clutter of nothing.

When we finally need them,
When we're reaching, hoping to find them,
When we're lying in the dark and wandering,
In quiet conversation when we long to
Share them,
Our little packages with nothing,
But broken dreams and hopes of starting.

Desire
Gugulethu Radebe

How Primitive are we to give into it?
She lies silently in my arms,
Deep breathes and nothing,
How Primitive am I to desire her?
In the midst of fear and darkness,
I dare to want her.

I dare to touch her,
She responds,
How primitive are we to make
Love during war?
To crave normalcy in
The belly of death?
To crave a moment of pleasure
In the midst of never ending pain.

How Primitive are we to give into it?
Daring to hold and be held like those
Who enjoy freedom would,
To allow ourselves to feel like
Nobody is hunting us?
How Primitive am I to desire her?
In the midst of uncertainty and fear,
I dare to want her.
I dared to look into her eyes and
Seek normalcy in the belly of death.

THE WRITER

Enesa Mahmić

I didn't know how to become a writer
Some things trigger you
A tree bared by the storm
And then everything was announced
After an abundant dinner
When heads and clerks
Dive into deep sleep
We're bleeding on paper
We waiting for the sky to become fair
My *dearling*, I'm telling you about my rage
How rage turns into sorrows
Folie à deux
There is a birds' comentary in my stomach.

MOTHER FREEDOM

Enesa Mahmić

You can find her in the poorer quarters
In the ghetto, in the factories
She passes through deserts, forests and oceans
She is washing dresses with peasant woman.
She is sitting in the conference room
You can feel the bitterness in her voice
Usually she reapeats: No!
                          I disagree!
                          I can't accept it!
She makes small traces for the brave steps
Her sleep is reflected in the deep lake
In prehistoric times
In ether.

Year 2027
Oscar Gwiriri

Upon the sky of my country,
Flies metallic eagles,
Freely dropping acidic droppings,
Scorching the lives
Of my people and environ.
In my prophetic dream,
I scream for our souls,
Realising we're already in war.
Year 2027, women and children hide,
A gruesome war awaits,
Someone is brewing to unleash.

The President
Oscar Gwiriri

Our President bows at the front yard,
Caresses the Calla lily inflorescence,
Leans towards the trumpet-shaped bract,
Peeps inside and suddenly withdraws,
A bee flies out ululating and saluting.
Neatly, he cuts the stalk with a secateur,
Smells the beautiful white trumpet,
Carefully puts the magnificent flower aside,
Pulls weeds on the forsaken flowerbed.
The caretaker rushes with a dish 'n' towel,
He doesn't wash the hands, leaves for office.
We stare through the dirty windows panes,
Suffering from self-inflicted punishment.

Peaceful Country
Samuel Nyachiro Kegwaro

Demonstrations are over
but your loathsome combatants roam the streets,
in military fatigue
to intimidate us with their ferocity.

Your irate and insolent men kill and maim us,
riddling our emaciated bodies with bullets,
as they defile and rape vulnerable women and children
then jeer them.
And you feign innocence as you ascend to power.

Journalists kidnapped and incriminated,
then slaughtered in cold blood
for being politically incorrect
and executing their duties diligently
and professionally.
They are silenced for saying the truth
and hindering you from gaining power.

Families evicted for their political allegiance
to your competitors.
Common masses crushed then alienated
and the elites cajoled
with prodigy children suppressed
Yet they do not know what politics is
in this "peace loving country."

ETHNIC MISCONCEPTION
Hélder Simbad

Rotten blood ball explosions
in the volcanic uterine chains
    [My sister terrorized by the monsters of the age

Mansions and luxurious cities
being born from my urine
the tip of the tongue kissing the absence of teeth
the fragile milk teeth Crushing Stone breads
    [First orgasms between measles and cholera

My mom
my poor mom
[AFRICAS of my lives
without dreams
dreaming on the cloudy cushion
our dreams
in the hands of a bantu breeder
resting on the chest of misconception

The Death Of My House

Samuel Nyachiro Kegwaro

My house is beautifully furnished,
with paraphernalia for a comfortable life.
Her living room is splendid,
her kitchen good for my health.
Her bedroom intrigues me.
Oh! my beautiful house.
The floor of my house is diaphanous;
complete with expert artistry.
Her walls burnished cream and brown,
Her roof beautifully festooned,
leaving me exuberant.
Oh! my beautiful house.
My beautiful house is now askew,
her former image irredeemable.
Her kitchen leaves me desolate,
her inexorable roof in disarray.
Oh! my beautiful house is sick!
Yesternight,
My beautiful house breathed her last,
without intimation.
Her incredulous death,
leaving me an orphan.
Oh! my beautiful house has caved in.

AFRICA OF MY FEELINGS

Hélder Simbad

Africa of my feelings
ancestral dream
between the light and darkness

Rise from the earth
floating and walking
among the flying cottons of Egypt
and the cities of stones of Kilimanjaro

Walking aerial
I absorb you in the breezes of Cape Verde
and I see you combing the dense hair
in Mayombes of vanities

Even today the waters of your Nilos run
between eternal hope and rivers of blood

I lived authentic festivals
in the early hours ofAngola-1992
Pyrotechnic exercises of gunpowder and projectile
Wandering walking convalescent
From the south to the north of death
Because of the fatigue of discords

I ignored alliterations of people and gunpowder
But perpetuate the eternal dreams Of a mortal god
And never gather the hot potatoes of the earth
In a feast of perceptions
I'd rather be north of life.
And travel to moon

LOST IN-BETWEEN

Ifeoluwa Ayandele

Father's father hung drum
On a nail in the corridor
To pick up the gun to war
Father dropped both for the bible
Now, stand I, nude,
On these paths pondering…

My wife-to-be is wearing
A new look,
She shouts aloud with streaming tears
Without her necklace, bracelet, earrings and
Her trousers.
To the altar of faith, she runs.
What faith!
"…Christ-like love," she tells me.

For love, I pick up the bible
But at the gate, I return
Wondering wild, off the pedals
Of the church.

To the deserted corridor
Of my grandfather, I return.
On my neck, I put the ancient drum
But cannot make a rhythmic noise
I drop it on the floor and leave

breakfast with a hippopotamus

James Bell

the whole body moves like
a rotund dancer on a sprung
floor high on rock and roll
to express how breakfast has
been interrupted

                     when grass
is still lush with dew at 8 am

the location in a nook of acacia
has the look of the habitual

we see from his dampness
he has bathed to refresh his flesh -
an early wallow somewhere
where there is mud and a deep pool

the intrusion on his routine
is reflected in an evil eye
his dance and roar represents

a very still malevolence that says
our time with him has now finished
time to start the motor and go

migration

James Bell

I must accept there is no word
for goodbye in Swahili
it's – see you when you return
when you come back one day –
Kenya has touched me
although I must migrate north again
like wildebeest and zebra
who travel in herds with that pull – that flow
man and beast know so well
so deep it is never acknowledged –
in spirit I cross the Mara river
that I wait beside as the water drops
to let me go
                      there are no demands
upon me – like the heron that stands
among a clump of reeds
the water so low now
the crocodile cannot stop me
the hippo has sunk into its own deep pool
go now then return someway somehow

The Land of a Thousand Hills
Matt Black

Immigration man asks -
what do you do? I'm a poet.
He wavers, frowns, smiles

Sunrise bush medley.
Birdsong orchestra crowned by
African chicken

Noisy moto-moto,
crazy bustle, red and yellow.
Oasis of hotel

Primitive straw rooves
banned. Sun beats, monsoon hammers
corrugated iron

Eyeball gorillas
for big money? No, I want
to meet coffee plant

Where you from? U.K.
That's good. Developed country.
Pause. Think. Theresa May

I ride with you on
your dangerous old moto,
number plate "My God"

Lift mattock, let fall,
lift, fall, lift, fall, all year till
long valley is tilled

Small mud house asleep
in sun. Family weeds beans.
On earth, bright clothes dream

Constance knits fingers,
tells her story, brave, strong, true.
Sad eyes catch old ghosts

If this can happen.
Questions flower, red and blue.
Too dark. Not again

Elephant with mobile
phone rings with international
lessons for the world

Bikes hold backies, sacks,
racks of sugar cane, planks, wobbling
towers of cabbage

Yellow cans heaved up
to huts, hills, lovers, doctors;
water for skin, tongues

Bare feet, dusty legs,
thin, aged 5, lugs heavy can.
Small angel smiling

Banana tree fans,
green fingers, leaves like feathers,
like frayed propellers

Ticking crickets stitch
a tune, pavement Singers hum
threads of afternoon

Dark, low market. Crowd
hear preacher's halleluliahs
sung from heaped garlic

Muzungus do good
in umudugudus, relax
in hotels, by pools

Pink sun, orange track,

purple shack, painted lizard -
if you like it, Crown It!

Roadside: Primus, Skol,
Airtel, Onetel, Rwandatel,
Guma Guma Bar

Roadside: women, kids,
bikes throng. Watch out, bus coming
at ninety miles an hour

Bus rides waves, up, down,
through land of a thousand hills;
valleys, old as Wales

Flat-topped hills in mist.
Fire-heart gorillas beat chests
astride volcanoes

Slow treks on hot tracks.
Worlds balanced on careful heads -
bananas, fish, doors

One cup porridge, one
bowl stew, nine hours teaching,
the daily menu

Akagera. Fast
hyena's flash of orange.
Flash back: land before

Crashed trees, elephants,
eagles, crocs. Gentle zebras
strut ancient catwalk

This hill, Congolese
refugees; that hill, young leaves
grow strong Yorkshire Tea

The Clash sing: "Breaking
rocks in the hot sun." Rwandans
break rocks in the hot sun

Bye Nyamirambo,
Chimoronko, Nabugogo.
Maracose Rwanda

muzungu (white person or outsider)
umudugudu (village)
maracose (farewell)
guma guma (painted on the outside of many bars, sponsored by Primusblager,
Guma Guma is the biggest music contest in Rwanda)

Good sports
Sinaso Mxakaza

You will find a piece of us in every mineral exported
The hands that laboured for this country
linger in these raw materials bleeding reconciliations
Waiting on land reclaims
To be heard when speaking their languages
of how the motherland is an orphan
Protesting the lives put at risk
for the wealth of her nourishment
to align her with capital countries
The dependency on development
as seen from foreign lands
Is freedom indeed for all?
Or manipulated economic relief
You'll find a piece of the people
In every tourist attraction spot
Cities divided into subsections of class
Urban areas hosting visitors on decorated cultures
Of a people that were and what they became
Poverty lurking the deeper you go in the ghetto
Political bonds tightened between continents
In sports, arts, business and skills development
But mostly gun trade and black markets
Which breed grounds for drug and human trafficking
We are new people with old battle scars
These are present times drenched in history
Time thought people to carry themselves with ease
After rusting in chained societies
To speak their mother tongues relishing change
Working to never house wars on any land
United by laws and humanity

The land of peace

Sinaso Mxakaza

Loss is deeply rooted in certain times
People carry their history with them
With hopes of laying claim to their ancestral land
They wish to rebuild and find dignity at home
Leave better legacies for their children
Not dwell too much on the pain of the past
If their homes are their own
Not owned by the banks or government
If their time is their own but is it?
They speak of fallen heroes in memory
Walk freely in countries with powers elected by people
Nations merge across borders
The past taught us the art of peace
Teach the young this history
That they may fight the good fight
School them in proper politics
Don't burden them with hate

Now we don't know the world any other way
Sinaso Mxakaza

We live in beautiful times
Easily connected at a touch of buttons
even when we know what lines never to cross
Leaders chosen with care
Travel, a leisure known to many
Libraries for us all
Sharing the same paths on streets
We don't know the world any other way
We might have found a common language in past pains
In hurting and being born generations
after the world found a new face
Botched up politics cut close to home
The world is forever watching
We cannot go back to yesterday
Separated by fear and class
Everybody has learnt to live where they are
Found refuge in another land
When they lost a part of their country
Some families carry two races in their DNA
Their family portraits thrive on no border restrictions
We live among each other beyond the politics of skin
Able to tell the tales of the past because the present is for us
And speak life into the future which our children carry

hyena

James Bell

so we finally meet
as you gnaw on a piece of vertebrate
to keep the habit and strengthen the jaws –
I look at those teeth as you stare back
with a practised eye
that in a moment establishes your place
in the food chain

      you are the one who cleans up
after the lion pride has feasted and taken a nap
and flies make you some guts of tenderised meat
so only bones remain on the Masai Mara –
scuttle to the next job like a Uriah heep
who does not ingratiate – does not look
for thanks as your hirpling shanks
move back into the bush to hide away
in a grove of acacia

      know you will never eat me
because I am not yet dead –
so clear is our understanding as I stare you out
as you gaze out from the leaves –
realise we could be friends
with no great ambition for more – our jaws
could go far though I prefer meat cooked –
see – we have meat in common –
it looks like our brief communion is finished
as you do not reply

AT MY MOTHER'S FUNERAL
(A performative poetry)
NURENI Ibrahim

Lend me an eye or more eyes to grieve with my broken spines
Lend me a mouth or more mouths to tell the tale of this ...
Lend me a soul or more souls to breathe at my mother's funeral
If you truly love me; please begin to grieve in tears, before the
Starving soil guzzles at my mother's corpse
On my head lies a gushing ocean; drowning in a spectacle of
sorrows
Tendered thunders threaten to tumble through my vault, drizzling
in the
Distillation of a diverse deftness; a wedge of weeping wounds
Doomsayers weave tales of my survival. Only the skeleton in me
cries
Heavily to the deaf ears of the mourners' conglomeration
Who will mend the grieving of my broken spines?
Mother!
I have seen the end edge of this world—who slew you too soon
Now, God! I am lonely like a porpoise, rushing to be delivered
From the nemesis' wombs of this motherless earth
Mother! Mother!! Mother!!!
I remember ...
I remember the ...
I remember the tale of tortoise you told me in twilight
You ... said
You ...said ... (silence)

OGUN

NURENI Ibrahim

When you get to Idanre

Tell Ogun that I have

Been mourning his silence

For so long?

For Geoffrey Philp
Rethabile Masilo

I should have cut a hole in the ceiling
to let my prayers out.
--Joyce Ellen Davis

It is a call from the edge of a cliff
like the one to prayer which the faithful heed,
though that's not all a poet needs;
there has to be sacrifice, a culling,
the thinning of a population, words must die
for ideas to fly, like Khotsofalang
and Maaparankoe, Marcus Garvey
and Ruth First, whose hearts were wrenched
out of history.
Whole lines of life-like swaths of land must burn,
boil to their essence, their stanzas sent
through Joyce's prayer hole in the roof,
until a little time only is left
at the depth of a poem, and we know
that we are going to take the leap.

Lovers
Rethabile Masilo

After coming, the lovers
are exhausted in that way,
in a shade under which
their shawl is sprawled,
a sun sieved to where
others have lain before,
a basket cradling fruit
near them. After coming,
the lovers are reminded
of laundry, chores to do
before light leaves the eye
(like a candle withdrawn
from a room). For Cupid
now has no more work
with them; love holds them
against the world's intent
in its ransom of the heart.
So they agree to return
to houses where bodies
are ghosts and ghouls
behind locked doors,
though their souls aren't
for pillows and eiderdowns
and doors; that place is only
where they surreptitiously
wait it all out until they can
return here to come again
and again, again and again.

Thoughts of home
Rethabile Masilo

I drag a dead suitcase through Maseru
looking for what could make me understand
the image in shop windows that says
I am what had to happen. All over Kingsway
four-ones weep for the promise of a time
when this nation finds itself, and hope
grows again like a mountain at night.

I bay for relief, and peace that may one day
find itself deserving. If winter is here
to conquer us, what happens can only be
in the way we hold ourselves to light,
even as words die on our lips
and we are reduced by delay past belief.
We must live with history, not push it
out of the way, or let it find us a surprise.

Voices from the ashes
Wilson Waison

I
Note that I was murdered to have risen transformed
Note that my flesh and blood was readily made dust
Note that my bones and skeletons got incriminated
Note that my impetuous voice echoes from the ashes

Note how I was silenced... to have risen transformed
Note how I struggled: from the liberational coercion
Note how I triumphed over the sceptre and bayonets
Note how I gamed over the war sceneries impeccably

II
Note that I was flawless, efficient, resilient, competent
Note that my energies were sapped during the event
Note that my knee crawled from valley to valley deep
Note that my aim was for the betterment of the kins

Note how I was enslaved* before and fought swiftly
Note how I become a guerrilla in motherland, savage
Note how I raptured apart the foes and the schemes
Note how I became violent and vigilant in my domain

III
Note that I was a victor before I got engraved deeply
Note that my wrath did grew with the evolution peak
Note that my beloved comrade back stabbed his own
Note that my bones has risen, the ashes mold vessels

And let my long gone blood reflow from the pool of
That Impetuous distant rivers, and rekindle the lost

Blazing flames of the Chimurenga wars... Magamba
Josiah Tongogara the barracks named after decades

IV

Denote when I rise from the ashes I vote mercilessly
Denote when my passions gather I will spit of venom
Denote when my strengths grew I will fight back fists
Denote when my courage reverberates I will burst out

Denote when I become potent, I will reign over again
Denote when I am with the mighty I will aside favours
Denote when I reign the Augustus house it will report
Denote when I speak order will reign, reconstructions

V

Denote how the muddled economy will reboot again
Denote how the incubators of corruption will vanish
Denote how the lost zealous and confidence bestows
Denote how the ills and evils will be driven to extinct

Denote how the brothers will cheer from the drums
Denote how the sisters will break a leg to Jerusalem
Denote how the fathers will fail conscience off brew
Denote how the mothers will pail the yield in joyous.

I have lived at a time
Tralone Lindiwe Khoza

I have lived at a time when buckets of dirty water had to be carried
by the wayside, so the breeze would fall into the house
I have lived a time when I cared to see my face upon the waters.
I have lived a time when souls, drifting with their shadows would
pass me, pass by so they can trade their dreams for money with the
Chinese.
I have lived at a time, when people believed quick-fixes who deliver
them from their anxieties.
 I have lived at a time when the tap would drip loudly for the
forgotten aunties and uncles who lived with us.
I have lived at a time; I dared to see Star with her majestic crown in
the big black sky,
Yet those that lived below failed to see their answers lay above
them.
I have lived at a time when men believed in the power of their
words.
I have lived at a time, when keys would be pushed under the door
so rightful seeker would find them later.
I have lived at a time, when the red chair sat beside the blue chair,
so the girl would sit beside the boy.
I have live at a time when we thought our freedom would never
bring down the shadow of Cecil John Rhodes.
I have lived a time when university was a door to finding your
purpose, not, a blood massacre for the 142 students at Garissa.
Who will comfort those who weep, who sold sugarcane and cows
for their offspring?
I have lived at a time.

*A statue of Rhodes erected in 1934 on the University of Cape Town campus,
on the lower part of Jameson Hall steps overlooking the university's rugby fields.*

This statue became the focus of protests in March 2015 calling for its removal. After weeks of student protests, a council meeting delivered a final verdict to remove the statue of Cecil John Rhodes from the University Of Cape Town (UCT). It was officially removed from the University of Cape Town on 9 April 2015. The calls to have the statue removed are not new, Afrikaner students demanded its removal in the 1950s.

*****

Terrorist attack at the Garissa University in Kenya, left 147 students dead on the 6th April 2015. This remains to be the deadliest attack in the nation since al Qaeda killed more than 200 people at the U.S. Embassy in Nairobi in 1998.

Inkanyeziyami
Tralone Lindiwe Khoza

She fought through eternity to find me
Always imposing her independence in fair laces.
She cuddles with Elves everywhere
She wants to go anywhere
Her purity lingers to the downtrodden
It took me a while to find her in the reach of my heart
She is my divine work of art.

These days we love with our eyes and our laughter.
She mimics stories from day mother
In the patter tone of one, who is almost three years in the world?
We recite surreal nursery rhymes, and matching song soothing hymns.
We play games, old and new and smell citrus leaves.
Orbit in circles as the earth is to the sun.
 She sucks the juice out of oranges and tangerines.
Until the apples of her cheeks are rosy.
She chases her brother in God's earth.
Until they are both out of breath
We put lilies in our hair.
Blow kisses to the air
She is a teacher to me.
It was meant to be.
And I am the one she loves.

Inkanyeziyami- Zulu for my Star

211

The Rhino of Hoxton Square

Troy Da Costa

No more comforting words than
He was born of Africa
Carved of her Granite hills
With the bled soil of a thousand warriors in his veins
And while they expected him to be ordinary
He could be anything but

In this place so far from home he began to sing
The song of a mother
Her child and a land stolen so many years go
It was the sound of rain rushing across the savanna
Of a wild and untamed romance in the setting sunlight

Finally, they heard his voice
In the darkness
Saw the fire he'd gifted them
And knew him as son and brother
The best part of who they were
And all that was good from the land we belong.

Harare
Troy Da Costa

She was the dark side of me
The music of my soul that tore it apart
And left me lying in her streets
Cause she knew how to get me high
And I walked away
Because the hurt without her was less than the pain she caused

I found someone else
She mended what she could
And nurtured what was left
A crooked tree that bore no fruit
But I dream of her
That women who never slept, that filled me with such desire
And would break me if she could.

Footprints at Heathrow
Troy Da Costa

Falling from thirty thousand feet was easy
Even the icy runway paled in daunt comparison
To showing a green passport
To any unjustly aggravated immigration official
It may as well have come with a return to sender note

It seemed simple enough for my forefathers
To turn up on the shores of Mozambique
With all but a sense of entitlement
To unburden on the locals
To satisfy their adventure thirst

Instead, the sense of dread loomed
Through the halls of Heathrow
Past busy Vogons
And pairs of fellow travellers desperate in their failing attempts
At convincing their inconsolable cherubs,
They had not arrived at the shores of Hades.

The immigration officer sat at a high desk
To make it easy to talk down to me
I gave her the papers she so craved
And she devoured the information with an uncanny distaste
Pausing only to probe for felonious intent
In my unguarded gaze

Finally, unreasonably angry, she spoke:
"Are you here to subvert the British culture or bring down the
government?"
A ruse to draw confessions of nefarious intent

"No" said I, unsure if she'd be convinced
Outmanoeuvred she slammed her stamp on my pages
and pointed indignantly to the door.

I'd made it, the new life sought beyond the sliding plates
The story unwritten in the swirls of ice and snow
Of a December unlike any
Among the civilised, the vogon and the desperate
I stepped across the threshold as if it were fresh and unbroken soil
And I the first to leave a footprint.

AFRICA, MY STORY
Chido J. Ndoro

Allow me to tell a story
Of my home,
My Africa,
My beautiful mother
Who is said to be beautiful
But filled with wretched children.
Separated from those she loved
At birth,
Hopelessly looking on
As she was stripped
Off all that glorified her.
My Africa,
My beautiful mother,
Your fate in the hands
Of greedy, inhuman devils.

Let me tell you a story
Of how my mother
Was torn from limb to limb
For the pleasure of patriarchal 'brothers.'
Violently separated from her children
By arrogant men,
Who sought worldly glories.
My humble mother,
My Africa,
Powerless
Against imperialism.
Her body divided between them,
Her fate in their hands,
Greedy, contempt devils.

I have a story to tell,
Of how my mother was raped
By wicked men,
Who were superior in their minds,
Who divided her jewels among themselves.
My beautiful mother,
My Africa,
Bearing headstrong offspring,
Her children abhorring
The hypocrisy of her rapists.
The spirit of rebellion
Alive in their midst,
Fighting for their fate,
From men who threatened
Subjugation forever.

I have a story weighing me down.
I have to tell,
Of how my mother was freed
By her children
From the devilish rapists.
Of how her children,
Free from the murderers, rapists, slavers
Have turned on each other,
Oppressing their fellow brothers.
The seeds of greed and corruption
Have been planted
In my dear mother,
My once beautiful mother,
My Africa.
Your children are thirsty for blood,
The blood of their brothers,

The brothers they fought with
For freedom.
Africa, your children forget
What you taught them;
"I am because we are."
Your children forget
The true meaning of democracy,
The true meaning of independence,
The true meaning of liberty,
The true meaning of love,
The true meaning of peace.

My mother,
My Africa,
I have been longing to tell a story
Of how we,
Your children with uncorrupted minds
Will not allow our fathers
To manipulate us with stories of war,
Stories of death in exchange for freedom,
When all we know now
Is freedom in exchange for death.
I will tell a story
Of how we,
Your hungry children
Fought our fathers
For true democracy,
And freed ourselves from their grip,
And once again
Gaze upon your beauty,
My beautiful Mother Africa.

Neighbourhood kids
(taken from 'The Africa in my House')
Andrea Mbarushimana

I showed you a photo of some kids I knew.
You described it back to me:
A picture of brown, African children
Kwashiorkor bellies distended under ragged
T-shirts stained with dirt
In adult jeans cut short to fit their tiny legs
Big brown eyes and naked feet.
"Poor kids" you said.

And in my shock. I forgot their names,
The games my husband played with them
The screams of their delight
And felt as though you'd taken out my eyes
Replacing them with TV screens.

The Human Animal
(taken from 'The Africa in my House')
Andrea Mbarushimana

Strawberry stained faces
Conversation foaming
She tells me proudly, how
settling in Uganda,
She set up a charity for animals.
Those poor puppies.

I too have seen orphaned creatures snap at fingers for food
Sniff from bags on street corners
And weep around their flies.

Mary Ellen, in 1872,
Was removed from abusive parents
Under a law against cruelty to animals.

Look how far we've come!
Cream puffed, Proseccoed,
Protecting white children
Alongside African dogs.

The African Markets
Tola Ijalusi

There was an Africa
Of gratis trade in gratis markets
With consensual prices among
sellers, buyers, clients
A differed structure yet similar capitalism.

This is the Africa I Know:

A feature of her soil, land
Is her market places
Evolved from junction in bush paths
To shades of giant trees
Now to the open markets
farmers, traders, hawkers
Free people buying and selling, rendering services
In peaceful coexistence embracing ideals
Embracing freedom of blacks, liberty of whites.

She has gained the freedom
Of her own lives, choices
And pursuit of happy-ness.

Colonials changed Africa
For the better;
                    Africa, oh motherland
Shall change the world
For the better.

Read Africa
Zongezile Matshoba

Read all
That is there about Africa

The only continent with an Anthem
The only continent with a public holiday

You will find religion
Its European roots quashing Africanism

You will find education
Dubbed civilisation by Europeans

You will find civil wars
Featuring colonisers and funders *(Belgium, France, Germany, Soviet Union, America, UK)*

You will find corruption and looting
Featuring the same smuggling state and natural resources

You will find poverty and sicknesses
With aid and Aids coming from Europe and America

You will find unemployment and poverty
Capitalism from Europe and US dominant

You will find entertainment along with binge
At the expense of African culture and custom

You will find drugs and sex trade
Imported as far as the East

You will find guns and Rambo knives
Helping Africans kill each other

Go to an African home
You will be greeted and welcomed anytime

Speak an African language
You will be cherished and made one of their own

Pizza-ingAfrika
Zongezile Matshoba

Pizza is not new
At least for Afrika
First made in around 1884-5
Somewhere in German's Berlin
Not by Debonairs and Romans
Colonialists flavoured and sliced Afrika

Fast-forward to the fast-food future
Africans guarding colonial interests
Becoming *mantshingilanas* scrambling for crumbs
Marching the yard, the borders
Always policing and soldiering it
Arresting, torturing and killing any resistance

Today Afrika fights black-on-black xenophobia
Language easily tell the colonial masters
Tyrannies fight about oil and land riches
Few turning farm land into gaming
For the sake of hunting the Euro and dollar
Living many dying of poverty and sickness

THE PLEBEIANS
Nwoke Theophilus

Loud
More
Than
The wailing cry of the Seagulls,
The
Plebeians
Bawl
Under
The
Brute boots
Of
The
Callous Captains
Of
Our
Sinking Ship of State.

Libation of Blood
Adjei Agyei-Baah

We have come to you with our gourd of tears
Take, accept and make us men of huge testicles
We have swam in our sweat as you instructed
And braced the harmattan with its cracks
On our lips and heels

Our hoes have tilled the same furrows that you made
Our fences going beyond the boundaries that you reached
But our harvest has always come with weevils

Must we pour you libation of blood
Before our voices climb up to your ears?

So Long a Shortlist!
Kariuki wa Nyamu

Beware Soul Brother
Of Chameleons and Gods
When Bullets Begin to Flower
Home Floats in the Distance
The Headline That Morning
Another Nigger Dead
Words That Melt a Mountain
Cut Off my Tongue
An African Thunderstorm
A Chequered Serenade to Mother Africa
This Land is Our Land
Song for the Sun in Us
An African Elegy
A Shuttle in the Crypt
Echoes Across the Valley
Flame and Song
Make it Sing
My Mother's Song
The Fisherman's Invocation
The African Saga
Labyrinths
Flowers in a Broken Smile
Horn of My Love
Give Me Room to Move my Feet
Building the Nation
A Nation in Labour
The Promise of Hope
Stubborn Hope
The Mad Man at Kilifi
A Pattern of Dust

A Thousand Voices Rising
Lament of the Silent
Village Voices
Echoes from the Mountain
Tensions
What if I am a Literary Gangsta?

An Epitaph for a dramatist-cum-politician
Kariuki wa Nyamu

Below this
gravestone,
lies late Rt Hon.
G. Maji Machungumno,
who had a brilliant career
as a socio-political dramatist,
But, politics attracted him, as he
created tragic heroes and heroines,
and so, later in life,
his playwrighting career
sadly came to an end! He
begged votes like anyone else,
and was elected to parliament,
vowed to exercise all his energies
and after polls, he was crowned
a Cabinet Minister, and so, he
devoted the rest of his life to
public affairs, but neither was
he an exceptional politician, nor an
incorruptible public administrator,
only he turned out to be one of villains
in his most acclaimed plays, and
walked on firm earth! Ugh! It's
only after I revisited his prize-
winning political satire,
that I understood
"Writing is one thing
and enacting is another!"
Fare thee well most prolific author,

Rt Hon. Dr G. Maji Machungumno,
BA, MFA, M. Phil, PhD. Pub Admin, EGH.

IT'S COMPLICATED

Mzomuhle Mkhabela

The world has fallen apart
Heartbreaks are the earth's mansion
Painted with shattered pieces,
Fenced with concrete blades.
Oh, what a stabbing world!
Souls are maimed
Now our hearts are in our mouths.

Hate carpets the planet floor
Hearts hold no smile,
Tears have the cutest smile.
Maligns are our wishes
And misfiring roll us in sheer ecstasy
It's complicated, where's love?

Immense hopes for tomorrow
Yesterday shakes our strength
And it's a hurdle we can't jump.
Irresponsibility remained an acid
To the skin of our passion,
Innocence peeled of the future
Now mistakes and regrets are dancing to every rhythm.

Living in a river of tears
Failures are swimming within
And we're drowning in quagmires.
Life is a book of shame
It's hard to Face this Book.
We connect to Pinterest,
Still can't picture our knots

It's really complicated
What's really up?

Surely, there're two worlds...
Kariuki wa Nyamu

I
I'm Mheshimiwa's wife
I've the benefit of
a seven-digit pay scale government job
I drive a limo worth millions
I report to work not on time
I vegetate in office
I ingest mountains of snacks
I snore at midday
I leave work before time
and hey
I don't care a damn!

Listen people
I live a very lavish lifestyle
in a castle with gold décor, pure gold!
Of course, that's away from city's poor dirt
I school my kids in the US
and whenever I catch a slight cold
I'm air-lifted to Cape Town
But, I must say
I'm dead inside!
For I see my billionaire husband
once in a blue moon
he insists, his job is too demanding!
He often jets overseas
deserting me in cold spell
but anyway, our people,
forget all ills

and let's just re-elect him
in order to maintain my
sky-scraping social class
after all, I know you take pride in me
whenever I make a fashion statement on TV!

By the way,
it's not that I'm proud or even selfish
look at it logically,
it's you people who'll benefit
when we re-elect him
for he'll labour to see to it that
electricity, tap water and telephone
all finds you in IDP camps
friends, look at it this way
(he'll make the camp better than you found it)
or don't you think
that all this
is for your own good, our people?

II
I'm the IDP camp's chairman's wife
I've a big heart in my thin body
I walk miles and miles
on peacekeeping deals
I toil and toil and toil
from sun up to sun set
eat cassava
rest not
and care a lot
for our people

Listen, listen people,

Did I tell you that I exist in a torn-paper tent
with my adoring husband...
where we share with a few fowls
our children learn under leafless trees
and now that I'm expectant,
I anticipate being wheeled to Level 4 hospital
And, I'm sure I'll be told
wool hasn't been procured, again!
Did money end up in people's tummies?
Ask me not
for I work not there!

By the way
Didn't I tell you that
I've never set eyes on Mheshimiwa?
He who assured us resettlement
upon being voted in?
Hmm... Yet I'm sure when
campaign time comes
he'll reappear to beg votes
and being law abiding citizens
we'll all desperately declare
"Mheshimiwa Tosha!"
and queue whole day
banking on the promise
of being resettled
Oi, damn the consequences!

But really Wanjiku
has your memory rusted?

Surely, there're two worlds...

Basahyeade
Adjei Agyei-Baah

Unlike Kubour, the soft strong
This ruler came
He saw
But alas, he scrambled

He came in a sheep sheen of humility
The spirit of countrymanship lead his path
And forced square pegs into round holes

He left behind a monument of debt
As corruption did blossom for harvest
And truth bowed to the ugly face of lies

Things really fell apart
As our glory of old
Yanked through the mire

Indeed he is gone
But we are left to gather
The chaffs from his winnowed grains

Some kind messiah
Do come and help us mend our broken china
Lest our glue hardens into an anthill of nothingness!

Basahyeade — an Akan word for a mismanaging fellow.

236

Pages of The Diary
Mandla Mvolwane

We all stood silent by the seashore
As we watched the sunset leave a
Merely visible shadow of ships,
Slowly sailing away.
Finally! The division of the
Magnificent African cake had ended,
The discord rhythm of gunshots,
Lashing whips with a stinging sound also
Sailed away with their owners.

Little did we know that today
Barbaric and ruthless oppression
Cloned itself into cunning mental manipulation
Disguised as a quest for civilisation.
Our ancestors' ways play a tug of war against
exotic ways.
An endless war which conceived
The notorious flesh abdicators
Preaching the restoration of the Ethiopian Sea,
A name recognized even by the Ashanti Empire.

Nature itself allocated roles,
Horse men were masters and soldiers,
Camel owners were tillers of the soil.
Paving way for the infamous stereotype
The "us" and "them" binary relationship
Sealed by the 20th century territory scramble.

Day by day, year by year
We long to resurrect Caesar's utterance

"ex Africa semper aliquid nov"
Something always new from Africa. L
Bearing a touch of coexistence,
fair trade, tranquillity and affluence.
Our ships sailing across the globe
Like a spider's unlimited access
to its web.
An ecosystem where horses and camels
Freely experience the Western winter and the African
summer.

Nostalgia
Beaton Galafa

Sending me back to where I belong is
Both hurting and honourable.
You could have sat on me as you have done
With thousands of ideas and rebellions
Which in your own words were retrogressive.
Squeezed tight in between rocks
I could've been suffocated to the underworld
Skull and bones crushed beyond recognition
There would be not a single trace of my being
On this fucked up paradise.
But you chose the human face of life.
Instead of twisting my bones and flashing the pile
Down an upper-class toilet hole towering over
Latrines and boys and girls scratching garbage
You chose to put me in a cage as you would
To your birds and the ebony Congolese girl
Leopold and his zombies put in a zoo in the times
Whose stories we are not permitted to discuss in
Public because we have to be woke men and women
Who will stand up to the new league of mandarins
Tossed forth and back from the Lancaster House
Right from the day we littered the streets dancing.

Do not judge her...
Amanda Sewani

Her tears have a story to tell
Her spirit is like a candle flame
Flickering in a winter wind storm
Her heart is broken to pieces of shrapnel
Surely, she was not ready!
Selfish? Perhaps
But it was her decision to make
Encapsulated in the emotional life of a nation in chains
A nation cursed by greed and corruption
A tyranny that had robbed her of her education
Reduced to vending
Her decision had been made
She was not birthing life
Into these pits of slavery.

MAKING OUR LOVE ETERNAL
Maria Menezes

Makingourlove eternal,
iwouldpaint in a coloured strip
sceneswe'velivedonourfantasy...
Andwithoutconsideritboldness,
iwould enlace itaroundtheworld.

Makingourlove eternal,
iwouldembosson a rainbow in thesky,
thedrawofyourhandon mine.
Yoursmooth skin on mine,
your body shaped to mine.

Makingourlove eternal,
iwouldwaterhappiness to life.
I wouldcallthewavesoftheseaandrivers,
andwiththousandwatersshining in threads,
iwouldweaveourcomplicity.

Makingourlove eternal,
iwould dance aroundthefireofpassion.
I wouldofferourwarmth to theworld,
andnotwoundingyouevenby a second,
youwouldalwaysbe in myheart.

The Trick
Niall Hurley

At the end of the rainbow:
that's where they keep their gold –
in pots – so I was told,
back when I was an Irish boy.
We chased those ribbons in the sky,
we children without colour,
hoping to cross the painted bridge,
slide down the other side,
and swim through a sea of coins,
ala Scrooge McDuck.
But what would meet us at the shore
of the world behind the world?

Might it be filled with Eire's missing creatures?
Bears in the forests,
Wolves in the valleys,
Snakes in the grass?
Would Banshee screams pierce the air?
Would fairies flitter, here and there?
Could we stay? Would we dare?
We never found out.
Because you can't reach a rainbow to begin with –
That was the leprechauns' trick.

And so we turned to other games,
and every rainbow seemed to mock us.
"Follow me", they seemed to say,
"Things are better over here",
My parents must've heard it too,
Because one day we started packing.

242

Like birds, we would fly down south,
to where Mandela did his dance:
Formerly, Suid Afrika.
Now, *The Rainbow Nation.*
That's how you reached it then: by aeroplane,
One long flight to freedom.

I watched my friends' tears blend with the raindrops
on the back window of our car,
as it left our driveway one more time.
I wasn't sure why they were sad.
Jealous maybe – that I would see the Colour Place
and they would remain in green and grey.
Or perhaps they knew what I would learn:
That there was no way back –
colour bridges aren't made to last.

In Johannesburg,
that's where they keep their gold –
Egoli – so I was told,
Back when I was an Irish boy.
My new home was bright, and loud,
Everyone shouting the same things:
"We're equals now; we know the truth,
We've reconciled; we're all the same."
If you squinted in the sunshine,
you could almost see their vision.
But if you opened your eyes wider,
you were taught a different lesson:
"We arrive in massive cars,
windows up to keep the air in;
They arrive in mini busses,
windows down to force it out.

They clean up the shit
of dogs trained to bite Them
in gardens bigger than Their homes.
We can't afford to suckle our children,
nor iron our own clothes;
They can't afford not to do it for us,
freedom and servitude, juxtaposed.

We live in The World;
They live in the one behind it.
You can call your maid a domestic worker
But she remains a maid.
You can say *Ngiyaphila* when she says *how are you?*
But you'll never speak her language.
We are White.
They are Black.
And that's all that really matters."

If you believed in this derision, you were carried by it,
between islands of wealth,
just fast enough to blur the masses,
who floundered in the township tide,
surrounded by water, dying of thirst.
And where was the gold in all of this?
It was all around me.
In our suburbs, in our malls,
our hospitals, and our sports clubs –
they all sparkled with *Mzanzi's* wealth
applied as a first-world sheen.

I saw that Whites were like the leprechauns,
and I myself was one of them,
My skin was forced membership,

My privilege, my induction.
We hoarded the country's gold.
And we said: "of course we'll share.
We'll use it to build the rainbow nation.
That would only be fair",
Knowing you can't reach a rainbow to begin with.
That was our trick.

Twisted
Niall Hurley

I see him crumpled by the roadside:
one brown twist of legs and arms.
We're on our way to the seaside,
one white blur of bourgeois charm.
We've no time to stop the car;
we've simply no thing to gain.
Our inclinations lie too far
from the Boy from Mitchells Plain.

Here's a padstal of expensive food;
not to buy some would be rude.
Here's a "funny coloured dude",
forced to pander to our mood.
Here's a stunning sunset view
that bleeds into an ocean hue.
I wonder, does it take its cue
from that Boy's lips – red and blue?

We order drinks – the family's thirsty.
We eat fish beyond our fill.
I tell myself His death was mercy;
His life was pain and now He's still.

But as the tide rolls back, and then back in,
so my thoughts return to Him.
I hear the thud before He fell,
I hear it echo in the shells.
His mother screams; His mother shudders,
while we unwind – the privileged others.

Now she plans His funeral rites,
while we take in the sounds and sights.

But to mention Him would spoil the fun
of gluttony by the setting sun.
Sobriety is a sin;
Here's my tonic; here's my gin.

Yet still,

I see him crumpled by the roadside
through all the Weskus charm.
He haunts me by the seaside:
one brown twist of legs and arms.

MIGRANTS
Maria Menezes

Daybydaytheydoss light sleep.
Light becausetheheavysoulgrinds,
duringthebadAutumn'slong time,
theearthsuffersandthe body hurts.
Wesleepwell, blessedgrace!
Butalertbecause a brotheristearingapart!

Thrownintothebush, seaorriver,
theywalkonfoot, go in a boator a canoe.
Launchedwandering in runny,
sincedawnuntilthemoonvanish.
Withhopeonlyby a thread,
fleeingfrom a country withonly streets.

Thereis no labor orbedsheet in theirlands,
mensurprisethemselvestearing.
Thelandofmercilessarmsandsun,
compelsinnocentchildren to drainone'sstrength.
Thereismistreatmentthereisunboundedmisery,
peoplesuccumbwithunparalleledpain.

Itisworthdoubtinganddreamingwithluck,
believing in peaceanddestiny in anotherland.
Betterthancertainty in death,
is to face opportunistconsciousness.
Itisworthlooking for a peacefulden, a joyfulbell,
intheSouthor in theNorth.

248

Play

Some Other Mother

AJ Taudevin

Some Other Mother premiered at the Traverse Theatre, Edinburgh on 7 June 2013. This is the text as it went into rehearsal at the Tron Theatre, Glasgow, on 13 May 2007.

CAST

Star Shvorne Marks
Mama Joy Elias-Rilwan
Billy/Dog Man Billy Mack
Janice/Sarah-Jane Pauline Knowles

Developed with support from *Creative Scotland, The Playwrights Studio Scotland, LINKES, A Moment's Peace, Ankur Productions, The Arches and Robin's Fund.*

WRITER'S NOTE

In 2006 my brother, Robin Taudevin, was working as a photojournalist documenting the lives of asylum seekers living in Glasgow. Robin and I grew up in Papua New Guinea and Indonesia, with summers spent at 'home' with my mother's family in the Isle of Lewis. Robin's work with the UN usually kept him working in Indonesia and in East Timor so the opportunity to see him in Scotland was too good to miss so I came up from London, where I was based at the time, to visit him. The people I met through Robin have become some of my dearest friends. I was introduced to a community that was not limited by geography, nationality, race, language, religion or class. I found a kind of solidarity and community I had never experienced before and this played no small role in my moving to Glasgow in 2007.

Shortly after the move, I started working at the LINKES women's group, a weekly drop-in at the high flats on Lincoln Avenue and have worked there ever since. I have facilitated and set up several similar projects across Glasgow. Through these projects I have met hundreds of women, men and children who have been traumatised by the UK's asylum system – regardless of the outcome of their individual claims. I have worked in communities united by a belief in human rights and a more just society, and communities ravaged by the kind of suspicion that is often a by-product of marginalisation. The structures of support for people in the asylum system are restricted when faced with the brutality of the UK's asylum model. The structures of support for people living in marginalised communities are equally restricted as austerity demolishes the welfare state and lived experience of societal solidarity dies out.

I've known for a long time that I wanted to translate my experience into theatre, but for a long time I struggled to know which story was mine to tell. *Some Other Mother* is entirely my own story in that it is a fiction. But what happens in it is absolutely plausible. Since 2007, I have several times been a support to or advocate for women asylum seekers pushed to the absolute limits of despair as their children have been taken into care by social work because the mothers aren't seen to be coping well enough under the pressures of the asylum system.

Dawn raids are still carried out, children are still detained indefinitely or taken into care whilst their parents are detained indefinitely and made vulnerable to deportation without their children, and, of course, deportations continue daily. People are being forced back to countries ravaged by wars fought in my name, plundered by the capitalist exploits of first-world conglomerates and devastated by the legacy of the British Empire.

251

This play has been inspired by the photographs of my brother who I miss and the stories, hope, joy and determination of my dear friends living in and around the high flats in Knightswood.

Some other mother

AJ taudevin

First published in 2013 by Oberon Books Ltd
521 Caledonian Road, London N7 9RH
Tel: +44 (0) 20 7607 3637 / Fax: +44 (0) 20 7607 3629
e-mail: info@oberonbooks.com
www.oberonbooks.com

PB ISBN: 978-1-78319-020-1
E ISBN: 978-1-78319-519-0

Characters
Star
a ten-year-old child
Mama
her Nigerian mother
Dog Man
her imaginary friend
Janice
her Glaswegian neighbour
Sarah-Jane
her mother's social worker
Billy
her other Glaswegian neighbor

Some Other Mother is set on a Glasgow high flat estate and within Star's imaginary world in 2011.

PROLOGUE

Star stares out of her bedroom window onto the unfamiliar high-rise estate on which she now lives. It is a Glasgow dawn in early summer.

Star: 'Once upon a time many hundreds of years ago, there was no land, only ocean. Above the world of water flew a great, white bird. A bird as white as the ocean froth, with wings as wide as the sun and eyes as round and deep as the moon. This bird was the wisest and oldest of all birds. It was the albatross. One day the albatross grew heavy. She flew up into the sky and called out to Yemaya, mother of the Orishas "Please ask Oludamare to give me a stretch of land on which I can make a safe home for my babies". Yemaya took the message to Oludamare who smiled on the albatross and granted her wish. And so, for the first time in ten thousand years, the albatross landed...'

Billy walks out onto his balcony. He stands and watches the sunrise. Star watches him.

Billy: We're still staundin, Billy Lithgow. Still staunding. Watched them pull doon the Gorbals wans last year. They say they'll be pullin wan o they Red Road wans doon next. But we'll stay staundin. Jist like the wans in the west. They'll soon be here with their scaffolding and their cladding and their paint and their...

Billy senses Star. He turns to see her. Their eyes lock.

Star: *(Suddenly)* Roar!

Star hides.

Billy: God knows I seen them house some strange creatures in these flats but I've never seen them house a baby lion! How on earth did they get her up here? Twelve landings in the sky. Hey wee lion? I know you can hear me. Your windae's wide open. Gonnae tell an auld dug like this wan your tale?

Star peers over the window.

Billy: What you saying to it? What sounds like four?

A lion says...

One two three...

Star: Roar!

Billy: Woof.

Star: Roar.

Billy: Woof!

Star: Roar!

Billy: Nice tae meet you too.

There are distant sounds; immigration vans arriving on the estate, the slamming of doors, the pounding of feet on the pavement. They watch.

Billy: Just you stay locked away behind that windae, hear me? Keep you safe from the lion catchers. See if you'd been here when I was a wean we'd've been down there playing dawn till dusk so we would. Nae bother about nothing. Not a care in the world. See they clatty windaes up the top there? They werenae always closed aff like that. Used to be open. Open to the wind. A blethering communal laundry so it was. All our mammies up in the clouds. Aye, back then it wis brilliant. Back then it was grand.

More distant noise, voices calling, crying, the march of boots, the slamming of car doors. Janice walks out onto her balcony, on the other side of Star's window from Billy.

Janice: *(Calling to those below)* Nae fuckin way out pals! Nae cunt fuckin escaping.

Billy: Watch your language, you've a wean for a neighbor now.

Janice: Welcome to block seven eighty young yin. Where life's wa long shitey symphony of fuck.

Billy: You're a disgrace, Janice Ucello.

Janice: Words are the only things we huv, Billy. *(Calling out below)* Isn't that right, pigs? Gonnae come up here and lock away my words?

Star: Roar.

Billy: Honest to God, I'll rip your tongue out with my bare haunds if I ever get close to it.

Janice: I'll jist staund here silent will I? Jist staund here and watch as they tear weans fae breasts o their mothers.

Star: Roar.

Janice: Just staund here and watch as they gang about robbin and rapin.

Star: *(Like a dog.)* Grrarrfk.

Janice: And pissin and shitein and / fuck fuck cunt fuckin…

Star: Mama!

Janice: …in this fuckin cunt hoor cuntish hell that we're stuck in.

Billy: Janice will ye fuckin shut it…

Mama enters Star's bedroom and shuts the window on Billy and Janice, shutting out the world outside and closing her and Star into the bedroom.

Mama: Shhhh. Irawo, Mama wan bi. Mase oyonu ololufe, Mama wan bi.

(*Shhh. Star, Mama is here. Don't worry darling, Mama is here.*)
Star: Mama? Se ole so si fun mi nipa itan Albatross?
(*Mama? Can you tell me more of the Albatross story?*)
Mama: (*Wearily*) Albatross? Albatross. Okay. 'Ni igba kan
wa...'
(*'Once upon a time...'*)
Star: 'opolupo ogorun odun loju'
(*'many hundreds of years ago...'*)
Mama: '...ibi rara aye...'
(*'...there was no land...'*)
Star: '...kan yoyo okun nlaagbami okun...'
(*'...only ocean...'*)
Mama: '...o ga ju aye igi okun nlaagbami...'
(*'...and above the earth of waves...'*)
Star: '...fifo eye fun fun to tobi.'
(*'flew a great, white bird.'*)

ONE

*Later the same day, inside Star's bedroom. It is a bare, drab room. The only
furniture is a bed and a packed suitcase on the floor which Star sits on. There
is a huge patch of damp in one of the walls. Dog Man stands, still and silent
inside the damp patch. Do Man looks exactly like Billy, but he is not Billy.
He is Dog Man.*
Star: '...many hundreds of years ago, there was no land, only ocean.
Above the world of water flew a great, white bird. A bird as white
as the...'
Star looks at Dog Man. They watch each other for a moment, silent.
Star: 'A bird as white as the ocean froth, with wings as wide as the
sun and eyes as round and deep as the moon. This was the wisest
of all the birds. It was the...'
*There is a loud knock on the front door. Star jumps up and grabs the suitcase.
She listens to the front door being unlocked and opened, then murmuring in the
hallway. Star crouches over her suitcase; an animal ready to flee.*

Star: One... Two... Three...

Mama enters with Sarah-Jane who is carrying a large file of papers.

Mama: Irawo? Sarah-Jane niyi. So 'Hello Sarah-Jane'. So 'Hello'. *(Star? This is Sarah-Jane. Say 'Hello Sarah-Jane'. Say 'Hello'.)*

Star: Hello.

Sarah-Jane: Hello. Aren't you just the cutest carbon copy of your mother? She looks like you. How old is she?

She consults her notes.

Sarah-Jane: Ten?! Goodness me you're tall. Tall but thin. We'll need to get you strong for starting high school next term, won't we? No rubbish. Just lots of good Scottish food all summer long. My kids would kill for a long holiday like you're getting, so, believe me, you are one very lucky young lady.

Your daughter is lucky. She has good luck. Lucky.

Mama: Thank you.

Mama goes to exit.

Sarah-Jane: *(Following Mama)* Shall we have a wee sit down in the...

Mama: *(Gesturing for Sarah-Jane to stay)* Please.

Sarah-Jane: It's you I'm here to see Mrs Yewande...

Mama: *(Going to exit again)* Thank you.

Sarah-Jane: Wait. Wait. Do you understand what I'm saying?

Mama: Please.

Sarah-Jane: *(Consulting the file)* It didn't... It doesn't say... Mrs Yewande, I'm terribly sorry. You see, there are supposed to be two of us for a first visit like this but, well...um...you've only got me today. And I have no note of you needing an interpreter. Which you clearly do. Don't you?

Comprendez-vous Anglais?

Mama: You. Help.

Sarah-Jane: Right.

Mama: Letter. Please. Help.

Sarah-Jane: I'll need to come back another day.

Mama: You help. Letter. Come today. Please.

Pause.

Sarah-Jane: Five minutes. I can give you five minutes.

Mama exits. Star stares at Sarah-Jane. Pause.

Sarah-Jane: I bet you speak English. Says here you were in London for six months weren't you? See? Not every fish slips through this net. Six months, eh? Must feel like half a lifetime when you're ten. That's a big suitcase you're sitting on. Don't you want to unpack it?

Star: They move us.

Sarah-Jane: You've only just got here, Stella. You need to start thinking of this as your home. I suppose ten's a bit too old to play games. It isn't? Do you want to play a little game then?

Star: Yes.

Sarah-Jane: Do you want to choose something in this room and describe it for me in English?

Beat.

Sarah-Jane: Go on.

Star points at the damp in the wall where Dog Man is hiding.

Star: Black.

Sarah-Jane: (*Slowly*) Damp. We use the word 'damp' for that. Or the word 'mould'. But you're right. It is black in colour. So well done. How about something else now? But maybe this time describe it in a full sentence?

Star points at Dog Man inside the wall.

Star: There is a man in there.

Sarah-Jane: (*Carefully*) You are right. There is a man in the flat next door. Have you met him?

Sarah-Jane opens the blinds and looks out of the window.

Sarah-Jane: Ah. I see. Your window looks right into his balcony. They're doing these flats up soon. Making them nicer. Cleaner. Better. And if the other schemes are anything to go by they'll be getting rid of all the balconies. So when you look out of this window you won't need to worry about seeing anyone. It'll just be you and the sky. Well, and that block in front there. I don't think they're pulling that one down. But at least it'll look nicer than it does now.

Mama enters with a letter and hands it to Sarah-Jane.

Mama: Letter. Please.

Sarah-Jane glances over the letter and hands it back to Mama.

Sarah-Jane: Stella, can you be my little helper? Just for today? Can you tell your mother that she needs to speak to her case worker about this. I can't help her with what's in it. It's not connected to my work with her. Can you tell her that for me?

Star: Umm. Leta rara di owun.

(The letter is not connected to her.)

Sarah-Jane: Tell her that she needs to ask her case worker for help with this. Okay?

Mama: Rara di ti owun? Il aye di. To ri leta yi lon ba mi sise!

(Not connected to her? Everything is connected. This letter is the reason for your work with me!)

Sarah-Jane: *(To Star)* Can you tell me what she's saying please sweetheart?

Star: She says it's all...um... It's all co...conn... It's all connect...

Sarah-Jane: It's all connected? Can you explain to your mother that I don't work for...

Mama: Wa da wa pada si ilu wa. Wa wo ilekun wa.

(They will send us back to our country. They'll break in our door.)

Star: They will send us back. They will break the door.

Sarah-Jane: I'm sure that won't happen.

Mama: Agbodo pada.

(We cannot return.)

Star: We cannot go back.

Sarah-Jane: I understand that. I do. But I can't help with this. Your mother's/case worker...

Mama: So mo ilu wa ti fo?

(Do you know our country is broken?)
Star: Our country. It is broken.
Sarah-Jane: I know sweetheart, I know. But this letter is from a completely different government/body from the one I work for…
Mama: Egbawa o! Bami fi omo mi obirin pamo fun mi.
(You have to help us. Help me keep my daughter safe.)
Star: You have to help…keep me safe…for my mamma.
Sarah-Jane: You are safe, Stella.
Stella is safe here.
Star: But the letter says…
Star takes the letter from Mama and tries to read the words.
Star: De-por-ta-tion…
Sarah-Jane takes the letter from Star and hands it back to Mama.
Sarah-Jane: Those words are not for you, okay, sweetheart? Mrs Yewande. This letter? Home Office. Me? No Home Office. Understand? Your case worker? Yes? She refer you to… Your case worker call my off… She… Um. She telephone me. She say:
Me, Sarah Jane,
help you,
be good
mother
to Stella.
Mama: *(To Sarah-Jane)*
Irawo.
(Star.)
Sarah-Jane: Sorry?
Mama: *(To Sarah-Jane)*
Irawo.
(Star)
Sarah-Jane: *(To Star)*
What's she saying?
Star: My name.
Sarah-Jane: I thought your name was Stella?

Star: Mama calls me Star. Irawo. I'm her Star.

Mama: Irawo. Oruku owun ni Irawo.

(Star. Her name is Star.)

Sarah-Jane: Does your mother always… Is her voice always so forceful?

Star: She is my Mama.

Beat.

Sarah-Jane: Will you tell her we can talk about this tomorrow when I will bring an interpreter.

Star: In…ter…?

Sarah-Jane: A translator. Can you tell her that for me, please? My little helper?

Star: I'owuro to bata.

(Tomorrow she'll bring trainers.)

Mama: Bata?!

Sarah-Jane: Yes. Bata. So we can talk.

Mama: Bata?

Mama and Star share a moment.

Sarah-Jane: (To Star) What does bata mean?

Star: Tr…trainers.

Sarah-Jane: What?

Star: Tomorrow you will bring us trainers.

Beat.

Star: Like Nike? Adidas?

Sarah-Jane: Thank you, Stella. Mama? Tomorrow I will bring someone to help with language.

To help us talk.

Your language.

English.

Communicate.

Okay?

Mama: *(Uncertain)* Thank you.

Sarah-Jane: That's okay. I'm going to go now. I will come back tomorrow.

Sarah-Jane and Mama exit.

Sarah-Jane: Bye, Stella. Thank you, sweetheart.

Mama closes the door behind them. Star sits on the suitcase and listens to the front door closing and locking. Dog Man emerges from the depth of the wall though, for now, he is still within its confines.

Star: One. Two. Three.

Dog Man: Grrrrrr.

Star: One. Two. Three.

Dog Man: Grrrrr…

Star: One. Two. Three.

Dog Man: Grraarrf.

Star: *(A new tact)* 'Once upon a time many hundreds of years ago, there was no land, only ocean. Above the world of water flew a great, white bird. A bird as white as the ocean froth, with wings as wide as the sun and eyes as round and deep as the moon. This was the wisest of all the birds. It was the…'

Dog Man: Albatross.

Star looks at Dog Man.

Star: 'One day the…albatross…grew heavy. She flew up into the sky and called out to Yemaya, mother of the Orishas…'

Dog Man: '"Please ask God to give me a stretch of land…"'

Star: 'Olodumare.'

Dog Man: '"Please ask Olodumare to give me a stretch of land on which I can make a safe home for my weans."'

Star: 'Babies'.

Dog Man: 'Weans.'

Beat.

Star: 'Yemaya took the message to Olodumare…'

Dog Man: 'Yemaya took the message to…'

Star: 'Olodumare'

Dog Man: 'Olodumare who smiled on the albatross and…'

262

Star: 'granted'

Dog Man: 'her'

Star: 'wish.'

Dog Man: 'And so'

Star: 'for the first time in ten thousand years'

Dog Man: 'the albatross landed and'

Star: 'made a home for her babies.'

Dog Man: 'But the weans soon grew hungry.'

Dog Man / Star *(Together)* 'Mother Albatross flew out across the ocean to gather food for her weans/babies. She swooped over the waves to find the silver white flash of fish on the ocean surface.'

Janice: *(Unseen, her voice emerging from the other side of the flat)* Ya cunting fucking bastard baws.

Dog Man begins to whimper like a dog.

Star: Who's that?

Janice: *(Overlapping, getting louder)* You arseholic cunts wi your forms and phone calls.

Star: Is that Yemaya?

Janice: *(Overlapping)* I jist want tae fuckin see him.

Star: Mama?

Janice: *(Overlapping)* Jist want tae know he's awright.

Dog Man begins to howl like a dog.

Star: Mama!

Janice: *(Overlapping)* You bastards care fer nae cunt!

Dog Man: Ggrrarrghhfk

Star: Mama? Where's my Mama?

Dog Man: Your Mama cannot help you. She cannot do a thing.

Janice: *(Overlapping)* Nae cunt gies a shite.

Dog Man: She doesn't speak the language. Closed off from everything.

Star: Mama?

Dog Man: She's a walking skinless eejit bird. Can't sleep, can't eat, can't understand words.

263

Star: Mama!

Star runs out of the room into the hallway leaving the door open.
Dog Man retreats.

Star: *(Hysterical)*
Ronmi Mama. Okunrin! Dog! Okunrin aja!
(Help Mama. Man! Dog! Man dog!)
Mama enters.

Mama: Irawo! Oto! Oto!
(Star! Stop! Stop!)

Star: Okunrin Aja! Aja! Dog Man Dog. Man. Aja. Aja. Man. Mama
(Man Dog! Dog!)

Mama: Oto, Irawo. Rara aja. Rara Okunrin. Kantan kantan leyi.
(Stop Star. No dog. No man. This is nonsense!)

Janice: *(Shouting loud and clear through the walls)*
Hoy! Whit the fuck is goin on in there?

Mama: *(Calling through to Janice)*
Ode buruku, kuroni iwaju mi! Fiwa le.
(Bloody fool, fuck off! Leave us alone.)

Star: Mama...

Mama: Mama wan bi, Irawo.
(Mama is here, Star.)

Janice: Dinnae lay a finger on that fuckin wean.

Mama: Olodumare O, egbawa o.
(Oh God, help us.)

Janice: You hear me in there? Dinnae lay a fuckin finger on her.

Star: Mama...

Janice: I swear I'll fuckin, I'll fuckin...

Mama: Shhh. Baby. Mama wan bi.
(Mama is here.)

Janice: Gi me back my wean, ya bastards.

Mama: Mama wan bi.
(Mama is here.)

Janice: Gi me back my wean, ya hoors.

Mama: Mama wan bi. Mama wan bi. Mama wan bi.

Mama wan bi.

Mama wan bi.

Mama wan bi.

A long moment of stillness.

Star: Mama. I made Yemaya angry.

Mama: Yemaya?

Star: The Orisha. The mother of sea and water.

Mama: Yemaya!

Star: I can make her forgive me though, can't I?

Mama: Irawo mi.

(My Star.)

Star: She can help us. Can't she? Se Yemaya egbawa?

(Can Yemaya help us?)

Mama: Be'ni. Be'ni. Yemaya egbawa.

(Yes. Yes. Yemaya helps us.)

Star: We just need to take her a present. Like something nice to eat. And then she helps us.

Mama: Telemi kalo, ololufe, od'aro.

(Come with me, darling, let's get you to bed.)

Mama gently puts Star to bed.

Mama: La ala to da, Irawo. Kini won npe ni ede geesi?

(Dream sweetly, Star. How do I say this in English?)

Star: You say…dream sweet.

Mama: Dream sweet.

Star: Mama? I promise I won't scream again tonight.

Mama: Irawo mi.

Star: Star. I'm your star.

Mama: Dream sweet, mi Star.

Mama kisses Star goodnight and leaves the room quietly.

Dog Man: Grrrrrr.

Star: Shhh.

Dog Man: Grrrrrrrrrrr…
Star: Shut up.
Dog Man: Grrrarfh.
Star: I'll feed you to Yemaya.
Dog Man: Grrmm mmmph.

As the light fades, winds begin to gently buffet and groan. Through the winds Yemaya, the voice of a thousand women, drifts faintly, barely decipherable, calling:

Yemaya: Gush the spring, gush the rivers, gush the ocean, gush the waters,
Swirl the waves, swirl the wind, swirl the bodies of my daughters.

TWO

Twelve days later. Star sits on the suitcase in her bedroom. Dog Man is still within the wall but he is almost breaking through it. They are more at ease with each other now.

Star: One… Two… Three…
Dog Man: What was that?
Star: One Two Three
Dog Man: Did you just hear something?
Star: OneTwoThree
Dog Man: There's someone at the…
Star: OneTwoThreeFourFiveSixSevenEight…
Dog Man: What are you counting?
Star: Nine Ten Eleven Twelve…
Dog Man: Ah. Twelve days since we got here.
Star: No. It's onto the next one anyway.
Dog Man: The next what?
Star: The next minute, mumu.
(idiot.)
Dog Man: Before what, wee Star?
Star: Before…

There is a knock on the front door. Star immediately grabs her suitcase; poised and ready to flee.

Star: Is it the letter man?

Dog Man: How should I know?

Star: Look.

Dog Man: I'll look if you promise to start talking to me all the time, not just when you need something from me.

Star: Mo leri.

(I promise.)

Dog Man: Promise.

Star: I did! Now look.

Dog Man becomes Lookout.

Star: What's Mama doing?

Dog Man: She's looking through the door flaps…

Star: She's not getting the clinkyjings?

Dog Man: She is.

Star: And opening the clangbangs?

Dog Man: Uhuh.

Star: Uhoh.

Dog Man: One…

Star: Who is it?

Dog Man: Two…

Star: Who's at the door?

Dog Man: Three…

Star: Dog Man! Who?

Dog Man: Grrrrr.

Star: Who is it?

Dog Man: Grrrrrrarrrrrfk

Star: Tell me!

Dog Man: It's that Sarah-Brain woman.

Star: She's already been twice this week.

Dog Man: She's alone this time.

Star: She hasn't she got Trainers with her?

267

Dog Man: Nope.

Star: Oh no, she'll want me to be her little helper again.

Dog Man: I'll do the talking.

Star: You can't.

Dog Man: Seriously, leave it to me.

Star: Don't you dare.

Dog Man: She's coming this way.

Star: Hide!

Mama opens the door.

Star: Quick!

Mama and Sarah-Jane enter Star's bedroom. Dog Man hides.
Neither Mama nor Sarah-Jane ever see Dog Man.

Mama: Stella? So 'Hello Sarah-Jane'. So 'Hello'.

Star: Hello.

Sarah-Jane: Hello. Still not unpacked that suitcase?
Mama, you really need to encourage Stella to make this place a home. We call it nesting here. Like a bird makes a home from twigs and things. A nest.

Mama: A nest?

Sarah-Jane: Yes, a nest. A bird's nest.

Mama: You English is too much fast.

Sarah-Jane: I'm sorry. But listen to you! Your English is pretty fast too.

Mama: Please!

Sarah-Jane: Sorry! Sorry! It's just really good to see how... Your English. It's better. It's good.

Mama: Thank you.

Sarah-Jane: Thank you.

Mama: You want tea?

Sarah-Jane: Thanks but I'm not here for long.

Mama: Yes?

Sarah-Jane: I just thought I'd pop in to let you know I've got someone for Stella.

Mama: Yes tea? No tea?

Sarah-Jane: Oh go on. Just a quick one then.

Mama: Please you stay here.

Sarah-Jane: I don't have long, Mama. mama: You friend to Stella.

Sarah-Jane: Of course I'm Stella's friend but it's you I need to talk to. You know this.

Mama: You stay. I bring tea.

Sarah-Jane: Okay. Okay. Remember to leave that door open.

Mama exits, leaving the door open.

Sarah-Jane: It's not long now till you start high school, is it? You've been so good at keeping up with your numbers.

Every time I'm in to see your mum I hear you practising.

How far can you count? Do you want to show me? One?

Star: Two...

Dog Man: Three...

Star: Three...

Sarah-Jane: Four? Five?

Dog Man: Grrrrr.

Star: *(To Dog Man)* Shhhh!

Sarah-Jane: Almost. It starts with 'sssss'.

Star: Six.

Sarah-Jane: That's right. What comes next?

Dog Man: *(To Star)* Seven.

Sarah-Jane: *(To Star)* Seven?

Dog Man: *(To Star)* Eight.

Sarah-Jane: *(To Star)* Eight?

Dog Man: *(To Star)* Nine.

Sarah-Jane: *(To Star)* Nine?

Dog Man: *(To Star)* Ten.

Sarah-Jane: Stella? Your mum and I have been doing lots of talking...

Dog Man: She's hungry, Star.

Sarah-Jane: And we thought you might like somebody of your own to talk to.

Dog Man: I can hear her tummy rumble.

Sarah-Jane: You can talk about things like, I don't know, what you like to eat.

Dog Man: She's going to eat you.

Sarah-Jane: Things like, dreams. Good dreams, bad dreams.

Dog Man: Eat you up and shit you out.

Sarah-Jane: Things like, what wakes you up at night.

Dog Man: *(Going for Sarah-Jane)* Grrraaffrgh Wrrarffghk!

Star: *(Lunging at Dog Man)* Rrrraaaaarrrrr!

Sarah-Jane: Woah there, tiger.

Star: *(To Sarah-Jane but still holding onto Dog Man)* Not a tiger!

Dog Man: Grraarrfghk.

Sarah-Jane: Oops. Not a tiger. Sorry.

Dog Man: Grrarrfghk.

Star: Rroaaaarrrarrrrffghk.

Mama enters, rushing to Star. Dog Man retreats into the wall immediately.

Mama: Irawo! Oto! Oto! Kili ndamu e?

(Star! Stop! Stop! What's wrong with you?)

Sarah-Jane: It's okay, Mama.

Mama: Kili ndamu e?

(What is wrong with you?)

Star: There's nothing wrong with me.

Sarah-Jane: She's just playing, that's all.

Mama: *(To Sarah-Jane)* Please. Every night she is screaming.

Sarah-Jane: It's perfectly normal for a child of her age to play like this.

Star: Mama?

Mama: You cannot imagine.

Sarah-Jane: These things take time.

Mama: She no eat.

Sarah-Jane: Have you made those changes to her diet yet?

Mama: She no sleep.

Sarah-Jane: Remember what we talked about the other day?

Mama: She has too much fear inside.

Sarah-Jane: The more rest you can get, the calmer you and Stella will feel.

Mama: I no can help her.

Sarah-Jane: You cannot help her?

Mama: She no sleep. I no sleep. I no can help.

Beat.

Sarah-Jane: Are you saying you are refusing to help your child?

Mama: Please. You help.

Sarah-Jane: I am.

Mama: You help her.

Sarah-Jane: I have. I am. I've arranged for someone to come visit her. But I think she's doing pretty well all things considered. You need to reconnect. You need to find a way to be calm and relaxed. And that is going to take a lot of hard work on your part. But a mother's work is never done, is it? Do you know this saying? It means, well what it says. A mother's work is never finished. It goes on and on and on and…and we wouldn't have it any other way, would we? We'll come by tomorrow morning, okay?

Mama: No. Please no morning tomorrow. We have signing. Go Home Office. Week and week and week. Signing name.

Sarah-Jane: Of course you do.

Mama: Please you come afternoon.

Star: Mama…?

Mama: Jo monbo.

(Hold on.)

Sarah-Jane: We'll figure something out. I'd better get on.

Star: Mama, Dog Man wan bi.

(Mama, Dog Man is near.)

Mama: Kantan kantan leyi.

(This is nonsense.)

271

Sarah-Jane: Be gentle with her.

Mama: Olua o!

(My God!)

Sarah-Jane: Gentle, Mama. Gentle. Gentle voice. Gentle face. Eyes. Gentle. Gentle.

Mama: Olua o egbawa o.

(My God help us.)

Sarah-Jane steps back. A beat.

Sarah-Jane: (Slowly) I'll show myself out. I'll see you soon.

Sarah-Jane exits.

Mama: Kili ndamu e?

(What's wrong with you?)

Star: Dog Man wan bi.

(Dog Man is here.)

Mama: Rara Dog Man. Woo! Iwo. Emi. Rara aja. Rara okunrin. Rara Dog Man.

(No Dog Man. Look! You. Me. No Dog. No Man. No Dog Man.)

Star: He says you don't know how to look after me properly. He says you don't know how to do it right.

Mama: Star! He is in you *(indicates her head)* ori. He no… ododo… He no…

Star: Real?

Mama: You say him 'You no real.' You say him 'Which kind back luck you make me craze so?' You say him 'Go away from me.' Huh? You say him 'Na. You nothing. I no need you. I am strong. Strong as lion.' Huh?

Dog Man: *(Emerging)* You tell Mama she can tae get tae fuck.

Star: *(To Dog Man)* Ode oshi ashewo.

(You stupid fuck whore.)

Mama: Stella!

Star: *(To Dog Man)* Stupid fuck whore.

Mama: Malo ede buruku!

(Don't use such bad language!)

272

Star: *(Wildly, barking at Dog Man.)* Grraaarrrfk!

Dog Man: Grrrarrghghk

Star: Rrraaaaaaarrrrrfghk!

Janice: *(As yet unseen)* Hallo?

Mama and Star freeze.

Janice: Hallo? Are youse awright in here? Ha-llo-o? Can anybody hear me?

Janice appears in the doorway to Star's room.

Janice: Thank fuck, I wisnae sure whit tae expect in here.

Mama: Out!

Janice: Your front door was staudin wide open, wumman, do they no tell ye ye cannae dae that here?

Mama: You dey craze?

Janice: You're awright, I'm no crazy. I'm jist checkin you're/awright.

Mama: You go now.

Janice: I'm goin. I'm gone. I'm jist glad youse are awright.

Star: You're the one.

Mama: Irawo!

Janice: I'm the wan whit?

Star: You're the one who shouts.

Janice: You and me both, wee pal.

Star: Mama wants to kill you.

Mama: Stella!

Janice: *(To Mama)* We've got plenty in common then.

Mama: She has too much young.

Janice: Ach, dinnae fash, hen, it's guid tae meet a lassie wi fire in her.

Mama: You go now.

Janice: I'm gone.

Janice hesitates.

Janice: What's your name by the way?

Mama: Mama.

273

Janice: Right. Does that mean something?

Star: It means mother.

Janice: Course it does. I'm jist a stupid auld witch, amn't I?

Mama: What is shchoopidowuche?

Janice: Wan day I'll make you a cup o tea and tell ye, how's that, sister?

Mama: My name is Mama.

Janice: I know that, sister. Now come on and lock the door behind me, you're no in the jungle noo. Ta ta, wee pal.

Janice and Mama exit. Dog Man slowly comes out of the wall.

They listen to the front door closing and locking. Mama walks back along the hallway into view. She is holding a new letter which she opens and tries to read the words. Only when she has spoken them does their meaning begin to land.

Mama: 'Application'

'Declaration'

'Asylum Claim'

'Legislation'

'Appeal'

'Exhausted'

'Deportation'

'Sorry. For. Your. Situation'.

Mama closes the door to Star's bedroom. From the other side of the door, Mama starts to cry. Dog Man begins to come out of the wall.

Dog Man: 'Mother Albatross flew out across the ocean to gather food for her weans.'

Star: 'She swooped over the waves to find...'

Dog Man: '...the silver white flash of fish on the ocean surface.'

Star: 'She gathered up the fish in her beak and...'

Dog Man: '...in amongst the silver white flash of fish were the silver white flashes of lighters and bottle tops and broken glass. The mother albatross, couldn't tell the difference between these new kinds of flashes and the flashes of fish.'

Star: No. Dog Man, no, 'She gathers up the fish in her beak and wings her way back to her babies. / The starving baby albatrosses sing for joy when they see their mother. They open up their beaks and flap their feathers and gulp down the juicy...'

Dog Man: 'The starving baby albatrosses sing for joy when they see their mother. With their paper thin bellies shivering with hunger they gulp down the silver white shards of glass and lighter and bottle tops. Their throats split as they swallow.'

Star: One...

Dog Man: 'Their stomachs rip and tear and the marble shards of dinners gone by crumble out of the babies' broken bodies filling their nest with the crunch of shredded guts and broken glass.'

Star: One two...

Dog Man: Have you looked in your food little star? Is your mama feeding you lighters and pen lids and razor blades?

Star: One two three...

Dog Man: Is she feeding you glass? Is she ripping you apart piece by piece without knowing?

Star: One.

Dog Man: What is that pain in your tummy little Star?

Star: Two.

Dog Man: Is that the first rip?

Star: Three.

Dog Man: The first cut of the blades?

Star: ROAR.

Star attacks Dog Man.

Star: I'll feed you to Yemaya. She'll have you for dinner.

Dog Man: She doesn't exist, ya doolally wee scunner.

Star: She does. She's the mother of the great Orishas,

Who keep the world turning and look after us.

There's Oyu. He rules wind and guards the gates of death.

There's Oshun. She rules fresh water and brings the rain to earth.

But Yemaya, she's the greatest. She rules the ocean and seas.

She's mother to every single thing. And she's always hungry.
The light fades and winds begin to whip and howl. Through the winds Yemaya, the voice of a thousand women, swirls, louder but still barely distinguishable, calling:

Yemaya: Rip the wind, rip the rain, turn my children's world to pain.
Flow the water over sand, flood the valleys, flood the land.

THREE

Fourteen weeks later. Star sits on the suitcase in her bedroom. Dog Man is no longer in the wall. They are entirely familiar with each other inside Star's bedroom now. There is the sound of construction work from outside.

Star: One...Two...Three...Four...Five...Six...Seven...Eight...Nine...Ten...Eleven...

Dog Man: Twelve thirteen fourteen weeks.

Star: I'm not counting the weeks, bawbag.

Dog Man: Oh. Are you counting the bangs from the diggers out there?

Star: Bang. Clang. Scrape.

Dog Man: I hate that scraping sound. Gies me the derubas.

Star: What did you say?

Dog Man: Derubas. It's Yoruba for heebeejeebees.

Star: Heebee...

Dog Man: Heebeejeebees. Mama taught me.

Beat.

Star: Onetwothreefourfivesixseveneightnine...

Dog Man: Don't you ever get bored?

Star: Don't you ever get eaten?

Dog Man: Apparently not.

Star: Stay with me long enough and you will.

Dog Man: You're lying.

Star: You're lying.

Dog Man: I can't lie. I'm an adult.

Star: You don't look like an adult.

Dog Man: I do. I look like Stupid old Witch.

Star: No you don't.

Dog Man: And I look like Sarah-Brain.

Star: You look nothing like either of them.

Dog Man: They all look the same.

Star: Witch is much uglier than Brain.

Dog Man: Shame you're not Brain's clever little helper anymore. It doesn't matter how many pictures you draw and cards you make for her, she still says you're not allowed to help.

Star: It's not because I'm not allowed to. She says it's because I'm not an apricot.

Dog Man: You mean she says it's not appropriate.

Star: I mean she says you should shut up because you don't know what you're talking about and you should get tae fuck. Don't you dare laugh at me. I'm strong! I'm strong as a lion! Stop laughing like that you...you...you...you nothing dog.

Dog Man: Wrrrf.

Star: You're pure mental by the way.

There is a knock on the front door. They look at each other, uncertain for a moment. Then assume the Lookout position. This is a routine they are very familiar with now.

Dog Man: Mama's looking through the letter flaps...

Star: Is it them?

Dog Man: It's not them.
She's getting the clinkyjings. And opening the clang-bangs.
Who could it be? One. Two. Three. It's... It's...

Star: Who? Who's at the door?

Dog Man: Grhmph. Witch.

Star: They're total bezzies now.

Dog Man: What's that about?

Star: Fuck knows.

There is a soft knock on Star's bedroom door and Mama enters,

Dog Man hangs back but does not disappear. Janice stands in the hallway.
Mama is much changed. She is exhausted after weeks of worry and uncertainty.
Mama: Stella, Jannie here.
Janice: Awright skinny malinky longlegs?
Dog Man: *(Quietly.)* Grrrrr...
Mama: Say 'Hello Jannie'.
Dog Man: Grrrrrrrrrr...
Mama: Say 'Hello'.
Janice: Ach, it's no bother. I wouldnae say boo to a goose when I was your age.
Mama: What is Bootoagoose?
Janice: They are words you do not need to worry aboot, sister.
Star: That's not her name.
Janice: I know that, you wally.
Come on, you. Let's have a look at the words you dae need worry aboot.
Mama: *(Leaving the bedroom)* I tell you, Jannie, they want to destroy me.
Janice: I know they do, hen. I know.
Mama and Sarah-Jane exit and close the door.
Star: 'One day the albatross grew heavy. She flew up into the sky and called out to Yemaya, mother of all Orishas...'
Dog Man: You do know you can't remember the end of that story.
Star: *(Honestly)* You do know you smell of wee.
Dog Man: That's hardly my fault.
Star: Lookia fudface, you're not real, so go away.
Dog Man: They're coming to get you. The letters have spoken.
They'll fly you both back to your land that is broken.
Star: Why are you speaking like that?
Dog Man: Like what?
Star: Like her.
Dog Man: Like who?
Star: *(Meaning Yemaya)* Like her.

Dog Man: But I'm you.

There is a loud knock on the front door. They freeze. Then assume the Lookout position.

Star: Is it them? Have they come for us?

Dog Man: Mama's looking through the letter flaps...

Star: They can't send us back, Dog Man. They have to let us stay here.

Dog Man: Shhh. I can't hear what Mama and Witch are saying.

Star: It can't be them. They take you in the morning. Or when you are signing.

Dog Man: They're getting the clinkyjings.

Star: We need to find Yemaya.

Dog Man: Opening the clangbangs...

Star: We need to find the way.

Dog Man: One...

Star: We need to ask her to help us.

Dog Man: Two...

Star: Before it's too late.

Dog Man: Three...

Star: Who is it? Is it them?

Dog Man: No. It's Brain.

Star: Sarah-Brain? Something's wrong.

Dog Man: Witch is leaving. Brain is coming in. She's asking lots of questions.

Star: Oh, please no, not again. What does she want? What is she asking?

Dog Man: Same as always. I'll be her.

I'll be Sarah-Brain.

Star: I'll be Mama.

Dog Man: 'How are you feeling? How are you doing?

How are you reeling? How are you pooing?

How are you coping? How are you reaping?

How are you hoping? How are you sleeping?'

Star: 'Spoonfuls.'

Dog Man: 'Spoonfuls of what?'

Star: 'Of sleep.'

Dog Man: 'I'm lost.'

Star: 'Night and night and night, awake with fear.'

Dog Man: 'You need to sleep, you need to persevere!'

Star: 'My life is like…'

Dog Man: 'What's it like?'

Star: 'Like…'

Dog Man: 'Like…?'

Star: 'Like…death.'

Dog Man: Death?

Star: That's what Mama just said.

Beat.

Dog Man: She just said the word death.

Was that the word she used?

That's not a word to use like that.

The Brain'll get confused!

Star: One…

Dog Man: It's pouring.

Star: Say one.

Dog Man: It's sleeting.

Star: Dog Man, say one.

Dog Man: And Mama…

Star: One.

Dog Man: is greeting.

Star: Say one!

Dog Man: One.

Star: Two.

Dog Man: Three.

Star /Dog Man: *(Together)* Roar!

A soft knock. Sarah-Jane enters. Mama stays in the hallway, she is falling apart.

Sarah-Jane: Stella? Are you okay in here?

Dog Man: Will I go for her? Will I take a wee bite?

Star: *(To Dog Man)* No!

Sarah-Jane: What's wrong? What's happened?

Dog Man: A wee chunk o her bum. Just tae gi her a fright.

Star: *(To Dog Man)* Don't do it.

Sarah-Jane: Don't do what?

Dog Man: *(Going for Sarah-Jane, who does not see him)* Grrrrrrraaarr. Wrrraaarrrfghk. Wrrrraaarrrfghk.

Star: *(Wildly, trying to distract Sarah-Jane from seeing Dog Man)* I made this, I made it for you. Look. I drew it all on my own. No help. Not one bit of help. Look!

Sarah-Jane: Oh! Another card. What is it this time? A pussycat?

Dog Man: Grrrr…

Star: No!

Sarah-Jane: A lion?

Dog Man: Wrrrarrfk.

Star: No no no!

Sarah-Jane: Calm down Stella.

Dog Man: Grraaarrrfk. Grrrarrrfk!

Star: Shut up.

Sarah-Jane: Stella, do I need to count to three?

Dog Man: Grrrr.

Star: He's a dog.

Sarah-Jane: Of course it's a dog. You always draw a dog.

Dog Man: It's going to eat you up.

Star: *(To Dog Man)* No it isn't, shut up.

Sarah-Jane: Stella?

Star: *(To Sarah-Jane)* Not you…

Dog Man: It's going to eat you up and shit you out.

Sarah-Jane: I'm going to count to three.

Star: *(To Dog Man)* Shut it.

Sarah-Jane: One…

Dog Man: Lion.

Star: *(To Dog Man)* Shut up.

Sarah-Jane: Two…

Star: *(To Dog Man)* I said shut up.

Sarah-Jane: Two and a half, Stella…

Dog Man: Lion!

Star: *(To Dog Man)* Shut the fuck up or I'll kick your fucking cunt in.

Sarah-Jane: Do not speak to me like that, young lady.

Star and Dog Man freeze.

Star: *(To Sarah-Jane)* Was that bad?

Sarah-Jane: You do not speak to people like that. Now apologise immediately. Apologise!

Dog Man: *(To Star)* I'm sorry

Star: *(To Dog Man)* I'm sorry.

Sarah-Jane: Stella, come on. You are better than this.

Star: Please don't take me away.

Beat.

Sarah-Jane: Can you come in here please, Mama?

Mama enters the bedroom, nervous, on the edge. Dog Man stays out of her way.

Sarah-Jane: Do you mind if I tell Stella a bit more about what it is you're agreeing to? Is that okay? Okay. We haven't been talking about taking you away, Stella. We've been talking about you taking a wee holiday. We all think you're doing brilliantly and that it would be great to give your mum a wee rest. A wee break. A holiday. Just for a couple of weeks.

Star: A holiday?

Sarah-Jane: Yes, sweetheart. A wee holiday in a place that is so good it's got a sand pit. A sand pit! And if everything goes to plan you'll be going there in the next couple of days. And you can make sandcastles for the rest of the summer, well what little is left of it Doesn't that sound good?

Star: What's sandcastles?

Sarah-Jane: A sandcastle is a castle made of sand.

Star: Will my mama have one?

Sarah-Jane: Your mother's going on a special holiday of her own. Isn't that right, Mama?

Mama: Please.

Sarah-Jane: You're doing really well, Mama.

Mama: We need to be together.

Sarah-Jane: This isn't a separation. It's a chance to get some rest.

Mama: In London last week they take woman in detention centre but not baby. People from your work they take her baby.

Sarah-Jane: I don't think that's true.

Mama: It is true. A woman from Sudan!

Sarah-Jane: That sort of thing doesn't happen.

Mama: Maybe they send this woman back Sudan without her baby.

Sarah-Jane: That won't happen.

Mama: You say you are not from Home Office.

Sarah-Jane: I'm not, you know I'm not.

Mama: So how can you know they will not send her back without her baby?

Sarah-Jane: Mama, we're getting sidetracked here. I'm not sending you back anywhere without Stella. I'm just suggesting you take a short break before the school term starts. It's not forever.

Mama: Thanks be to God!

Sarah-Jane: It's the only thing I can do for you that will ensure you get some rest, Mama.

Mama: Maybe yes this sleep drug holiday make me have day and night no thinking. Maybe yes this fun time holiday make my baby laughing. But there is too much fear inside. If we are not together the fear become too much strong. It break us.

Sarah-Jane: Respite. You need respite. You'll find it so much easier to cope.

Mama: But when still the letters come?

Sarah-Jane: They won't come as long as you're in the hosp…
As long as you're on holiday.

Mama: And come the day the holiday finish? Next day I look to the door? Again letter. Again. Again. Again. Refuse. Refuse. Refuse.

Sarah-Jane: You know I can't change that.

Mama: We cannot go back. For us this is like death. We wait for the letter from them that say we can stay. You say you cannot make this good news letter come.

Sarah-Jane: I can't.

Mama: You say it is good for me I go holiday. Sleep holiday from my baby. Sleep holiday from bad news letter. Okay. But the day this holiday stop? We waiting again for good news letter. Again we waiting. Again night and night and night we fear. Again night an night and night we no sleep. Again you come back here. Again you say I am not this coping.

Sarah-Jane: Mama. You're not coping. You've said so yourself. You know that's why I'm here.

Mama: You are here because this good news letter not come. You are here because we live inside fear. You want I take sleep holiday from this fear? Okay. Maybe then you see that this not coping is not from me bad mother. Maybe then you see that this not coping is from fear. We live inside fear. This holiday? It cannot stop this fear.

Sarah-Jane: You're doing the eye thing you do, Mama.

Mama: You say my child is suffer. Yes. My child is suffer. But not from me bad mother. My child is suffer because the fear is too much strong it get in her head, in her heart, in her body. You tell me how I can get out this fear from her when this same fear is too much strong in me? Huh?

Sarah-Jane: Stop doing the eye thing.

Mama: You tell me how you can help me be good mother when you cannot make better this fear? Huh?

Sarah-Jane: Your eyes, Mama.

Mama: These are my eyes. I cannot stop them being my eyes.

Sarah-Jane: They are frightening to the child.

Mama: This is my child. My baby. My life. I am not this fear for her.

Sarah-Jane: Your voice is extremely aggressive.

Mama: This is my voice. How can I make you hear it?

Sarah-Jane: You are frightening Stella.

Mama: Stella, baby, comia to mummy.

Dog Man: Grrrrrrr.

Mama: Stella? Baby?

Star does not go to Mama. Beat.

Mama: Her skin. It is not like your skin. No oil and it go dry. It go white. Like bird feather. You take her this fun time holiday, how you stop this feather skin fly away? Huh? How you stop this feather skin fly away in the wind?

Sarah-Jane: It's only for a couple of weeks. I urge you to agree, Mama. It will make things so much easier.

Mama: Irawo, comia to Mama.

Star: Does Mama get a sandy bit?

Sarah-Jane: What's that, sweetheart?

Star: The thing you make the castles in. Does Mama get one?

Sarah-Jane: Pit. A sand pit. It's a pit. With sand in it. It's a holiday thing. A play thing. A fun thing.

Dog Man: She's thinks we're doolally.

Sarah-Jane: Doesn't that sound good?

Star: We're not stupid.

Sarah-Jane: I know you're not stupid.

Dog Man: The lion catcher's a liar.

Star: Why do you speak to us like we are?

Sarah-Jane: I don't.

Dog Man: Lying Liar.

Sarah-Jane: I...

Dog Man: Aye?

Sarah-Jane: I...

Dog Man: Aye?

Sarah-Jane: I... I need to go. I have more visits to do.

Dog Man: One...

Sarah-Jane: You need to agree, Mama. This is your best option.

Dog Man: Two...

Sarah-Jane: It's only a few weeks till she starts high school.

Dog Man: Three...

Sarah-Jane: You'll both come back relaxed. Rested. Ready to face what ever is ahead.

Dog Man: One...

Sarah-Jane: I'll lend Stella a plastic bucket of her own to make sandcastles.

Dog Man: Two...

Sarah-Jane: Are we agreed?

Dog Man: Three...

Mama: Okay.

Star: Four.

Mama: What more can I say? Okay.

Sarah-Jane: Thank you. They start work on this block tomorrow. You'll come back and they'll have put a nice thick layer of cladding on the outside. New paint on the walls. No more of that horrible damp. It'll be like, I don't know, like paradise. Compared to what it is now, anyway. You know, things are so much better than they used to be for people in your situation, Mama. Only four, five years ago, things used to be very, very difficult. And the more we communicate, the more we work together, people like you and me, the easier things become. For all of us. I should be able to wrap things up in time to move on this tomorrow. You will find it easier to cope after this rest. I promise. Bye bye Stella. Sleep well tonight. Come on, Mama, see me to the door. That's it.

Sarah-Jane and Mama exit, closing the door behind them.

Dog Man becomes Lookout to watch them go. Star stays sat on the suitcase; still and silent.

Dog Man: She's saying goodbye to Mama. She's ready to go.
She's closing the door… Three two one… Kabloomo!
Goodbye Shite-pie. Just you get tae fuck.
There is the faint sound of Mama crying.
Dog Man: It's raining.
It's sleeting.
And glaikit Mama's greeting.
Star: Right. That's it. There's no more time to waste.
I'll write a letter to Yemaya and take it to the Orisha place.
Dog Man: You'll never get there. You don't know the way. And
it's not long till bed time, till the end of the day.
Star: Perfect timing, she'll be up. Watching over the world.
We'll give her a letter to take to God and offer her in return
A gift of things she likes to eat…
Things like rare, unusual meat.
Star opens the suitcase and starts rummaging, throwing her things around the room.
Dog Man: What are you doing? You can't unpack. Didn't you hear
her? You're not here to stay.
And what if they come for you in the morning? And you don't get
your holiday?
Star: We'll write 'Dear Olodamare, how's it going? Can you help us?
The Brain's a bit confused about what's really in those letters.
Like the albatross, we need a safe place we can be.
But somewhere we're together, my Mama and my me.'
There is a knock on the front door. Dog Man freezes, expecting Star to assume the Lookout position, but Star is too busy looking for pen and paper. Dog Man completes the routine on his own.
Dog Man: (Hushed voice) Mama's looking through the flaps…
Is it them?
It's not them.
She's getting the clinkyjings. And opening the clang-bangs.
Who could it be? One. Two. Three. It's… It's…

287

Janice: (Calling) It's Janice.

Dog Man: Huh. Fannychops.

Star is totally unaware of Dog Man as she sits on the suitcase writing the letter to Olodumare. Unimpressed, Dog Man returns inside the wall. Janice enters.

Janice: You awright wee pal?

Star hides the letter.

Janice: It's jist me. Your mammy's through there getting the kettle on. Nothin like a good bang o the gums to make you feel better. What about yoursel? Gonnae gi your ain gums a wee bang for us?

Star looks to Dog Man. Janice follows her gaze.

Janice: Do you know something? I have a photie somewhere of me when I was younger. I'm sittin at the windae, right? My wee Davey on my knee. And the wall behind me in the photie is just beginning to go black wi the mould. I mean, imagine that, eh? Imagine that wall there, what, ten year back. Imagine it being mare paint than damp. Can you imagine that?

Star: I hear people call you things. What do they call you?

Janice: Folk call me all sorts o hings. But my name is Janice.

Star: What do I call you?

Janice: You can call me aunty. If you want?

Beat.

Janice: See, Star, it's hard being on your ain wi a wean. You'll no doubt learn that yoursel wan day. But jist think, what if we were femily? What if we all ganged the gether? Stood up against they folk in charge? Looked oot for wan another? Heart to heart. Like family, aye? Like sisters. Like brothers. You've got nae uncles here have ye? Nae aunties?

Star: Just me and my Mama.

Janice: Well, as your Scottish auntie, I am givin you full permission tae call me whatever the fuck you like. Now, I don't know about you but I've got a right drouth. Gonnae come through and say night-night tae your mammy?

Come on then, wee pal. Hey. It's all going to be okay.

They exit. Dog Man stays in the wall, uncertain. Star runs back in, still holding the letter for Yemaya.

Star: Dog Man? You still there?

Dog Man: Aye.

Star: We'll find the Orishas and Yemaya tonight.
Will you come? Please. I need you.

Dog Man: Do you? Oh.
Alright.

Star: Promise?

Dog Man: Promise.

Star: Good. Now don't go anywhere.
We'll go after I've kissed Mama goodnight
So she doesn't get worried and scared.

Star exits.

As the scene fades, the winds begin to rip and roar and Yemaya, the voice of a thousand women, howls:

Yemaya: Gush and swirl and rip and flood
My children fish in pools of blood.

ROAR

Much later that night. Star and Dog Man are in the world of the Orishas, looking for Yemaya. It is a strange and constantly shifting world which looks more and more like Star's bedroom as the scene progresses.

Star: Hello? Is anybody there?

Dog Man: Nope. Naebody. Let's go home.

Star: Not yet. We've got all night.

Dog Man: This place gi's me the derubas.

Star: *(Shouting)* Is there no one else in this whole world that can hear me?

Dog Man: *(Howling)* Halloooo!

The wind begins to rip through the Orishas' world – like a storm at sea. Yemaya, the voice of a thousand women, is never seen.

Yemaya: Who's your me?

Star: My Me?

Dog Man: She's me.

Yemaya: Who?

Star: Me.

Yemaya: You?

Dog Man: We.

Yemaya: Who?

Star: We?

Dog Man: She.

Yemaya: If she is 'me', then who is he?

Star: Mama.

Dog Man: I'm not Mama! She's Mama!

Yemaya: Bye bye birdie. Off you fly.

Star: What? Where are you taking her?

Yemaya: That's classical information. Say good bye.

Dog Man: If it's Mama you're after, that's her right there.
Mama's nose. Mama's skin. Mama's eyes. Mama's hair.

Star: Oh no, no no no no no.

I'm not Mama. I'm… I'm…

I'm…

A plastic bucket appears.

Dog Man: Say 'Hello Stella', say 'hello'!

Star: *(Into the plastic bucket)* Hello Stella.

Dog Man and Star begin to tap and bang on the side of a plastic bucket.

Star: Hello Stella!

Hello Star!

Are you happy so far far far

far far far far away?

Are you happy on your fun time holiday?

Dog Man's tapping builds until he is bashing and banging the plastic bucket around the room.

Dog Man: Are you happy, Stella oh Stella oh Star?

Happy on your sand pit holiday?
You don't need to come back for morning time
They will only just take you away
Back to the land that is broken and fucked
The land the letters tell you is safe.
Stay where you are, Star, you're much better off
Sarah-Brain has always been right.
You don't need your Mama to look after you
You're far too clever and bright.

Dog Man's banging of the bucket becomes the sound of people banging on the front door. Mama enters Star's bedroom, in real time. Star is still in the world of the Orishas and Mama tries to bring her back into reality.

Mama: Stella?

Dog Man: Mama!

Star: *(To Dog Man)* Stay! Dog Man! Stay!

Dog Man races wildly around the room, howling, wild, bewildered, lost.

Mama: Stella! Stop! Oto! Stop!

Star: *(Turning on Mama)* You crazy fuck nut bitch.

Mama: Stella, baby.

Star: You lying monster mother.

Mama: Stella. My baby. My Star.

Star: You thieving bastard voodoo witch!

Mama: Mama wa nib, Star. Mama is here.

Star: You can't be a mother.

Mama: They have come, baby. They are here.

Star: You can't be anything.

The banging on the front door is louder. Janice's voice can be heard over the banging, shouting from inside her flat.

Janice: *(Her voice, through the walls)* Ya mother-fucki cuntinfucks lay aff my sister's door.

Star: Olodumare doesn't exist.

Janice: Have you nae mothers? Nae family?

Star: And Yemaya's a stupid whore!

Janice: Have you nae weans?
Star: I'm going to eat you. On the count of three.
Mama: Star. My baby.
Janice: Have you nae hearts?
Mama: God. You destroy us.
Star: One…
Janice: Shame on you!
Mama: Please help, God, please.
Star: Two…
Janice: Shame!
Mama: We are on our knees!
Janice: Shame!
Mama: Our skin is flapping.
Star: Two and a half…
Mama: Flapping in the wind.
Janice: Shame!
Star: THREE

There is a crash as the front door is smashed in. All of Star's imaginary torments, including Dog Man, vanish completely.
A brief moment of calm.

Star: Mama? They are here, aren't they?

Mama cradles Star.

Mama: Mama wa nibi, Irawo.

Mama is here.

Mama wa nibi.

Mama wa nibi.

Mama wa nibi.

Mama wa nibi.

EPILOGUE

Later the same day. As in the prologue: Star's window, Billy's balcony, Janice's balcony. Star is not at her window. Her room is strewn with the rubble of last night. Billy walks out onto his balcony. The sounds of construction is constant.

294

Billy: Get a whiff o that, Billy Lithgow. Woooft. That is the stench of a dying era. Nae hearses yet, though, Billy. No fae the likes of us Mare's the pity. Knock em doon. That's whit I say. Knock us all doon and bury us all.

Janice walks out onto her balcony.

Billy: Was that you this morning Janice? Banging and shouting and screaming? Given up the good samaritan act, have you? Knew it wouldnae last. A craikit bell'll never mend. And your bell's craikit right through in't it? In't it? Hey? What you sayin tae it? Not like you tae gi that tongue o yours a rest.

Janice: I cannae find it, Billy.

Billy: There is a God!

Janice: The photie.

Billy: He's answered wur prayers and ripped oot her tongue!

Janice: Billy! The photie! I cannae find it.

Billy: Hallelujah!

Janice: The photie, Billy, the photie. It's the only wan I've got o my wee Davey.

Billy: Ach, change the record, ya auld witch, the Wee Davey wan's been playin ten year.

Janice: We're sitting at the windae. The wall behind us jist beginning tae go black wi the mould. And see, the photie is that dark, it could be anyone sitting there. Any mother. Any wean. But I cannae find it. I want to see if that mother is me or if it aye could be some other. Some other wean upon the lap of some other mother.

Billy: You were born spoutin shite, Janice Ucello.

Janice: They've took them, Billy. They're gone. The mama and th wean. They've sent them back from where they came. We'll never see them again. The sounds of construction builds.

Billy: Well cryin and hallooin like that's never goin tae change a thing.

Janice: *(Shouting)* Words are the only things I huv, Billy.

Billy: Cannae hear you ower that racket, Janice. Cannae hear a word.

Janice: *(Calling out to those below)* Aye, go on ya herd o shiteflaps. Jist you seal us intae silence. Jist you seal us intae toxic walls, jist you make us look aw nice and white. So nae cunt'll know the truth aboot whit's goin on inside us.

Billy: Dinnae bother wi that paint, pal. Knock us doon! Bury the lot o us.

Janice: Jist you lock us in and wall us aff so you'll think we're aw awright. While they bastards whit own us dae whit ever they like tae folk whit live beside us. Nail ower wur doors. Paint ower the cracks. There's nae body we can tell. Whit cunt'll listen tae me? Inside this castle of sand. Inside these walls you're paintin sae white against the grey sky black.

Blackout.

RAGE OF THE DEVILS (An extract)
Tendai Rinos Mwanaka

Characters

Komurade Hokoyoi: Youth leader of the ruling Jongwe party and a political thug

Mbuya Wa Shereni: old village lady forced to attend rallies from Border's village farm

Keresenzia: Mbuya Wa Shereni's niece

Mbuya Mukotsanyera: an old lady of the village, a friend of Mbuya Wa Shereni who would accompany her to the rallies, from Border village farm

Mbuya Wa Matikiti: an old village lady, a friend of Mbuya Mukotsanyera and Mbuya Wa Shereni, forced to attend these rallies, from Border village farm

Mbuya Wa Chenhamo: an old village lady, a friend of Mbuya Mukotsanyera, Mbuya Wa Matikiti, and Mbuya Wa Shereni, forced to attend these rallies, from Border village farm

Kanzura Katipedza: rural councilor of the area

Povho: people

CDE MP Chirowangoto: Member of Parliament for the constituency, of Jongwe party

Headman Shamba: Vicious village headman of Mapfurira village, one of the villages of this constituent

Komurade Ndande: Youth leader of the ruling Jongwe party, a political thug

Mbuya Takataka: an old lady of Mapfurira village, a member of the opposition party, DALP

Sekuru Mukaka: and old man of Mapfurira village, a wife hoarder, spy and traitor

Baba Samaboreke: a grassroots activist and local leader of the opposition DALP

Kule Ngosana: Mbuya Wa Shereni's brother.

EPISODE ONE

Komurade Hokoyoi: Gogogoi! Gogogoi! Gogogoi! *He shouted with vigour (Gogogoi is a Shona entrance call for someone arriving in people's compounds. Komurade Hokoyoi is one of the youth members of Jongwe party. This youth league member was one of the notorious black bombers (National Youth Service trainees) who had graduated from the notorious training camps.)* Today, at 10 O'clock, I said today, there will be a rally at Nyatate shopping centre; the MP for the constituency is coming. Do you hear me people? Be there for your life...at 10 O'clock. *He said that before even greeting the people in their homes.*

Mbuya Wa Shereni: Run Keresenzia, run Kere, run, go and tell Mbuya Mukotsanyera and others. *She says that full of fear.*

Keresenzia: Alright Mbuya. *Keresenzia runs to the next household to tell Mbuya Mukotsanyera the news, who would then tell the others.*

They haven't started on the cooking so they have to do that faster, to make it to the rally in time. It is already nine and they have just come from the fields.

Keresenzia: Good morning Mbuya Mukotsanyera. My grandmother has sent me to let you know there is a rally at Nyatate shopping centre at 10, and that you have to let others know. Grandma also said that you should come through home and pick her on your way to the rally.

Mbuya Mukotsanyera: Imwewoye Vasikana, mwaka uno tingorimashe? *(Hey girls, are we going to farm this year)* These thugs are just wasting our precious time, moreover, they have nothing substantial to offer us anymore. They are still talking of Chimurenga to this day, are they the only ones who fought Chimurenga? We even participated more than them as they hide from Smith's bombs in foreign capitals whilst we faced these everyday, but they now make a lot of hot-air as if they own it. Maybe we have always got it backwards; the river must flow the other way.

But she knew she had to pass the news and prepare for the rally. There was no excuse, not even old age would matter to those young comrades.

Mbuya Wa Matikiti: Maiwe kani! *(Oh, my mother!)* When are we going to rest? We are old people, at our age we are not supposed to be walking such long distances, especially for such empty campaigns. Now, we have to walk through Gomo Remadindingwe *(Cheaters' Mountain, a mountain that was rife with cheaters)*. It's such a difficult mountain to climb, and then we have to wade cross Nyahukwe, Chitsoko, and Nyajezi Rivers to Nyatate shopping centre where the meeting will be happening. How about our fields we will be abandoning for these stupid meetings, who is going to plough and plant them for us, Mbuya Wa Chenhamo. *Nyatate is at least 15 kilometres from their resettlement areas, at Border's farm.*

Mbuya Wa Chenhamo: If it was only going to be this long journey we would have to face up to, then it was going to be easy, but we would also have to endure the heat, as well. It's so hot these days, Vasikana *(girls)*.

These old ladies whined to each other but they knew they had to comply or else they would invite wrath on their families. They knew they would be denied food, farming and many other donations by their headman. Their fields would be confiscated and be given to Jongwe party people, and that their houses would be set on fire, even they might be killed. All the villages and villagers surrounding Nyatate were being forced to participate in these marathon rallies. Even teenagers were being forced to attend these rallies. Schools were being closed off for the day, way before close-off time to allow school-going children to attend the rallies. So these three old ladies had to forego eating their breakfast so that they could make it to Nyatate, even though, in actual fact, they never made it in time for the start of the rally, which always invited warnings from the notorious youths. They had to travel by foot, barefooted, for they couldn't afford lifts to Nyatate, and the lifts were far fewer and unreliable. It was about midday when they arrived, and councillor Katipedza, a corrupt, vicious, strong supporter of Jongwe party was addressing the rally.

Kanzura Katipedza: Excuse me, people of Nyatate ward! We are gathered here specifically to hear the message from our honourable Comrade MP, Wa Chirowangoto. But before we give him the stage we need to welcome him mumusangano *(the Jongwe party)* way. We ask the youths to lead us in the chanting of the slogans and some dances.

Komurade Hokoyoi: Pamberi naMudhara wedu! *(Forward with our Old man). That was the nick-name given to the president of the Jongwe party*

Povho: Pamberi! *(Forward!)*

Komurade Hokoyoi: Pamberi nemusangano! *(Forward with Jongwe party!)*

Povho: Pamberi! *(Forward!)*

Komurade Hokoyoi: Pamberi nokutora ivhu! *(Forward with the land grab!)*

Povho: Pamberi! *(Forward!)*

Komurade Hokoyoi: Pasi nevarungu! *(Down with the whites!)*

Povho: Pasi navo! *(Down with them!)*

Komurade Hokoyoi: Pasi nezvimbwasungata! *(Down with the white apologists!)*

Povho: Pasi nadzo! *(Down with them!)*

Komurade Hokoyoi: Pasi na Tsungirirai imbwasungata! *(Down with Tsungirirai, a white apologist!). Tsungirirai is the president of DALP, the opposition party to Jongwe party.*

Povho: Pasi naye! *(Down with him!)*

Komurade Hokoyoi: Pasi nezvimbwasungata DALP! *(Down with white apologists, the DALP!)*

Povho: Pasi nayo! *(Down with it!)*

Then he started the new war cry for Jongwe party, a song that praised Mudhara and the land reform he had carried out, how they took the land from the whites and how people had to continue being strong as the country experienced economic problems, resultant of the land reform exercise.

Mudhara murambe makashinga here
Old man stay strong is it
Shingirirai, gadzirirai, Zimbabwe ndeyedu
Be more stronger, prepare, Zimbabwe is ours
Baba murambe makashinga, Zimbabwe ndeyedu
Father stay strong, Zimbabwe is ours

Makashingaa,
Strong
Rambai makashinga
Stay strong
Rambai makashinga
Stay strong

Makashingahee
Stronghee
Rambai makashinga
Stay strong
Makashingaa,
Strong
Rambai makashinga
Stay strong
Baba murambe makashinga, Zimbabwe nde yedu
Father stay strong, Zimbabwe is ours

Ivhuirii

301

This soil
Takaritora nehondo
We took it back through war
Takaritora nehondo
We took it back through war

Neshungu neshungu
With passion with passion
Ticharima neshungu
We will farm it with passion
Ticharima neshungu
We will farm it with passion

The people danced as they sang the song. Even the old ladies had to dance, despite the fact that they were old and others hadn't eaten anything since last night's supper, everyone had to dance, artificial appreciation was far much better than doing nothing. When the song was expended Kanzura Katipedza continued.

Kanzura Katipedza: Now, it is time for the MP to give us what he has in store for us. All those with opened umbrellas, bloody close them up! Make sure there is no loitering. For men, you know that culturally, if an elder is speaking, you mustn't have something on your head. So, remove all those mushrooms on your heads! Thank you, thank you people, over, over to you our honourable, the great Comrade MP.

CDE MP Chirowangoto: Zimbabwe shall never ever, ever, ever..., be a colony again, pasi naTsungirira, chibwasungata, he is a puppet! He is a dog, even a dog is better than him. Always licking the white man's ass, licking and licking, such a bloody dog! We are going to deal squarely and physically with him and all those who do not conform to the Cock. Take note of muvengi *(enemy, specifically the DALP supporters)*, put them on a list, create lists in your cells of

302

these traitors and submit them to the councillor Katipedza. We are going to beat them and show them the way to Jongwe. We went to war. We won this country through the barrel, not through a pen. Only through the barrel would this land be taken away from us again. Never, never, never, noooo...

Mose mose murambe makashinga here
All of you stay strong is it
Shingirirai, gadzirirai, Zimbabwe ndeyedu
Be more stronger, prepare, Zimbabwe is ours
Baba murambe makashinga, Zimbabwe ndeyedu...
Father stay strong, Zimbabwe is ours

CDE MP Chirowangoto: This is our country. This year, after winning the election, of course with your vote, I'm planning to bring lots of developments to this constituency. I will give you food, lots and lots of food. Your tummies will be bigger than mine, full of food. Mudhara, our president is going to donate lots of computers and text books into all the schools in your wards. Women... you have to group yourselves for some many projects, like sewing and poultry. The funding will come from the provincial leadership. Men and youths, you have to develop your sports talents like soccer through some tournaments. The party will be funding these and many other projects. There is a rich mining company in the Marange diamond fields that has promised to give us money to have these sporting tournaments. I will give you the details of everything later, after we have swept off the bastards DALP out of our homes. A lot of things are already in the pipeline and the donors are ready to go, so you have to vote for me, so that I can be able to do all that for you in the next five years.

Mudhara murambe makashinga here
Old man, stay strong is it

303

Shingirirai, gadzirirai, Zimbabwe ndeyedu
Be more stronger, prepare, Zimbabwe is ours
Baba murambe makashinga, Zimbabwe ndeyedu
Father stay strong, Zimbabwe is ours

Makashingaa,
Strong
Rambai makashinga
Stay strong
Rambai makashinga
Stay strong

The poor and miserable ladies danced until the place was a cloud of dust. From 10 O'clock through to 6 pm, the rally was defined with chanting of slogans, dancing and insulting of Tsungirirai and the Westerners. People had to risk their lives by travelling back home in the darkness than leaving the rally before dismissal time because they were afraid of incurring the wrath of the comrades. However, those who were quick to think, who knew the reality about everything, started questioning these empty promises. The very same MP had been in office for nearly thirty years and there was no physical project he could point to as his own. He was also the minister of education, but in the whole constituency, he did nothing to show that he was interested in the education of his people. All what people could remember of him was the removal of Cambridge examinations and replacing them with ZimSec, a useless board; full of corruption, bungling of examinations and leaking of exam papers. The other thing he was remembered for was suggesting for a single school uniform across the nation, an idea that was rejected for its stupidity and absurdity. He wanted to make the whole of Zimbabwe's education into one school!

Then it was the time for the headmen of the villages surrounding Nyatate ward to address the meeting. That day it was the fearsome Headman Shambarishakwata (it's his nickname that became a name, it means 'he washes hands before the food is done cooking'), and people had shortened it to

Shamba. He was a vicious buckthorn. He was the headman of Mapfurira village, but addressing the meeting on behalf of the village heads.

Headman Shamba: As you all know, next Wednesday is Election Day, so everybody in my village and all the other villages must go and vote for The Cock *(the symbol for Jongwe party)*. If you vote otherwise, you will be evicted from our villages. I personally will take your fields and give them to our people, and moreover, you will be beaten, kwamupfiganebwe chaiko *(to the graveyards)*. The country was liberated through blood; it came through blood, so through blood we will win this election. We will beat the bloody hell out of you all if you fight us on this. We will kill you. We will maim you. We must go together to the polling stations, as villagers with its headman, and vote for The Cock. Nobody will vote without their headman. All the suspects, I have your records. If you think you are not a suspect, you have to prove yourself innocent on this Wednesday by voting for Jongwe. Jongwe is the country, the country is Jongwe. Have I made myself clear? *He said that with authority as the headman, his face serious and sharply creased in wrinkles and creases.*

Komurade Ndande: All those without membership cards should make sure that by sunset today they have the cards or else we will kill you. Remember, I am collecting 10 billion dollars per head *(the currency was by then in bearer cheques and the inflation was very bad but the amount was difficult to secure those days)*, in preparation for the celebrations of the victory of our party after this Wednesday election.

Headman Shamba: Yes, you heard well, there. Comrade Ndande is right...we need to make our comrade MP win, and then celebrate in style, so we need the monies now.

Komurade Hokoyoi: Yes, headman VaShamba is right. We want the money, right now.

Komurade Ndande and Komurade Hokoyoi were the most notorious of the youth members of Jongwe party, in the Nyatate area and, were the ones who had devised torture and beatings, even killings of the opposition party members in this area, so everyone was afraid of them. There were graduates from the notorious National Training Camps. People started mumbling silently but no one would voice aloud what they were complaining about because they were afraid of being killed. Some were asking each other what kind of victory was that. Some were asking each other why they had to be forced to pay the money. Some even questioned why Jongwe party was already talking of celebrations, as if it had won the election. But no one could voice all these grumbles, other than Mbuya Takataka.

Mbuya Takataka: Excuse me, Headman! I am a widow and I have no way to get that 10 bhiriyoni *(she pronounced the billion in Shona)*, what are you going to do about me? *The youths knew all along that Mbuya Takataka was of the opposition party. She had come to this meeting out of fear, so had come out fear, Baba Samaboreke, who was the underground leader of DALP party in the Mapfurira's cell. They had been informed about the activities of these two by Sekuru Mukaka, who was their informer. Sekuru Mukaka would be telling them what those would discuss as they go back home, later that night. But headman Shamba shouted Mbuya Takataka down.*

Headman Shamba: Your problems won't make me suffer old lady. Go and figure! You can be a lady of the night, you can steal, you can buy some Tokoloshis to accrue wealth for yourself, oh..., you can sell those two goats of yours...I don't give a damn! I just want my money hey! Clear! Everyone is now free to go home.

Komurade Ndande didn't bother to help headman Shamba in scaring Mbuya Takataka. Comrade Ndande, who stayed in the Tenga village, would go to Sekuru Mukaka's home, to be briefed, and then he would call other youths including Komurade Hokoyoi who stayed in Border farm. The youths would then visit Mbuya Takataka and Baba Samaboreke's place, by the middle of the night and deal with them. They were becoming a threat in Nyatate villages, recruiting all the youths to DALP party. So, Komurade Ndande closes off this meeting.

Komurade Ndande: Before we go, we should hammer the slogan, once more. I suggest Mbuya Takataka to lead us to show that she is willing to work for Jongwe by raising the required 10 billion, she should start doing that by leading us in celebrating Jongwe through the slogan. Mbuya Taka, lead us!

Mbuya Takataka: Pamberi neJongwe! Pamberi neJongwe! Pamberi neJongwe! *The old lady shouted, with no conviction.*

Komurade Ndande: You old witch, stop it! You piece of shit, where did you learn that stupid bullshit slogan? We are not in the fucked up sixties. It's "Pamberi neJongwe yaMudhara" *(Pamberi with Mudhara's Jongwe party, as if Mudhara owned the party!).* Be careful old lady. You should also raise your stupid hand fisted, not an open palm. The open palm is for zvimbwasungata, DALP party.

Mbuya Takataka had to redo the slogan correctly. She didn't want to incur the wrath of these dangerous comrades. After the slogans people moved silently back to their homes but nonetheless contemplating on how this young fellow could reprimand an elderly person who even qualified to be his granny that disrespectfully. When walking in the pitch black darkness of the summer night, hungry as a desert, stumbling, those four old ladies couldn't help discussing their day.

Mbuya Mukotsanyera: It was better for us had we remained under the British colonial yoke because we were oppressed but free. Now we are free but oppressed. It's not a better life, all that we hear of is theoretically the promises for better life, all through these years we have been under this new galling yoke. What was that stupid MP talking of? Rubbish, rubbish, trash, trash. You can almost Heimlich yourself listening to his stupidity. He is the man who has destroyed the education of our children. All he cares about is history this and history that, do we eat history, Vasikana.

Mbuya Wa Chenhamo: Had it been the proper history, it was better. Everything is about Jongwe this, Jongwe that. Chikwambo here Jongwe yacho? Inga inyama wani. *(Is Jongwe a Tokoloshi? After all its food. A Tokoloshi is a small half human, half animal goblin used to help the owner in getting easy wealth especially money in the African traditional world.)* And in their blasted history they never talk about how they have killed each other. Chitepo, Mahachi and Gezi are never mentioned. They think we are fools, we don't know; one day they will tell us the truth about those deaths.

Mbuya Mukotsanyera: These guys are blood suckers and liars. As you know nothing fools us better than the lie that we lie to ourselves. They are so thickly enmeshed in their own lies, they don't know anymore when to tell the truth. They think since we live in the villages we are stupid. We know those killings were not road accidents but that they have been killing each other. Sometimes they say it's through the road accident but they don't even show the place where it happened and which truck has hit these cars to make them overturn and kill these people. We know it's their monster Puma vehicles they use to kill with. Sometimes they go and put people on the road then they start shooting photos to hoodwink us like they did with Cain Nkala, manufacturing an accident! Kuita mutambo neupenyu hwemunhu nhai! *(To make theatre out of someone's killing!).* Now they have started killing us recklessly...remember Matipedza, he was killed in broad daylight, a couple of weeks ago...and they lied it was a Tokoloshi that killed him. Everyone knows he was killed because he was the head of youths here for the DALP.

Mbuya Wa Chenhamo: Don't be surprised very soon to hear that president Tsungirirai has been involved in a road accident. They are the monsters mentioned in the bible and after killing someone they are not ashamed to declare the person a National Hero. Look at what happened with Mahachi? They will make such a beautiful story about the person at their dirty Heroes' Acre, and offer a lot of support to the bereaved family, simply to cover up the whole thing. And after burial the family is ignored and wallow in poverty, whilst they move on to the next target.

Mbuya Wa Shereni: This old man has troubled us; we do not know why God still stays him.

Mbuya Wa Matikiti: They are making us hate them all the more with these ill treatments. When are we going to be with our families now? It will be midnight by the time we reach home. We didn't even eat the whole day. Why are we being punished like this? Come election time, we will just vote pa chanzapo *(we will vote for the palm, the symbol for DALP party).*

Mbuya Wa Chenhamo: Zviri nani hondo idzokere tavhotera Tsungirirai pane kusungwa mbiradzakondo ngeharahwa dzodekufa idzi. *(It's better to have the war after voting for Tsungirirai than to be enchained by these old and dying men.)*

These old ladies were forced to share these emotions after a tiresome and frustrating day. They couldn't think of their problems with their legs though, which still needed to take them home. On the other side of Nyatate, a threesome, were also discussing the same issues as they made their way homes in this pitch black night.

Sekuru Mukaka: Heyi, heyi, heyi, zvakaoma Mbuya Takataka. KaMudhara aka kotiita kunge mahachi *(Hey, hey, things are tough Mbuya Takataka. The old man is treating us like horses). Sekuru Mukakanhaka was the oldest person in Mapfurira village but an informer, a wife hoarder (Mukaka) for he had 10 wives. He was good at claiming nhaka (taking over his brother's wives after the death of these brothers), and so the village disrespectfully called him Sekuru Mukaka, short-cut name to his nickname, because of his deeds. He pretended to sympathize with Mbuya Takataka who had been treated like a child by comrade Ndande, but deep* down he wanted to invoke Mbuya Takataka to say trash against the president and Jongwe party, and thus entice baba Samaboreke to join in, in this bashing of the president. These two didn't have a whiff of what truthfully Sekuru Mukaka was trying to do. They thought he was one of them, so Mbuya Takataka started into the lion's den, her tongue always the sharper like a magpie, said.

Mbuya Takataka: Tati taoneyi hedu, uku kutanga (We haven't seen anything, this is just the beginning), we are going to suffer more than this Sekuru Mukaka. We are already slaves in our own land, being slaves to our own people. Better mabhunhu adzoke havo (it's better for the whites to return back and re-colonize us).

Baba Samaboreke: What really has happened to our nation? One family shouldn't own the village like that. Komurade Ndande is the nephew of the headman so this village is theirs to do as they wished. Is there anyone who was born with the land in his hands? Is there anyone who has ever been pregnant and gave birth to a land? These people called chiefs and headmen, who ordained them to those responsibilities? Why can't we vote for their positions, as well? Baba Samaboreke delved in, as Sekuru Mukaka drooped with saliva in his mouth, just contemplating the amount of money he was going to make when he makes his report to the young comrades. He almost chocked himself when saliva took to the wrong pipe but coughed it out, and aimed his ears to more from these two as he faked comradeship and empathy with these two.

Sekuru Mukaka: Eeh, eeh, eeh, wakuda kufa manje! (You are now looking for death). Most of them have Tokoloshis who would spy for them. We might be walking with one of those Tokoloshis, listening to what we are discussing. Lighting might strike us in broad day light without the sky raining a single drop of water, or even having any clouds at all, baba Samaboreke. Remember what happened to Matipedza last week. Remember he was always against headman Shamba. These people hunt for devilish powers to kill those who want to overthrow them from power. Don't you see the way they are now killing each other within their own party? He was this

310

convincing, and baba Samaboreke continued with his tirade against those in power, unknowingly that he was creating his own undoing by this tirade.

Baba Samaboreke: These monarchies are very oppressive, Sekuru. We fought for freedom but it now seems we fought the liberation war for tyranny. We just hear of Hitira Hitira *(Hitler)*. We now have our own Hitira here. We are now old people, Mai Samaboreke is in her early fifties, and I am in the late fifties. We have failed to conceive a single child in our twenty years-plus marriage. We have visited every faith healer we could think of, or hear of, every Sangoma, Sekuru, but everything failed us. But all that has helped us to get closer to each other, we have become closer and closer the more we have failed. We now exist for each other, and for this dream we have for the country. We are grassroots activists for DALP *(Democratic Alliance Labour Party)*. You know of it Sekuru, do you?

Sekuru Mukaka: I have heard of the party..., I believe it's a good cause that they are fighting for... I will be joining it, as well, so do tell me more, baba Samaboreke. *Inside he was bursting with happiness that baba Samaboreke had given him enough already to make a killing. He was just looking after himself, his large family needed food. That was his workplace.*

Baba Samaboreke: They have been a lot of hair rising situations working for this party, Sekuru; fighting for this party, for our beliefs, for the other people's beliefs..., we have come up acres. We have survived beatings, injuries, attempted killings as we did our jobs. Sekuru, the logs kept falling in our paths, forcing us to keep jumping, even when we could barely walk. It is two years since we joined this party; we joined it in early 2001. Things are now haywire throughout the country now as you can see. We have had stolen elections, some beatings, force has been used to make us attend rallies before, and now the game has been upped....there is too much strife as we head towards this election... it's so painful, Sekuru.

Mbuya Takataka: Even if we vote against them, it is a useless exercise in Zimbabwe for they will simply rig the vote. Our votes always fill up the air like the sounds of left-over dry corn stalks in the August winds! Maybe voting will be meaningful for future generations when Zimbabwe would have real multiparty democracy. *Mbuya Takataka interjected in, but Sekuru Mukaka wasn't interested in Mbuya Takataka... so he didn't even try to encourage her. She was a useless pony in this chess game of politics.*

Sekuru Mukaka thought to himself as he parted with these two fools that avoiding those logs was possible, he has had to join the other party in order to avoid those logs, but it was unthinkable to these two stupids. He thought they were fools, and fools deserved to die. He would make a lot of money out of these fools' deaths tonight, he thought of the money; salivating his mouth again. By this middle of the night, as Sekuru Mukaka gets paid, the three old ladies were just arriving home.

Mbuya Shereni: Keresenzia, what do you have for us to eat tonight? I just want to eat and go to bed, I am so exhausted.
Keresenzia: Granny, we haven't cooked anything, there was no relish and the maize meal flour is finished.

The old lady felt so hopeless and irresponsible. She had to disregard her body and try to find food for her family in the middle of the night. She had to find food for her niece who was going to school early the following morning at Tendanayi primary school, about 10 km walk from home. Then she remembered she had hidden some rice grains somewhere for future use.

Mbuya Shereni: Boil that rice your Mother sent from South Africa! It's in the locked middle shelf. I can't think of anything else to eat tonight. It's all because of those idiots whom we had to listen to for the whole day at that stupid rally. I hope you have taken care of all livestock today, I hope they are safe and secured.

312

Kule Ngosana: Yes, we did that, Tete *(Auntie).*

Mbuya Shereni: Vahanzwadzi *(brother)*, can you please go and ask for some relish from Mbuya Mukotsanyera. I can't swallow this dry rice; I have to take some medication for my BP. *Kule Ngosana ran like some wild hare to Mbuya Mukotsanyera's homesteads.*

Kule Ngosana: Hello, Mbuya Mukotsanyera, Auntie is asking for some relish.

Mbuya Mukotsanyera: What relish? Hello Kule Ngosana. We have had roasted maize cobs for super. What does your auntie want to do with the relish, at this time of the night?

Kule Ngosana: As relish for the rice!

Mbuya Mukotsanyera: Good for you! We don't have any relish, no maize meal flour, not even rice, so I can't be of any help. I am sorry, Kule.

Kule Ngosana: Ok, I will tell Auntie you don't have anything. I will leave you. Sleep well!

As those four ladies and their family made do with what they had for supper...and go to sleep, on the other side of Nyatate, Baba Samaboreke was facing up to something devastating and inhuman.

At the sound of the knock of the door.

Baba Samaboreke: Who is it?

Komurade Hokoyoi: Open the door!

Baba Samaboreke: Who is it, what do you want?

Komurade Ndande: We said open the fucking door, Samaboreke.

Baba Samaboreke: It's the middle of the night, can't you see we are already asleep. Why don't you come back early in the morning?

Komurade Hokoyoi: Hey Samaboreke, you heard what we said. Open the door or else..., just know that you will regret it. *Samaboreke knew what they meant. He knew he would be burned inside the house if he continues refusing them this. Who could these people be? What did*

313

they want in the middle of the night? Did this have something to do with what's been going on throughout the whole country? He could only do as he had been told to do. He pushed the blankets to his feet, aimlessly rose from the bed, and so did his wife, Mai Samaboreke.

Baba Samaboreke: Stay inside, Mai Samaboreke, please. *He whispered to her softly.*

Mai Samaboreke: No, I am not staying inside...I am not leaving you to face that alone. *She whispered back and pointed at the door.* After all, they will be coming inside the house, anyway, to check there is no one else inside.

He tried to plead with her as she put on clothing, but she now refused to even look at him, afraid he might dissuade her. She avoided his gaze as she accompanied him to the door. She knew she could only frighten him if he were to see the fear deep down her eyes. They walked slowly to the door, unsure, like two young people who have suddenly aged, wondering why the problems always beset them, even when they thought they have done enough toward solving them or to just come to terms. At the door, Samaboreke heaved a heavy sigh as he prepared to open the door. He started opening the door slowly, trying to figure out what awaited him, but he was taken by surprise when a heavy boot smashed heavily on his left jaw from the left side, draining the oxygen gaspingly out of his lungs as he thudded on the floors like a bag of maize grains.

Mai Samaboreke: Yowe.ee..eee, maiwe kani, what's the matter, baba. *Samaboreke's legs were outside and the rest of his body was still inside, piled on top of his wife. Mai Samaboreke cried in alarm and fear for her husband. She was also trying to raise herself from her husband. The lights blinkered dangerously from an opening sky. It was a clear sky Samaboreke was seeing, even though it was, in actual fact, a dark night. The stars were coming down in a fast, fierce, transcendental traditional beat of the Jiti music hitting on the climax. They were swirling, round around, like the swirl and dazzling acrobat drifts of the monkeys on tree's branches. But, before the stars could touch him, he gave in to the absorbing darkness, which ensnared him soothingly.*

Komurade Hokoyoi: Bloody-sucking traitors...you deserve to die...

Komurade Ndande: We are going to teach these nonconformists a great lesson. We are preaching for One Party state yet the likes of these dogs are going all over the country, misleading our people. What is DALP to Zimbabwe; traitors, zvimbwasungata...

Other young comrades: Yes, let's kill these traitors....they deserve to die *They shouted, all over this household. They were over thirty youths from Jongwe party who had been causing mayhem all over Nyatate area. They knew they could do as well as they liked because there was no recourse to the law for the victims. The country was simply ungovernable with the police, security and army silent spectators, sometimes instigators.*

And then, still deeper into this darkness, he felt the crack in his side body, and jolted back into consciousness as another boot slammed into his side, that hurt like he has never been hurt before.

Baba Samaboreke: Yoweee...you are killing me....please have mercy on me...I was just trying to do my job....I am so sorry....please have mercy on me.

Komurade Ndande: Go and ask mercy from your president...you are a bloody traitor, Samaboreke...you are dying today. If I were you I would be asking for absolution from your creator...that's where you are going..., kwamupfiganebwe nhasi *(into the grave tonight)... Samaboreke hallowed with pain, complementing to his wife's wails. She had been crying as she begged them to stop beating her husband. Nobody seemed to hear their cries; nobody came to help them. They knew the next neighbourhood were hearing their cries but they also knew nobody was coming for the people of the next household were of this party. They knew they could only cry...or hope God would get into the minds of these thugs and stay them away from a killing orgy, but they also knew it was a futile hope.*

Komurade Ndande: You are going to be a lesson to the other DALP party supporters. We thought you were going to stop when

315

we killed your youth chairman, Matipedza, but you have continued to defy us... here is a kick for doing that...

Komurade Hokoyoi kicked Samaboreke on his stomach, and another kick from another Komurade whammed his face, as if kicking an inflated ball. The teeth came down from his gums like blooded gemstones as he grabbed his mouth trying to keep them inside his mouth, but he knew he couldn't. He needed to release the pain inside his mouth, so he puked the teeth in a ball of blood, teeth, mucus and spit as another boot kicked the air out of his lungs, devastating him with pain as he fainted again. He started drifting from being conscious to out of consciousness as they continued beating him. He was no longer angry with these monsters, only bewildered. How could humans be these monsters? These animals, these monsters, must reside with us, only that we just don't see them. Humanity in these humans was just a pile of humus. For long minutes he drifted in and out of consciousness as he still felt the cries of his wife, now being beaten, as well, as she hallowed with the pain he now knew she was feeling, all over her body. As one group continued beating him he knew the other group were beating his wife. He knew there was nothing he could do about that, neither his wife. He came to the sad realisation that he had reached his endpoint in life. He was dying, but he had no regrets. He had faced the reality of his existence. He had tried all the best to achieve on the things he believed in. He knew the struggle would continue. It wouldn't end with their killings. As he folded for the last time he knew he was happy.